Beyond the Stadium

BEYOND THE STADIUM

How Sports Change the World

ANDREW BERTOLI

STANFORD UNIVERSITY PRESS
Stanford, California

Stanford University Press
Stanford, California

Library of Congress Cataloging-in-Publication Data
Names: Bertoli, Andrew, author.
Title: Beyond the stadium : how sports change the world / Andrew Bertoli.
Description: Stanford, California : Stanford University Press, 2026. | Includes
    bibliographical references and index.
Identifiers: LCCN 2025022680 (print) | LCCN 2025022681 (ebook) |
    ISBN 9781503645257 (cloth) | ISBN 9781503645493 (paperback) |
    ISBN 9781503645509 (ebook)
Subjects: LCSH: Sports--Political aspects. | Sports--Social aspects.
Classification: LCC GV706.35 .B47 2026 (print) | LCC GV706.35 (ebook) |
    DDC 306.4/83--dc23/eng/20250615

LC record available at https://lccn.loc.gov/2025022680
LC ebook record available at https://lccn.loc.gov/2025022681

Cover design: Tim Green, Tiny Giant Co.
Cover art: Pexels and Shutterstock

The authorized representative in the EU for product safety and compliance is: Mare Nostrum Group B.V. | Mauritskade 21D | 1091 GC Amsterdam | The Netherlands | Email address: gpsr@mare-nostrum.co.uk | KVK chamber of commerce number: 96249943

CONTENTS

LIST OF TABLES AND FIGURES

Tables

Figures

PREFACE

My early life largely revolved around my passions for sports and politics. I viewed these as entirely separate matters. At school, I focused on developing the skills and knowledge that I needed to become a political science professor. Meanwhile, I devoted much of my free time to watching and playing sports. I even got a job as the head coach of a large youth summer swim team in 2009, which I greatly enjoyed for three summers despite my concern that it would distract me from my career.

In 2013, when I was in my fourth year of graduate school, an exciting new idea came to me. I would change the focus of my research from military conquest, the topic I had studied in my first three years of graduate school, to how the World Cup affects international relations. With much enthusiasm, I shared this decision with a number of academics who were kind enough to indulge my interests. The reactions of many of them surprised me. Some of these scholars saw merit in the topic but viewed it as so far outside mainstream political science that focusing on it would likely be a career-ending mistake. Others seemed confused about how I thought sports could plausibly impact important political issues in meaningful ways. This second reaction puzzled me at the time. After years of study, I now understand that it fits into a broader tradition of how some very intelligent people have viewed sports and politics, as I will explain in the coming pages.

What I could not argue with back then, however, was that researching sports and politics would likely make landing a job as a political science professor immensely challenging. In fact, up until 2017 the leading political science and international relations journals had published hardly anything on sports.[1] Further, while I could identify a few political science professors who had done side projects on sports and politics, I struggled to find any who had made sports their main focus.

Much has changed in the last decade. I have greatly enjoyed witnessing the wave of interest in sports and politics that has swept the field of political science starting in 2017. Not only did I publish my article about the World Cup and interstate conflict that year, but the *Journal of Politics* also published two other articles on sports and politics.[2] Meanwhile, Thomas Gift and Andrew Miner wrote an article in *World Affairs* advocating for political scientists to take the effects of sports much more seriously.[3]

Since 2017, numerous articles on sports have appeared in some of the field's leading journals, including *American Political Science Review, International Organization*, the *Journal of Politics, Comparative Political Studies*, the *Journal of Peace Research*, and the *Journal of Experimental Political Science*.[4] These studies have explored a variety of questions, including how sports victories and defeats affect leader popularity, how sports impact attitudes toward refugees and immigrants, how authoritarian governments use sports for political gain, and how sports influence levels of conflict within countries.

It is hard to know what caused this explosion of research. It certainly drew inspiration from earlier work about sports and politics by pathbreaking political scientists such as Robert Elias, Michael Mandelbaum, Jennifer Ring, Victor Cha, and Jules Boykoff, whose contributions typically appeared in journals outside of political science or in book form.[5] Much valuable and inspiring work had also been done by historians, sociologists, economists, sports studies scholars, and academics in various other disciplines. Further important and insightful analyses have come from journalists, especially Dave Zirin and Simon Kuper, and former coaches, athletes, and others with extensive first-hand experience in the sports industry. These contributions have taken the form of books and articles, as well as many films, documentaries, interviews, and lectures. Beyond providing inspiration, these experts have given political scientists a strong foundation to explore fascinating questions and expand their own footprint in this critical research area.

My own experience appropriately illustrates this point. As I worked to become an expert on sports and politics over the last decade, I found myself with an ocean of valuable resources that could provide a wide range of insights into the social and political effects of sports. However, I also realized that exploring this vast terrain would take significant time and commitment, and doing so might not even be possible if I wanted a career in political science.

A fortunate development allowed me to devote myself to this endeavor in a way that few other political scientists could. In 2018, I was hired to teach political science and international relations at IE University in Spain, where I have worked for the last six years. My colleagues and supervisors at IE University have valued my passion for sports and politics and encouraged me to immerse myself in the subject. In particular, my former colleague Henry Pascoe suggested that I create my own sports and politics course, which I first taught in 2022. Over the last several years, this course has brought me into many fascinating and thought-provoking discussions with students who are passionate about the topic and approach it from a wide range of perspectives.

Beyond the Stadium is my attempt to take many of the important and surprising lessons I have learned and package them in a way that any reader can absorb in a few hours. I also advance some novel insights and present new empirical analysis that demonstrates how sports can impact society and politics in significant and often remarkable ways. I believe that this book will serve as a valuable resource to political scientists who are interested in the social and political effects of sports and might even be thinking about conducting their own studies on the subject. The content of this book will also likely appeal to readers from many other backgrounds, whether they be academics, athletes, sports fans, or those simply interested in learning about the profound impact of sports on modern societies.

ACKNOWLEDGMENTS

This book would not have been possible without the help and support of many people. I would especially like to thank my two main advisors in graduate school, Ron Hassner and Jasjeet Sekhon. These two scholars were wonderfully supportive of my risky decision to study a topic that, in the mid-2010s, fell well outside mainstream political science. In particular, Ron and Jas helped me pitch my research to a political science audience at a time when it felt like much taboo surrounded the study of sports and politics. Beyond the valuable guidance I received from these two scholars, they were both very generous with their time. They are each the type of scholar and advisor whom I strive to be.

There were many others who gave me advice related to this book. In particular, I would like to thank Aila Matanock, Allan Dafoe, Robert Trager, Michaela Mattes, Daniel Sargent, Thad Dunning, Laura Jakli, Jason Klocek, Benjamin Bartlett, Tara Buss, Rochelle Terman, Alice Ciciora, Caroline Brandt, David Broockman, Josh Kalla, Baobao Zhang, Alexander Theodoridis, Sebastian Rosato, Michael Desch, Keir Lieber, David Kang, Brian Rathbun, Jonathan Markowitz, Benjamin Graham, James Lo, Andrew Coe, Brett Carter, Daryl Press, Benjamin Valentino, Jennifer Lind, Bill Wohlforth, Kathleen Powers, Stephen Brooks, Jason Lyall, Andrei Markovits, Nicholas Sambanis, Patrick James, and Paul Avey.

Thanks also to my current and former colleagues in the School of Politics, Economics, and Global Affairs at IE University in Madrid, Spain. In particular, I am very grateful to Daniel Kselman, Henry Pascoe, Daniel Flynn, Patricia Gabaldon, Nikitas Konstantinidis, Nina Wiesehomeier, Pedro Gete, Evan Liaras, Elsa Voytas, Zuheir Desai, Guillermo Toral, Xiaoyan Qiu, Carlos Lastra, Michael Becher, Irene Menéndez, Vicente Valentim, Emmy Lindstam, Charlie Kushner, Waya Quiviger, Stephanie Lackner, and Tim Foreman.

I would especially like to thank Dan LoPreto, Alan Harvey, Thane Hale, Emily Smith, Melissa Jauregui Chavez, and the rest of the team at Stanford University Press for their support throughout the publication process. In particular, Dan LoPreto's suggestions at critical moments in the book's development proved invaluable for helping me expand and sharpen my analysis. I am also especially grateful to Jennifer Gordon for her exceptional work in editing the manuscript. In addition, the two anonymous reviewers provided insightful and constructive advice. Further, I would like to extend my appreciation to the team at Oxford University Press for their help with including the parts of Chapter 1 that I adapted from my previously published research.

I greatly benefited from my many conversations with Aleksandra Smajevic and Thandiwe Keet, who challenged me to think in new ways about the social effects of sports. I am grateful to all the students who have participated in my sports and politics courses at IE University, in particular Lukas Koppermann, Kathryn Walton, Alejandro Gimeno, Sofía Guilbert, Michael Duffy, Catalina León Alonso, Jason Massouh, Denise Rubenstein, and Mehrunnisa Chaudhry. The lessons and insights that emerged from our discussions have shaped this book in important ways.

I am also very grateful to the many scholars whose research on sports and society made writing a book of this nature possible. Foremost among them, I would like to thank David Goldblatt, Jules Boykoff, Barbara Keys, James Druckman, Elizabeth Sharrow, Allen Guttmann, Jessica Luther, Kavitha Davidson, Victor Cha, Robert Elias, Thomas Bunting, Jennifer Ring, Michael Mandelbaum, Andrei Markovits, Lars Rensmann, Eileen McDonagh, Laura Pappano, Earl Smith, Harry Edwards, J. A. Mangan, Simon Kuper, Stefan Szymanski, Dave Zirin, Welch Suggs, John Hoberman, Paul Oyer, and Matthew Andrews. Their groundbreaking contributions served as a major source of inspiration for this book.

Others who provided invaluable support include Salvador Carmona, Manuel Muñiz Villa, Enrico Letta, Marco Giarratana, Marco Trombetta, Daisy Escobar, Cuqui Cabanas, Ángel Alonso Arroba, Borja Santos, and Julio de

Castro. I am also grateful to Kosuke Imai, Miriam Golden, Catherine de Vries, Austin Carson, Dylan Forrester, Anthony Bertelli, William Clark, Kevin Arceneaux, Stephane Wolton, Kenneth Scheve, Maria Carreri, and Connor Jerzak for fascinating discussions related to this book.

Lastly, I would like to thank my parents, who provided me with a childhood immersed in sports and who gave me endless support throughout the process of writing this book. I also thank my sister Kristen and my brothers Kyle and Bryce. Our many conversations gave me much deeper insight into the effects of sports on society.

While I am grateful to all these people, the views expressed in this book are my own, backed primarily by my research and a wide range of scientific studies about how sports impact the world.

Beyond the Stadium

INTRODUCTION

Sports captivate the world unlike anything else. More than a billion people watched the final game of the 2022 World Cup.[1] The Summer Olympics typically attract an audience of more than 3 billion people, with many world leaders attending to see their national athletes compete on the global stage.[2] In the United States, more than 120 million Americans tuned in to the 2025 Super Bowl, making it the most-watched single-network telecast in U.S. history.[3] In fact, nine of the top ten most-watched broadcasts in American history have been Super Bowls.[4] Without question, sports have become a central feature of global culture. Arguably, they have replaced religion as the most dominant cultural force of our time.[5]

Playing sports is also one of the main sources of exercise and social engagement for a large portion of the world's population. These people range from professional athletes to the many casual players who are just looking for fun and exercise.[6] In between, there are millions of athletic hopefuls aspiring to climb to the elite ranks, often devoting hours a day to their sport for little or no pay, and sometimes even investing a great deal of money in their athletic aspirations.[7] For many of these individuals, sport is one of the most important commitments in their lives.

How does the global obsession with sports impact the world? Two prevailing schools of thought underpin the way that many people think about the social and political effects of sports. These viewpoints each have some merit, but both ultimately oversimplify the impact of sports on modern societies.

THE BREAD AND CIRCUSES THEORY OF SPORTS

A commonly held view is that sports are merely the new opiate of the masses, distracting societies from important political and social problems.[8] This notion dates back to Roman times. The first-century Roman poet Juvenal claimed that the Roman population, which had achieved so much, had become distracted and placated by sports.[9] As Juvenal explained around 100 ce, "the people who once upon a time bestowed military commands, high civil offices, legions, and everything else, now restrains itself, and instead, eagerly hopes for just two things: bread and circuses."[10]

This *bread and circuses theory of sports* has had a lasting impact on how people view the relationship between sports and politics, including within academia and in the field of political science in particular.[11] In fact, political scientists have largely avoided studying sports until very recently. As Victor Cha put it in 2009, "Indeed it is astounding that a phenomenon that matters so much has been so little studied by a field that purports to explain relations among states and human beings around the world."[12]

This hesitancy to take the political effects of sports seriously is rooted in the widespread habit both inside and outside academia to simply view sports as a trivial distraction.[13] According to this way of thinking, sports are just one of many distractions, such as video games or reality TV, that when consumed in excess can degrade the quality of democratic society. It thus follows that sporting events do not merit serious intellectual inquiry, except possibly in studying their potential to distract from more productive endeavors.

No doubt, sports certainly can divert people from important social and political problems. Many cases demonstrate that major sporting events can placate the masses, sidetrack attention away from government corruption, and reduce civic engagement. For instance, governments sometimes announce controversial policy decisions around major sporting events, when much of the public is too preoccupied with watching the competition to protest.[14] One recent example was the Russian government's announcement on the opening day of the 2018 World Cup that it would increase the national pension age by about five years.[15] The controversial decision was widely unpopular within Russia but was largely overshadowed by the competition on the playing field.

Indeed, various other authoritarian leaders have tried to use sports to distract the masses. In the context of Caribbean baseball, the repressive dictator of the Dominican Republic Rafael Trujillo (1930–1961) bluntly explained, "It's good to have people [watch] baseball [so] they don't pay attention to politics."[16] In Spain under Franco, the government used televised soccer matches to keep protestors off the streets on International Workers Day.[17] This method of diversion was similarly employed by military dictatorships throughout South America during the Cold War.[18] The notion of authoritarian governments using sports to distract the masses has almost become a cliché, depicted in popular classics such as Aldous Huxley's *Brave New World* and Suzanne Collins's book series *The Hunger Games*.[19]

In the democratic context, a fascinating recent study published by political scientists Matthew Potoski and Robert Urbatsch found that U.S. voter turnout on Election Tuesdays tends to be lower when *Monday Night Football* games the prior evening have higher-quality teams, closer point spreads, and higher expected scores.[20] The researchers examined data from 1970 to 2014 and found that higher-quality *Monday Night Football* games reduced voter turnout by an estimated 2.1–8.0 percentage points the following day among likely voters.[21] The authors explain the finding by pointing out that spending about three and a half hours watching a football game greatly reduces the free time that individuals (or their partners) have the following day, thereby decreasing their likelihood of going to the polls.[22]

Aldous Huxley commented in 1958:

> In regard to propaganda the early advocates of universal literacy and a free press envisaged only two possibilities: the propaganda might be true, or it might be false. They did not foresee what in fact has happened, above all in our Western capitalist democracies—the development of a vast mass communications industry, concerned in the main neither with the true nor the false, but with the unreal, the more or less totally irrelevant.[23]

This fear about society's obsession with "the more or less totally irrelevant" seems even more urgent today given the rise of sports broadcasting around the globe, not to mention the many sports talk shows, websites, and podcasts that capture so much public attention.

However, despite there being some truth to the bread and circuses theory, it represents an overly simplistic view of sports.[24] The impact of sports on politics is far more extensive and interesting, as this book will show. In fact, sports and politics are deeply intertwined. Three main reasons explain why this is inherently the case. First, as modern sports emerged between the mid-1800s and early 1900s, leaders in the sports world sought to use sports for overtly social and political purposes.[25] In particular, major sporting events like the Olympics and World Cup were created with the stated purpose of influencing politics, as we will discuss in Chapter 1.[26] Second, many governments, athletes, and other actors have tried to harness the power of sports for their own broader goals.[27] Third, sports tap into humanity's hopes, passions, and desire for group identification. As such, they have many unintended social and political consequences.

A fascinating example appears in Robert Putnam's influential book *Bowling Alone*, and it turns the bread and circuses theory on its head.[28] For background, this book stands out as one of the most important studies published in the social sciences in the last fifty years. Putnam's work explores the social science concept of *social capital*, roughly defined as the social connections between individuals. Like physical capital (such as a factory) or human capital (like computer programming skills), social capital provides societies with many important benefits.

If you live in a community where you know and trust your neighbors, you will be able to ask them for favors, like lending you a ladder or watching your home while you are on vacation. On the other hand, if you live in a society where you hardly know or trust anyone, you will likely need to go to the store any time you need something, as well as buy an expensive alarm system for when you go away. For these reasons, strong social connections can greatly benefit society. Countries with high social capital have major advantages over countries that are more socially disconnected.

Why is Putnam's book *Bowling Alone* named after a sport? It has to do with a story about a sixty-four-year-old Black man named John Lambert from Michigan who needed a kidney transplant. He had been on a waiting list for three years when a thirty-three-year-old White man whom he met through his bowling league volunteered to donate one of his kidneys.[29] As this example shows, sports can strengthen social ties between individuals in ways that are highly beneficial to society. Thus, even though sports can sometimes be a pernicious distraction, they can also provide the glue that helps hold communities together.[30]

To be sure, sports are not the only way that communities can build social capital, nor are they necessarily the best way. We will consider this topic more in the coming chapters. However, there is no disputing that people do often make important social connections through sports, as the *Bowling Alone* example demonstrates. This notion that sports could provide valuable benefits brings us to the second popular but problematic view about how sports impact modern societies.

THE GOSPEL OF SPORTS

While the bread and circuses theory of sports represents one oversimplification of how sports impact society, another influential but erroneous view is what I call the *gospel of sports*.[31] In a nutshell, the gospel of sports posits that sports are almost always a powerful force for good in the world. According to this view, sports advance racial and gender equality, encourage world peace, teach important life lessons, and bring out the best in humanity. Such lofty claims run rampant in modern society and are advanced by many politicians, political organizations, sports fans, and members of the sports industry.[32]

The United Nations has played an important role in promoting the gospel of sports. In the 1990s, it joined forces with the International Olympic Committee (IOC), with UN Secretary General Kofi Annan declaring in 2000 that "Olympic ideals are also United Nations ideals: tolerance, equality, fair play and, most of all, peace."[33] The UN went on to release a document in 2014 called "Sport and the Sustainable Development Goals" that suggested myriad ways that sports might help build a more just and sustainable world. According to the document, sports can reduce poverty and hunger, have beneficial environmental impacts, improve gender equality, and promote more peaceful societies.[34] While the United Nations has tempered its claims about the benefits of sports in recent years, its website still praises them as "a powerful tool to strengthen social ties and promote sustainable development and peace, as well as solidarity and respect for all."[35]

The UN is just one influential actor to endorse this very optimistic view of sports. The idea of the gospel of sports has also motivated many "sports for development and peace" (SDP) programs that aim to improve societies around the world, often in communities lagging in education and health services where that money might be better spent.[36] Similarly, whenever a major sporting event like the Olympics or World Cup occurs, one need not look hard to find politicians, celebrities, and journalists praising the presumed benefits of sporting mega-events.[37]

Although many speak as though the intrinsically beneficial nature of sports is a self-evident truth, this notion contradicts some traditional views about sports, games, and other leisurely pastimes. These more critical attitudes are captured in the ancient fable, "The Ant and the Grasshopper," attributed to the legendary Greek storyteller Aesop.[38] The fable draws a contrast between an ant who works hard during the summer gathering and storing food and a grasshopper who spends his summer playing and having fun. When winter comes, the ant has plenty of food to survive, while the grasshopper gets caught unprepared.

Various governments throughout history have viewed sports through this prism.[39] English authorities tried banning early versions of soccer beginning in 1314, partly because they feared that such activities would distract young men from archery, which was critical for the national defense.[40] Even as late as the Victorian era, sport was viewed by many as an activity that corrupted character and undermined work ethic.[41] The Ottoman Sultanate also tried banning soccer, in part fearing that it would divert young students from their education.[42] Likewise, some European missionaries shunned sports when spreading Christianity abroad, instead focusing on teaching their converts more practical activities like building schools and homes.[43]

Authorities certainly did not always view sports as a pointless pastime. Besides Rome, sports received political backing in many pre-modern societies, including the ancient Greek and Aztec civilizations. In such cases, sporting events often constituted pagan rituals meant to honor and entertain the gods.[44] At the same time, some ancient thinkers also credited sport with promoting positive virtues in athletes.[45] This view provided an early antecedent to modern-day claims about how sports can develop resilience and character.

This notion that sports build character became very influential in England's prestigious public boarding schools in the mid-1800s.[46] These institutions were the key starting points for the development and spread (via the British empire) of both soccer and rugby football, which later evolved into American and Canadian football.[47] In the 1800s, schoolboys at these institutions learned early versions of soccer and rugby from the English working classes. The boys demonstrated a great passion to play these games. Rather than suppressing these new activities, the schoolmasters thought the games could provide an outlet to channel the boys' adolescent energy, promote social skills, and keep the boys busy so that they would stay out of trouble.

Like the bread and circuses theory of sports, the gospel of sports idea does have some merit. Sports can provide many valuable benefits. The example from *Bowling Alone* is one inspiring case, and many people who play and watch sports, including myself, can point to a variety of ways that they improve our lives. In particular, sports provide people with opportunities to exercise and make social connections, which together can help people live longer and happier lives. However, the impact of sports can also be surprisingly negative, as this book will document. Most importantly, the negative consequences of sports are especially likely to arise when people engage with sports in an overly optimistic and uninformed way—that is, when they naively accept the gospel of sports instead of being critical thinkers. On the other hand, the better we understand sports and the more intentional we are about how we engage with them, the more likely sports are to bring value to our lives.

I argue that political scientists should take a leading role in studying how sports impact modern societies. Sports affect many important issues that political scientists care about deeply, including how people think about their identities, how countries try to brand themselves on the world stage, how citizens view their political leaders, how dictators advance their corrupt agendas, and how marginalized groups advocate for social change.[48] The study of sports and politics therefore needs to be a major research program in political science, not on its periphery. This book will make the case for giving sports serious thought and attention, and it will outline a number of research programs to which political scientists and other scholars can contribute along the way.

ELITE VERSUS GRASSROOTS SPORTS

As this book explores important ways that sports and politics interact, we will see a key theme emerge that relates to how we can best approach sports both as individuals and as communities. This core lesson is worth discussing now, because it will help readers draw deeper connections between the different topics that this book covers. It involves a struggle that has divided the sports world going back to the 1800s. It has been fought by various actors in a wide range of historical contexts, but it ultimately features a conflict between two competing approaches to sports. The first is the *elite sports model*, also called the "champion system."[49] In this model, individuals advance as far as they can up the athletic ladder, with the vast majority failing out and, in many cases, then shifting their main relationship with sports from being an athlete to being a fan. The second approach to sports is the *grassroots sports model*, or the popular participation model. In this model, people play sports for fun, exercise, and to make social connections.[50]

The elite sports model emphasizes excellence in sports. Such excellence is rewarded in a variety of ways, from high school varsity jackets (and the prestige they bestow) to high-profile awards like the Heisman Trophy and Olympic gold medals. Notably, athletes in the elite sports model often focus on mastering a single sport, although other sports are sometimes used for cross-training. Occasionally, exceptional athletes like Deion Sanders excel at the highest level in more than one sport, but such cases are exceedingly rare.

In contrast, the popular participation model does not seek to determine who is best or incentivize individuals to develop elite skills in a specific sport. An individual's goals in the popular participation model are typically linked more closely to their personal health and well-being, since winning matters little. In fact, the goal of winning is subordinate to these other goals and can be viewed as instrumental in that trying to win is necessary for game play. It is hard to imagine, for instance, a casual basketball player doping to gain a competitive advantage in pick-up games or playing through a serious injury to secure a win.

Historical Links to Capitalism and Socialism

Historically, the elite sports model has been associated with capitalism, whereas the popular participation model has been associated with socialism.[51] However, scholarly research casts significant doubt on these relationships.[52] In particular, grassroots sports organizations have flourished in many free-market capitalist societies.[53] Meanwhile, many socialist countries have recognized the prestige that success in elite sports can bring on the world stage and have thus invested heavily in the elite sports model.[54] While such socialist countries may publicly espouse the popular participation model, they essentially use it to discover talented young athletes and then train them to bring glory to the nation.[55] Further, in both socialist and capitalist countries, elite sports often receive substantial government subsidies.[56] Therefore, the link between the elite sports model and capitalism, on the one hand, and the popular participation model and socialism on the other, is tenuous at best.

Tribalism

In fact, the primary force underpinning the elite sports model for both capitalist and socialist countries is tribalism. Tribalism involves positive feelings towards one's in-group combined with negative feelings toward out-groups.[57] Tribalism tends to have a negative connotation because of its tendency to worsen relations between different groups. We will see many examples of this in Chapter 1. However, the more positive side of tribalism—in-group bonding—can have important benefits, a subject that we will examine in Chapter 2.

In the realm of international sports, which will be the focus of the first three chapters of this book, tribalism typically takes the form of nationalism. The synthesis of sports and nationalism makes international sporting competitions of great interest to both fans and governments. As we will see in Chapter 3, it can turn sporting events into symbolic warfare between nations, transforming a seemingly frivolous sporting contest into a perceived yardstick to determine which country has a better economic and political system.[58] The marriage of nationalism and sports also leads to serious dilemmas in the international sporting realm. For example, it requires international sports organizations to decide who counts as a nation, as well as to judge whether nations that violate international laws and norms should be allowed to compete. We will discuss these issues more in the next chapter.

At the international level, success in sports, whether measured in victories or merely the staging of an impressive tournament, can bring prestige and respect to a country. This point relates closely to Joseph Nye's concept of soft power.[59] Nye describes soft power as "the ability to get what you want through attraction rather than coercion or payments."[60] No doubt, this can be one reason why countries seek to elevate their reputations through sports, as we will see in this book.

However, soft power is not the only reason why countries strive for excellence through athletic competition. Another key reason is that many countries view prestige and respect as ends in themselves, even when obtaining them does not lead to political or economic advantages.[61] It is hard to overstate the human desire to excel and be recognized for achievement. Indeed, anthropologists and sociologists have documented the widespread tendency for humans to seek such recognition for themselves and their tribes.[62] This impulse helps account for the prevalence of sports, as well as other types of games and contests, that is so universal across cultures.[63] In the context of our modern-day tribes—like universities, cities, and countries—the pursuit of group pride and social status can cause communities to invest immense resources in elite sports and to take winning very seriously.

Corporate Capitalism

Besides tribalism, a second powerful force that underpins the elite sports model is what we might call corporate capitalism—that is, the drive of corporations to maximize their profits through both economic competition as well as their connections to government.[64] In the popular participation model, ordinary people engage in sports as a casual pastime. This approach does not require any large organization to oversee and manage a particular sport. In contrast, the elite sports model molds sport into its corporate version. It turns most people into spectators who provide the economic basis for a much more costly (yet sometimes profitable) sports system, while a small percentage of elite athletes rise to the top.[65] Further, various businesses, especially construction companies, profit from the creation of new stadiums and other infrastructure, increasing their revenue often at the taxpayers' expense.[66] Meanwhile, other corporations use elite sports to market various products to spectators, further spurring consumption and increasing corporate profits.[67]

Because of its corporate underpinnings, the elite sports model becomes heavily influenced by market dynamics. For instance, the strong preference among fans for watching men's instead of women's sports has led to a large gender pay gap in athletics. Such market dynamics can create other seeming injustices, with governments rarely, but occasionally, getting involved to redress them (e.g., Title IX in the United States).[68] As the scholars Jessica Luther and Kavitcha A. Davidson explain, "Sports are big business, and with that comes the dirtiness of any major moneymaking thing that holds cultural significance."[69] As we will see in this book, in particular in Chapters 4–6, market dynamics create a wide range of controversies and seeming contradictions in the world of elite sports. Government involvement has proved at best contentious in addressing some of these issues. Meanwhile, other problems in elite sports appear to lack any solution that will satisfy the vast majority of athletes and spectators.

No doubt, the elite sports model does bring some benefits, as this book will document, despite the significant and seemingly unresolvable problems that it also creates. Given its popularity, it is also highly unlikely to disappear anytime soon. Therefore, this book will propose some ideas that could allow spectator sports to have a much more positive impact on the world. Some of these changes can easily be made by individuals reading this book. Other changes would need to take place at the societal level. Some of these reforms are modest, others more ambitious. However, they all point to ways that sports might serve as a more powerful force for good in the world.

To make such recommendations, however, we must first utilize the tools of social science to understand how sports impact the world currently. Quantitative methods, case studies, and critical analysis are all powerful assets that social scientists can use to gain a better understanding of the global phenomenon of modern sport. We will begin by investigating one of the oldest and most controversial questions about how sports affect politics: Do international sporting events encourage peace between countries?

1

INTERNATIONAL SPORTS AND INTERSTATE CONFLICT

Do international sporting events like the Olympics and the World Cup make countries more peaceful or more violent? Many believe that international sports foster peace by teaching states fair play and providing an outlet for nationalistic aggression.[1] However, others contend that competition on the playing field actually intensifies rivalries between countries, much like it often does for universities or high schools.[2]

This debate has important policy implications. If international sporting events act as a pacifying force, then we could hold more of them to reduce tensions between countries. On the other hand, if they tend to make international conflict more likely, then we might consider cutting back on them, especially when they are most likely to cause international conflict.

THE ARGUMENT FOR PEACE

The notion that international sports encourage peace goes back to the ancient Greeks, who used to grant safe passage to athletes and religious pilgrims for the Olympic Games—a tradition that came to be known as the Olympic Truce.[3] In 1896, the French academic Pierre de Coubertin revived the Olympics with the stated goal of encouraging peace between countries.[4] Earlier in his life, Coubertin had actually promoted sports for militaristic purposes. Specifically, he viewed them as a means of preparing the French population to avenge their defeat in the Franco-Prussian War, which he witnessed as a young child.[5] However, as he grew older and traveled internationally, he became a proponent of the idea that international sports could serve as a forum to foster mutual understanding among nations.[6] He also claimed that countries were predisposed to engage in nationalistic violence, and that international sports could provide a peaceful way to release this energy.[7]

This last notion is rooted in a theory about aggressive behavior that psychologists now call the "drive-discharge model" or the "catharsis hypothesis."[8] Inspired by the ideas of Sigmund Freud, this theory posits that aggressive desires build up in the mind and need to be released through peaceful channels.[9] Although the drive-discharge model was once very popular, it has been disconfirmed by a series of studies in psychology over the last several decades.[10] In fact, experiments have found that prompting subjects to vent their aggression actually makes them more likely to behave violently in the future.

Nevertheless, the idea that sports can channel aggression has persisted.[11] For example, in a 2009 interview, the renowned political scientist Benedict Anderson asserted:

> [E]ven though these Olympic games are ugly in the jingoism that we see, nonetheless, it's a hell of a lot better than murdering people and going to war. If these aggressive impulses have to be expressed somehow, it's much better if they're expressed in a football stadium at a football match.[12]

Despite his brilliant academic contributions to the study of nationalism, Anderson seemed to be unaware of the research on the drive-discharge model and its implications for international sports.

The founder of the World Cup, Jules Rimet, also championed sports as a way to foster international peace. He claimed that international sports would bring countries together in a spirit of healthy competitiveness, which could make them more willing to cooperate in other areas of international relations.[13] This theory has become a very popular idea in world politics. In recent years, several U.S. presidents have praised major international sporting events for bringing countries together, including Ronald Reagan, George W. Bush, and Barack Obama.[14] Many other prominent leaders have made similar claims, including Tony Blair, Nelson Mandela, and Pope John Paul II.[15]

Rimet's idea closely resembles a theory about international relations called neofunctionalism, which suggests that participation in one area of international relations can spill over and increase cooperation in other areas.[16] However, one could also say that international sports really involve competition between states. Therefore, these events could result in the spillover of rivalry rather than cooperation. Nonetheless, many defenders of international sports argue that they do involve an important element of cooperation between countries. For instance, the historian Cesar Torres claims that the competing nations must recognize one another as fellow participants and follow the rules.[17] Similarly, the philosopher William Morgan argues that international sports facilitate meaningful dialogue and encourage the participants to see one another as legitimate.[18] Therefore, the idea that these events generate positive spillover effects is plausible but uncertain.

In sum, many people champion the idea that international sports encourage world peace, and in fact this idea was a stated motivation for founding both the Olympics and the World Cup. As such, athletes were expected from the beginning to compete as representatives of their countries. This decision was not the only one that could have been made. Athletes might have just participated as individuals. Alternatively, they could have represented other entities, such as cities, continents, or religions.

This early decision left a lasting legacy that has created some complex challenges in international sports.[19] On one hand, athletes are sometimes expected to represent countries with which they have strong political disagreements, an issue that we will explore in Chapter 5.[20] There is also the problem of what to do when a country engages in blatant human rights abuses.[21] Should that country (and therefore its athletes) be banned from international sports, even when the athletes oppose their government's actions?

The nation-centric approach to sports also puts international sports organizations in the awkward position of having to decide who does and does not count as a nation.[22] During the Cold War, the IOC had to deal with intense controversies involving East Germany, North Korea, and Taiwan.[23] Indeed, China boycotted the Olympics from 1956 to 1976 to protest Taiwan's presence.[24] They were also outraged by Taiwan calling itself the Republic of China, since the government in mainland China viewed itself as the only true Chinese state and considered the government in Taiwan to be illegitimate. The IOC eventually made Taiwan change its name at the Olympics to Chinese Taipei.[25]

Most apparently, the focus on nations has also led international sporting events to become celebrations of nationalism.[26] We witness this tradition in the form of national colors, flags, and anthems that continue to be nearly ubiquitous at these events. Given Coubertin's theory that sports provide a peaceful outlet for nationalistic impulses, riling up nationalism makes sense—the more that people can vent their nationalistic passions, the better.

The idea that competition on the playing field encourages peace has also formally underpinned numerous competitions between rival countries since World War II.[27] The most famous example is the ping-pong diplomacy between China and the United States in the 1970s, which many scholars claim helped pave the way for cooperation between the two countries.[28] This example has served as an inspiration for many other competitions, including cricket diplomacy between India and Pakistan, soccer games between North and South Korea, and wrestling matches between the United States and Iran.

THE ARGUMENT FOR CONFLICT

Despite the popularity of the idea that international sports encourage peace, many scholars claim that they actually often worsen relations between countries. George Orwell made this argument after the Moscow Dynamo Soccer Club traveled to Britain in 1945 to play a series of games against British teams. The games were intended to strengthen British-Soviet relations, but they were marred by fights and allegations of cheating.[29] George Orwell responded to the incident by writing an essay called "The Sporting Spirit" in which he argued that sporting events have a detrimental impact on international relations. As he explained:

> Even if one didn't know from concrete examples (the 1936 Olympic Games, for instance) that international sporting contests lead to orgies of hatred, one could deduce it from general principles. . . . On the village green, where you pick up sides and no feeling of local patriotism is involved, it is possible to play simply for the fun and exercise: but as soon as the question of prestige arises, as soon as you feel that you and some larger unit will be disgraced if you lose, the most savage combative instincts are aroused. Anyone who has played even in a school football match knows this.[30]

Since the publication of his essay in 1945, Orwell's view has received support from studies across the social sciences. For instance, research from psychology has found that sports competitions can cause people to harbor feelings of ill will and resentment toward the other side.[31] Similarly, numerous articles from sociology have shown that international sports often make the national discourses within countries more hawkish, with reporters describing games in military terminology and comparing wins and losses to past battles.[32] More generally, research in political science has found that nationalism from other sources, such as national holidays, tends to make countries more likely to take military action against other states.[33]

In addition, many scholars since Orwell have pointed to numerous cases where tensions from international sporting events led to military or political conflict between countries.[34] The most famous example is the 1969 Soccer War between El Salvador and Honduras (also called the Football War or the 100 Hour War).[35] This war was sparked by a series of soccer riots that exacerbated an already tense political situation between the two nations.[36] Prior to the war, the Honduran government faced serious economic problems. To protect its native-born citizens, it decided to give them land belonging to the Salvadoran immigrants living in its country. This controversial policy led to clashes between Honduran and Salvadoran nationals and a media war between the two nations.

Amidst this tumultuous political atmosphere, Honduras and El Salvador were scheduled to play World Cup qualification games that would ultimately decide who would go to the 1970 World Cup. The night before the first game, Honduran fans congregated around the hotel where the Salvadoran players were staying and created disturbances to interrupt their sleep. Honduras won the first game 1–0. Salvadoran fans did not find the tactic amusing, and they retaliated when the Honduran team traveled to El Salvador to play the next game. As the journalist Ryszard Kapuscinski describes, "This time it was the Honduran team that spent a sleepless night. The screaming crowd of fans broke all the windows in the hotel and threw rotten eggs, dead rats and stinking rags inside."[37]

The next day, the Honduran players had to be driven in armored cars to the stadium, which resembled an active war zone. The army showed up in force, with soldiers on the field carrying submachine guns. Outside the stadium, Salvadoran fans assaulted Hondurans and also attacked the consulate. These acts sparked retaliatory violence against Salvadorans living in Honduras, leading many to flee back into El Salvador. While the game resulted in a 3–0 victory for El Salvador, the political violence became the main story.[38]

Nevertheless, because the countries had won one game each, a tiebreaker was necessary to determine which team would go to the World Cup. They played this match twelve days later in Mexico City. Unfortunately, the game did not diffuse tensions or promote understanding between the two sides. Rather, the two countries broke diplomatic ties just prior to the game, and less than three weeks later El Salvador invaded Honduras. The war killed or injured about 6,000 people. Rather than encouraging peace, nationalism from the games acted as a catalyst that caused an already tense political situation to devolve into an international war.

The 1969 Soccer War was not the first time that Latin America experienced a nationalistic uproar between two countries over sports. In fact, a similar incident took place in 1940 over a Caribbean baseball championship game. The game was tight, with Venezuela winning on a close call that the Dominicans disputed. The situation quickly turned into an international controversy. As the political scientist Robert Elias describes:

> [T]he Venezuelans offered to replay the game. The Dominicans refused, hurling insults against their opponents and then against Venezuelans generally. Offended, the Venezuelans staged rallies and demanded action. Their government severed relations with the Dominican Republic, but many Venezuelans wanted war. Cooler heads prevailed, but diplomatic relations were not restored for several years.[39]

Recent history provides numerous examples from other regions of the globe. In November 2009, a political dispute broke out from a soccer game between Egypt and Algeria. The game was played in Cairo, and it would decide which of the two countries would go to the 2010 FIFA World Cup. The media stoked tensions in the lead-up to the game. The situation then destabilized when Egyptian fans attacked a bus carrying the Algerian national team, injuring three players.[40] The incident quickly escalated into a major international dispute, with violence erupting between Egyptian and Algerian nationals.

Hosni Mubarak pulled the Egyptian ambassador from Algiers, and Egypt also tried to send a plane to Algeria to rescue Egyptian nationals, although Algeria did not allow it to land.[41] As James Montague wrote for CNN, "What had been billed as a crucial game between Arab and Muslim brothers ended in violence, recriminations, diplomatic intrigue and a trail of broken glass and burned-out cars from Cairo to Marseilles."[42] Christopher Hitchens gave this description of the event: "Before the match in Khartoum, Egypt and Algeria had no diplomatic quarrel. After the game, perfectly serious people in Cairo were saying the atmosphere resembled that following the country's defeat in the June 1967 war."[43] In response to the incident, the Arab League encouraged politicians from its member states to avoid attending sensitive sports games because of the potential hostilities that these events might provoke.[44]

Another incident occurred in October of 2014, when the Albanian national team traveled to Serbia to play an important qualification game for the 2016 UEFA European Championship.[45] Trouble started when a small drone, carrying a hyper-nationalist Albanian flag, flew into the stadium during the game. When the drone got closer to the field, a Serbian player tried to rip the flag down. Fights quickly broke out among the players, and Serbian fans rushed the field to attack the Albanian team, who barely escaped back to the locker room. Meanwhile, the Serbian crowd chanted, "Kill! Kill! Kill the Albanians!"[46]

The incident proved to be a major setback for relations between the two nations.[47] Prior to the game, tensions between Serbia and Albania had in fact been easing. The prime minister of Albania was scheduled to take an important diplomatic trip to Belgrade the following week, which would be the first of its kind in sixty-eight years, but he rescheduled it to allow passions to cool.[48] He finally made the trip on November 2. The visit quickly turned adversarial, and the opportunity for reconciliation between the two nations was lost.[49]

A 2016 UEFA European Championship game in France between England and Russia also suggests that international sports can worsen relations between countries. Three days before the game, the Russian military sent an attack submarine into the English Channel in a move that the defense editor of *The Sun* described as "an attempt to intimidate the UK ahead of the Euros."[50] Fights broke out between English and Russian fans the following day, injuring over thirty-five people. A top-ranking Russian soccer official, Igor Lebedev, tweeted, "Well done, lads. Keep it up!"[51] According to *The Guardian*, high-ranking British officials suspected that Putin sent Russian soldiers to France disguised as fans to attack English supporters.[52] Putin denied this accusation, but he added, "I don't know how 200 Russian fans could fight several thousand of the British."[53]

Table 1.1 lists these examples along with several other cases wherein scholars argue that international sports increased tensions between countries. Bodyline (1932–1933) featured a heated dispute between Britain and Australia over cricket that strained relations between the two countries for years to follow.[54] Mussolini hosted the 1934 FIFA World Cup with the goal of generating support for fascism and the Italian war machine, as we will discuss in Chapter 3.[55] Hitler followed his example with the 1936 Nazi Olympics two years later.[56] The Soviet-Czechoslovak hockey riots (1969) occurred following the Soviet invasion of

Czechoslovakia in 1968. After the Czechoslovak team defeated the Soviet Union twice in international hockey, tens of thousands of people took to the streets in Prague, vandalizing Soviet buildings in the occupied city.[57]

However, despite all of this evidence, the critics of international sports have largely been unable to persuade the optimists. This debate persists in part because it is really about the *net* effect of sports on international conflict. Even if everyone could agree that international sports sparked conflict in a few specific cases, such as the Soccer War, sports may still have an overall pacifying effect if they encourage peace most of the time. To address this issue, what is really needed is a large statistical test involving many countries. Such a test would be able to capture the *average* effect of how participating in international sports impacts the likelihood that countries will engage in military conflict. By doing so, it could shed light on whether international sports tend to be a force for peace or conflict in international relations.

This research idea caught my attention after I had finished my third year of graduate school at UC Berkeley. The topic brought together two of my greatest passions in life: sports and politics. In addition, I knew that the World Cup had created a remarkable and rare type of natural experiment that would allow me to get a clear answer to this question using statistics. I describe this natural experiment in the next section.[58]

TABLE 1.1. Incidents of military/political conflict
resulting from international sports events

Case	Year
1. Bodyline cricket dispute between Britain and Australia	1932–33
2. FIFA World Cup in Italy	1934
3. Nazi Olympics in Berlin	1936
4. Venezuelan-Dominican baseball championship dispute	1940
4. Moscow Dynamo soccer trip to Britain	1945
5. Soccer War between El Salvador and Honduras	1969
6. Soviet-Czechoslovak hockey riots	1969
7. Egyptian-Algerian soccer dispute	2009
8. Serbian-Albanian drone conflict	2014
9. English-Russian Euro riots	2016

DESCRIPTION OF THE TEST

Before devising any statistical test, it can often help to think of what the best possible research design might look like. In this case, the ideal test would be an experiment where we took a large number of countries and randomly selected some to attend a major international sporting event and others to stay home. We could then track the aggression levels of the treatment and control groups before and after the sporting event, much like we were medical researchers testing the effect of some new drug through a randomized controlled trial. These experiments are the gold standard for establishing causal relationships in many academic fields,[59] so the results from this type of study could significantly improve our understanding of how international sports affect state aggression.

Unfortunately, we could never conduct such an experiment, because doing so might start a war. Ethical considerations like this often arise when studying questions related to international conflict. However, in this particular case, an unusual historical process unfolded that puts us in a fortunate position. The World Cup created a natural experiment that closely resembles the ideal study described above. As I will explain in the following pages, the format of the World Cup qualification process resulted in a large number of countries qualifying (or missing qualification) in a somewhat random way. This natural experiment gives us a clean test of how the World Cup affects state aggression.

The Natural Experiment

The type of natural experiment created by the World Cup is called a regression discontinuity (or RD for short). RD was first discovered by two psychologists back in the 1960s.[60] These psychologists wanted to investigate the relationship between academic recognition and future scholarly achievement. They had data on a group of students who had taken a test where anyone who achieved above a certain score received a certificate of merit. They wanted to learn if receiving the certificate increased the likelihood that these individuals developed plans to go to graduate school.

The psychologists could not simply compare the people who got the certificate to the people who fell short, because those two groups would differ in many important ways. For example, the people who got the certificate probably had, on average, higher IQs, came from more affluent families, and placed a higher value on scholarly achievement throughout their childhoods. If many more of them decided to go to graduate school compared to the people who did not receive the certificate, it would not prove much of anything. It would be a mere correlation, and as every statistics teacher will tell you, correlation is not causation. The reason is that, in most cases, the group that receives the factor of interest differs in many important ways from the group that does not. This makes it difficult to tell whether differences in outcomes are explained by the factor of interest or other differences between the two groups.[61]

How these psychologists overcame this problem is what made their study legendary. Rather than comparing everyone who received the certificate to everyone who did not, they compared the people who barely scored enough points to get the certificate to the ones who barely missed getting it. The idea is that it should basically be random which of these students got the certificate and which ones barely fell short. It is almost as though someone ran a randomized experiment on this particular group of people. Therefore, the two groups should look pretty similar across important baseline factors. The people who scored just high enough to get the certificate should, on average, not be much smarter, wealthier, or academically driven than the people who just fell short. In fact, the only major difference between these two groups should be that one group got the certificate whereas the other group did not. Thus, if the two groups differed notably when it came to their plans to go to graduate school, we could attribute that difference to the certificate rather than to any baseline differences between the two groups.

RDs occur when there is a scoring system with a cut point, and everyone who surpasses the cut point gets a treatment while everyone who falls short does not. Provided there is some randomness in the scoring process, it should be largely random who gets the treatment. This randomness should ensure that the group who scored just above the cut point should be pretty similar to the group who scored just below it, except for the treatment. Thus, the RD provides the opportunity to see the causal effect of the treatment by comparing the outcomes of the group that barely got it and the group that barely fell short.[62]

The World Cup created an RD because its qualification process is based on a scoring system. Most countries qualify for the World Cup by playing a round of games against other states and earning a top position in the standings (see Table 1.2 for an example from Europe for the 1994 World Cup). It is therefore possible to compare the group of countries that barely qualified to the group that barely fell short. These groups should be similar except that the qualifiers went to the World Cup and the non-qualifiers stayed home.

TABLE 1.2. An example of the final standings from a 1994 World Cup qualification round (Group 1 from Europe). This sample consists of countries that barely made (Switzerland) and barely missed (Portugal) qualifying for the World Cup.

Rank	Country	Score	Qualified
1	Italy	16	Yes
2	Switzerland	15	Yes
3	Portugal	14	No
4	Scotland	11	No
5	Malta	4	No
6	Estonia	1	No

Using data from the first qualification round in 1934 to 2014, I selected pairs of countries that were separated by no more than two points in the standings, provided that the winner scored at least five points. This procedure gave me a total of 142 countries that barely made or barely missed the World Cup. Various statistical tests confirm that these countries were balanced across a wide range of political, economic, and demographic factors, which supports the pretty close to random assumption or the idea that this data is comparable to experimental data. In short, the two groups looked similar except that the qualifiers went to the World Cup whereas the non-qualifiers did not.

Measuring Aggression

Before we can run the test, we need a reliable measure of state aggression. Fortunately, international relations scholars have constructed a dataset of cases where countries started military disputes against other nations.[63] This dataset is commonly used in security studies to investigate the causes of international conflict, since wars happen too infrequently to be a useful measure in most statistical tests.[64] The dataset has about 2,500 total military disputes over the period from 1816 to 2014. For the purposes of our analysis, we will focus just on the military disputes involving the countries that barely qualified and barely missed the World Cup.

FINDINGS

The results suggest that going to the World Cup increases aggression substantially. Figure 1.1 tracks the aggression levels of the qualifiers and non-qualifiers. Prior to qualification, the two groups had very similar records of aggression. However, the qualifiers experienced a large spike in aggression during the World Cup year. The difference in the aggression levels of the two groups is statistically significant, meaning that such a notable difference is very unlikely to have occurred by chance. In fact, if the World Cup had no effect on state aggression, the likelihood of seeing a divergence like the one in Figure 1.1 by chance is only about 1 in 150. To publish a finding, researchers typically just need to show that this number is less than 1 in 20, so the difference between the two groups is well past the normal threshold for statistical significance.

The effect wears off in the years following the tournament. This long-term effect may seem surprising. However, it is likely explained by the qualifiers starting many disputes around the time of the World Cup that made the

FIGURE 1.1. Comparing aggression before and after the World Cup for countries that barely qualified and barely missed qualification. Note the spike in aggression for qualifying nations in the time closest to qualifying and in the years immediately after the tournament.

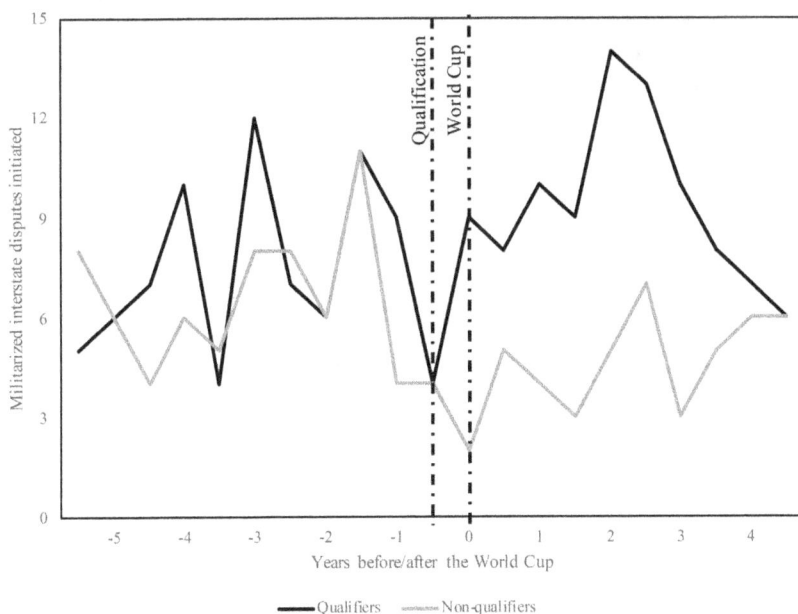

chances of future conflict more likely. Put simply, when a group of countries experiences a large spike in aggression, it should affect their aggression levels for several years, since some of the disputes that they start will likely lead to additional conflicts. Thus, this feedback mechanism could partly explain the longevity of the effect.

Not only did the qualifiers start more military disputes than the non-qualifiers, but they took more violent actions in their disputes. Twenty-nine of their disputes involved the use of military force, compared to just eight for the non-qualifiers. Similarly, the qualifiers started seven disputes that resulted in fatalities, whereas the non-qualifiers only started one. Further, 72 percent of the qualifiers' disputes were intended to revise the status quo (as coded in the Militarized Interstate Dispute dataset), compared to only about 53 percent for the non-qualifiers.

Notably, these results are entirely driven by countries where soccer is the most popular sport. In fact, countries where soccer is not the most popular sport—such as the United States, New Zealand, and Jamaica—experienced no change in aggression around the time of the World Cup. The fact that these countries seem immune to World Cup fervor points to an important caveat of this analysis: the results found here likely apply only in cases where countries take the international sporting event very seriously. This result also offers some assurance that the effect in Figure 1.1 is real. If the World Cup really does increase state aggression, we should expect it to do so for countries that care greatly about soccer.

Lastly, in the article that I published in 2017 presenting this data, I analyzed a case from the dataset that illustrates how nationalism from the World Cup can lead to a military dispute. In 2001, Senegal qualified for the World Cup for the first time in its history. The country's leader, President Abdoulaye Wade, was on a diplomatic trip to France at the time, but he cut short his visit so that he could return home and join in the celebrations. As he described, "[I]t's the most important thing that can happen to any country, and I will join the team and the nation in celebrating by reducing the amount of time I was expected to stay in Paris."[65]

When the World Cup started the following summer, Senegal did surprisingly well. It defeated its former colonizer France in the group stage. It then made it all the way to the quarterfinals, tying the record for the furthest that an African country had ever gone at the World Cup. The country was elated, and widespread celebrations and dancing broke out in the streets throughout Senegal. Meanwhile, the day before Senegal's final World Cup game, the Senegalese military started a military operation against a rebel group in the southwestern part of the country.[66] About fifteen days into this operation, the Senegalese military initiated a military dispute against Gambia, which it had previously accused of supporting the rebels.[67] This military dispute, which came roughly two weeks after Senegal's historic World Cup run, was the only military dispute that Senegal was involved in between 1993 and 2013.

One question that I have often been asked about these results is this: How can we conclude that the World Cup causes conflict when the United States, which cares little about soccer, engages in more military conflict than practically any other country? What must be remembered here is that many factors besides sports influence the likelihood that countries will take military action abroad, such as economic power, ideology, and alliance commitments. These other factors are what drive the United States to engage in military conflict, not soccer. What my results show is that going to the World Cup tends to make countries that really care about soccer more likely to start military disputes against other states.

OTHER NOTABLE SPORTS RIVALRIES

This tendency for sports to cause conflict between the opposing sides is nothing new. Rather, it stretches back much further in history. The earliest documented evidence that I have found goes back to the Roman empire. The most popular spectator sport was not gladiator fighting, as is commonly believed, but chariot racing.[68] The Romans staged about 1,500 chariot races per year in the Circus Maximus, a stadium that could hold around 200,000 people. Four main chariot factions competed in these races: the Reds, the Whites, the Blues, and the Greens. Each team had its own large contingent of supporters in the stands.

These chariot rivalries were intense. It was not uncommon for fans from one team to recite curses that called for the chariot drivers of other teams to crash and die.[69] At times, the emotions became so heated that they sparked violence, as seen in fan riots at chariot races in Alexandria.[70] This example demonstrates that as far back as the Romans, the passions evoked by sports were enough for spectators to wish serious bodily harm on their opponents.

Another case of serious rivalry in sports comes from Ivy League universities. When most Americans think of major college football universities in the

United States, they think of Alabama, Ohio State, and Clemson rather than Harvard, Yale, and Princeton. In the decades before World War I, however, it was these latter universities that developed American football and caused the United States to favor that sport rather than soccer. In particular, students at Harvard strongly resisted the soccer movement that gained ground in the northeastern United States in the 1870s, including at Yale, Princeton, and other major American colleges.[71] With the U.S.'s flagship university sticking with Britain's rugby version of football, other schools realized that they needed to field similar teams if they wanted to compete with Harvard. Thus, Harvard students put the United States on the path to become a football nation rather than a soccer country.

The term "Ivy League," now mainly known for its academic prestige, originated from the football competitions between elite northeastern American universities. These universities developed many of the early rules of football that distinguished the game from rugby, but they also had their own bitter rivalries. Controversies arose because of disputes over the rules, refereeing decisions, and disagreements about what constituted "fair play."[72] For instance, at a 1926 game, Harvard students distributed a satirical newspaper that falsely reported that Princeton's head coach, Bill Roper, had died. Roper had a history of serious illness, so this attempt at a joke was not taken lightly by the Princeton side. Princeton won the game and then severed all its athletic relations with Harvard. The two football teams would not play for the next seven football seasons. The scholar Mark Bernstein describes, "Harvard and Princeton have twice severed relations over football, while lesser disputes have soured relations between Brown and Dartmouth, Yale and Columbia."[73]

Another particularly notable example occurred outside the Ivy League, at a game between West Point and the U.S. Naval Academy in 1893. During the game, a dispute between an Army brigadier general and a Navy rear admiral became so heated that the two military officers challenged each other to a duel.[74] The annual rivalry game between the two academies was subsequently banned by President Grover Cleveland and did not resume until 1899.[75]

Youth sports also have the power to generate rivalries, so much so that they have played a prominent role in the development of an important branch of psychology called realistic conflict theory. This research program began in the 1940s with the psychologist Muzafer Sherif.[76] In one famous study, Sherif and his colleagues had two teams of eleven-year-old boys compete in various contests for about a week, including baseball, football, and tug-of-war.[77] The boys did not know one another before the games started, except for meeting their own teammates and engaging in cooperative activities about a week before the competitions began. After the contests concluded, the boys viewed their teammates favorably while harboring aggressive feelings toward the members of the rival team. These biases were enduring and only dissipated after the entire group engaged in team-building exercises. This context is slightly different because it focuses on people who themselves participated in sports instead of fans. Nonetheless, it attests to the power of sports to cause division between the opposing sides.

ARE THERE EXCEPTIONS?

An important point to note is that the statistical analysis done in this chapter examines the *average* effect of going to the World Cup on state aggression. However, not all countries respond to international sports in the same way. As mentioned earlier, some countries do not care that much about soccer, and we see no effect in the data for those countries. At the same time, there are some countries where soccer is very popular, but their sports culture makes international games lighthearted fun rather than intense competition. A classic example is Iceland, whose fans try to use international soccer games to show off their country's friendliness and cooperative nature.

In an insightful 2022 book called *Nationalisms in International Politics*, Dartmouth political scientist Kathleen Powers explains that there is not just one type of nationalism.[78] In some cases, nationalism can be rooted in equality and respect for other nations rather than chauvinism. This type of nationalism can actually promote international cooperation rather than conflict. Even within a given country, nationalism can mean different things to different people. In such cases, international sports could affect different individuals within the same country in contrasting ways. Therefore, it is important to remember that the findings discussed in this chapter do not hold all the time. Frequently throughout this book, we are looking at broad trends across many actors, and when it comes to human behavior there are almost always exceptions to any tendency.

POLICY IMPLICATIONS

There are several policy implications that follow from these findings. First, we should stop confusing the most powerful international sports organizations with humanitarian actors and movements that really do make the world more peaceful. In a 2011 article, "The Myth of Sport as a Peace-Promoting Political Force," historian John Hoberman argues that FIFA and the IOC differ greatly from organizations like Amnesty International and the Red Cross. As Hoberman puts it, "neither the IOC nor FIFA have met the minimum ethical and humanitarian standards required for international organizations to have credible peace-promoting effects."[79]

Rather, organizations that stage high-profile sports competitions between nations create what Orwell aptly described as "war minus the shooting."[80] In fact, the historian Barbara Keys suggests that the obvious connections between international sports and war could explain, from a sociological perspective, the origins of the dubious claim that international sports actually encourage world peace. As Keys puts it:

> Because [sport] showcased physical prowess at a time when military power depended on the health and fitness of human bodies, sport was intertwined with militarism from the earliest days of international sports competitions. The promise of peaceful outcomes sublimate and distract from sports ties to war. It might even be said that the close relationship of international sport and war makes claims of peace necessary to legitimize sport as entertainment.[81]

Second, international sports organizations could try to revise their rules so that their competitions would be less likely to generate nationalistic animosities. For instance, FIFA currently uses goal differential as a tiebreaker in many situations, like when two countries are tied in the standings in the World Cup group stage. The problem with this approach is that it often incentivizes countries to trounce their opponents as much as possible. For instance, a country would be better positioned if it won its first group stage game 6–0 as opposed to 3–0. Moreover, there are often massive disparities between competing countries in terms of population and economic resources. It is therefore common, for instance, for a much larger country to humiliate a smaller country. The rules in fact incentivize running up the score. FIFA could fix this issue by modifying the tiebreaking criteria. For instance, instead of looking at goal differential, FIFA could keep track of the amount of time a country was winning by at least one (or two) goals and use that as the tiebreaker. If such a rule was employed, countries would be incentivized to score quickly early in the game and then play conservatively rather than running up the score on weaker opponents.

Another commonsense reform would be to stop trying to reduce tensions between rival countries by arranging games where the two sides play each other head-to-head. These competitions could worsen the underlying political disputes and possibly even lead to violence. Exceptions could be made, of course, for sports that the two sides do not take seriously, since such sports are far less likely to incite nationalistic antagonisms.

International sports organizations could also revise their rules so that countries with any realistic chance of military conflict would be less likely to play against each other. For instance, they could try to decrease the chances that countries like China and Japan, Serbia and Albania, and Turkey and Greece compete head-to-head. Ideally, the countries most likely to play each other would be geographically far apart and unlikely to have any political conflicts.

An ambitious version of this approach would be to revise the major international sports leagues so that countries do not play their neighbors on a regular basis. Soccer seems like the key arena in which to do this, since it is the most popular sport in the world by far. Currently, the international soccer leagues are based on continents, like UEFA (Europe) and CAF (Africa). A different option would be to have two global parallel divisions with three leagues each: one for the best teams in the world, one for the middle-tier teams, and one for the least competitive teams. Countries could move up or down in the leagues based on their performance. With two divisions, policymakers could try to prevent major political rivals from playing in the same league at once. This format could help reduce the chances of conflicts like the Soccer War. It would also lead to better matchups, since the teams playing against each other would be of more comparable skill. One downside would be the additional travel, so this possible reform might require advances in cheaper and cleaner transportation options.

Another option would be to merge countries at sporting events so that they compete as groups of exceptional athletes rather than as representatives of opposing countries. This practice of integrating players from different countries is already present in many domestic sports leagues, such as the National Basketball Association and the National Football League. The social scientists

Andrei Markovits and Lars Rensmann argue that such integration can promote cultural respect and understanding, especially when fans admire players from other countries.[82]

In fact, this strategy has been employed in the programs FIFA sponsors to
decrease animosity between Israeli and Palestinian children. The players are
split up so that each team consists of children from both national groups.[83]
This practice seems to suggest that FIFA recognizes that having a team of Israeli children play against a team of Palestinian children would likely make
the two sides dislike each other more. However, FIFA regularly pits national
teams against each other on the international stage and suggests that doing
so will encourage feelings of goodwill, and this idea is accepted by many politicians, media personalities, and even academics. Historical examples, statistical analysis, and basic common sense all point in the opposite direction:
head-to-head competition tends to make the opposing sides dislike each other
more.

CONCLUSION

This link between international sports, nationalism, and conflict contrasts
sharply with both the bread and circuses theory and the gospel of sports. Athletic competitions between countries are neither a mere distraction from politics nor an unproblematic force for good in the world. Further, the findings in
this chapter highlight the importance of utilizing the tools of social science to
better understand how sports influence modern societies. Doing so is necessary if we hope to grasp the social and political effects of sports and how we
might improve their impact on the world.

One question that arises is whether one could apply the regression discontinuity approach used in this chapter to another international sporting event.
Unfortunately, the Olympics do not have a qualification process like the one
used for the World Cup. However, some regional soccer tournaments like the
European Football Championship and the African Cup of Nations do have similar qualification processes. When I tested how these competitions affect state
aggression, I found similar results to the ones presented in this chapter. The
sample size is smaller—there were only seventy-eight countries that barely
made or barely missed their regional soccer tournaments. However, it does
appear that these international sporting events caused the qualifiers to ex-

perience higher levels of military aggression compared to the non-qualifiers, similar to what we saw for the World Cup.

Lastly, one major limitation of the analysis in this chapter is that it focuses on conflicts between countries, and international sports may have an entirely different effect at the domestic level. That is, they might encourage unity within countries while simultaneously fueling international rivalries. If so, then international sports might provide benefits at the domestic level that outweigh the negative impact that they have on international relations.

However, do sports really unite countries internally? Further, is national unity, particularly when it is caused by nationalism from sporting events, really something desirable, even when it does not lead to interstate conflict?

2

INTERNATIONAL SPORTS
AND NATIONAL UNITY

Do international sports encourage unity within countries? Numerous examples suggest that they can: the "Miracle on Ice" in 1980, the Rugby World Cup in South Africa in 1995, and the Ivory Coast's qualification for the 2006 World Cup, which some people credit as having helped end the First Ivorian Civil War.[1] On the other hand, the power of sports to bring people together within countries might be greatly overstated. In fact, emotions from international sporting events might cause divisions within countries rather than creating unity.

Various factors might impact how sports affect countries internally. For example, whether the country performs well or poorly could matter greatly for the likelihood that an international sporting event will increase national unity. It also depends on the subnational groups in question. At the international level, the major actors are countries, which is why we focused on international conflict in Chapter 1. However, there are several different actors to look at when thinking about national unity.

In fact, we could think about national unity on three different levels. First, we could consider how individual citizens within a country treat one another. A country with high rates of crime and violence among its citizens would qualify as internally divided along this dimension. In contrast, a country with low crime rates and few cases of interpersonal violence would count as united.

Second, we could examine the relationship between citizens and their governments. A country can be thought of as more unified when its political leaders enjoy high approval ratings and fewer anti-government protests. Third, we could look at relations among the different ethnic, religious, and ideological groups within a country. Even if a country's leaders are popular, it could still be internally divided if its subnational factions harbor resentment toward one another.

RELATIONS BETWEEN INDIVIDUALS

When it comes to this first dimension of national unity—relations between individuals—international sports often make people feel closer to their fellow citizens through the shared experience of rooting for their nation.[2] Spectators usually watch games together, and the thrill of an exciting win can cause many of them to high five or hug complete strangers.[3] Even a loss is a loss experienced together.[4] As the scholars Andrei Markovits and Emily Albertson explain, "Sports fandom has been a remarkable vehicle for including the most varied and disparate social groups into a common whole . . . . [B]y dint of their inclusiveness and ubiquity, sports have created ties across class, ethnic, regional, cultural, religious, and age lines that few, if any, other forces could even approximate."[5] Even for women who tend to follow sports less closely, Markovits and Albertson find that many who are not avid fans still view important sporting events as valuable opportunities for social gathering.[6]

Importantly, Markovits and Albertson highlight that major international sporting events capture public attention in ways that few domestic sporting events can match. As they put it, the power of nationalism "transforms every sport's existence and augments its value beyond any other measure and imagination."[7] Markovits and Albertson explain that during the Olympics, "millions of viewers are captivated by sports and athletes about which they have no clue but for whom they develop emotional affinities and allegiances, solely based on the shared commonalities of their passports."[8]

This sense of community that comes from the shared experience of watching major international sporting events provides tremendous benefits, which are perhaps most dramatically captured in data on suicide rates. In his seminal 1897 study on why people attempt suicide, the sociologist Émile Durkheim discovered that social isolation can be a central motivating force.[9] This finding suggests that people might be less likely to commit suicide when they feel more connected to their communities. The reporter Simon Kuper and economist Stefan Szymanski tested this theory in the context of international sports, with the help of Greek epidemiologists Eleni Petridou and Fotis Papadopoulos. Their research was partly motivated by the fact that some people mention the failures of their sports teams in their suicide letters, raising speculation that major sporting events might actually increase suicides.[10]

However, the researchers found exactly the opposite. They looked at suicide rates in twelve countries during summers when European national teams were playing in major international soccer tournaments. They found that the typical international soccer tournament during their study period appeared to "have helped save several hundred Europeans from suicide."[11] Interestingly, the effect appeared to apply to both men and women, and whether a country won or lost did not seem to have much of an impact on suicide rates.[12] Their finding also has analogs in the U.S. context, like the tendency for suicide rates to be lower on Super Bowl Sundays compared to other Sundays.[13] It also accords with the tendency of countries to experience drops in suicide when they go to war.[14]

While international sports create a sense of shared community amongst fans, they can also undermine national unity by increasing tensions between people. One of the main reasons is that spectator sports tend to cause increased alcohol consumption, which can have many unintended negative consequences.[15] Historically, alcohol has been an important part of sports.[16] As recently as the early 1900s, alcohol was actually considered to be a healthful sports drink that improved athletic performance.[17] Fortunately, sports professionals now understand the myriad of adverse health consequences that alcohol can cause, ranging from depression of the nervous system to dehydration.[18] As such, alcohol is typically no longer considered a performance booster. Nevertheless, it remains a major part of the spectator experience.

Much research shows that sports increase drinking rates among spectators.[19] This link between sports and alcohol may not be surprising given the extent to which beer companies target the sports market. Further, experimental research has shown that exposure to beer advertisements during sports games can lead people to have more favorable attitudes toward alcohol.[20] This present-day link between sports and alcohol is particularly ironic given that people tend to associate sports and athleticism with health and fitness, whereas alcohol has many known health repercussions.[21]

Building on the connection between sports and alcohol consumption, research suggests that sporting events can lead to increased assault rates. This pattern seems to hold true for the World Cup,[22] NCAA football games,[23] NHL games,[24] and MLB games.[25] In general, the research suggests that larger sporting events like World Cup games can more than double assault rates, whereas smaller sporting events like college football home games appear to typically increase assault rates by about 10 percent.[26] Increased alcohol consumption likely explains much of this effect.[27] However, other factors like emotional stress from watching sports and fans congregating to watch games could play an important role.[28]

Relatedly, sporting events also frequently appear to cause spikes in domestic violence. Numerous studies confirm this link.[29] The disturbing finding shows up time and again, including for every World Cup from 2006 to 2018. While research from NFL games suggests that increases in domestic violence are only associated with upset losses, research on the World Cup has found spikes in domestic violence after both wins and losses.[30]

Therefore, international sports appear to cause disunity when it comes to assaults and domestic violence. Although rooting for the national team can make many fans feel more connected to their communities, the research suggests that violence between individuals actually goes up, particularly for important international soccer games. This finding is tragic, but it is important to recognize if we want to understand sports on a deeper level.

GOVERNMENT POPULARITY

Research on how sporting events influence government approval ratings suggests that sports can affect citizens' attitudes about their leaders in two primary ways. First, sports outcomes can impact citizens' general levels of happiness, which can indirectly improve their attitudes toward their current leaders.[31] Strangely, people's emotions from sports often subconsciously influence their beliefs and attitudes in other areas of life. Thus, wins in sports can cause them to feel that times are good, which can then make them more supportive of their current leaders. Losses, meanwhile, seem to do the opposite, causing people to perceive that times are bad and transferring those feelings onto their leaders. Second, international sports victories can affect people's views of their leaders more directly by making them feel more closely tied to their nations, especially after wins.

General Happiness and Leader Approval

The first statistical study on how sporting events affect government approval was conducted at Stanford by the social scientists Andrew Healy, Neil Malhotra, and Cecilia Mo.[32] These researchers looked at how the performance of college football teams in the United States prior to elections affected the likelihood that voters would choose to keep their current politicians in office. The researchers suspected that a recent victory on the football field would make voters more likely to favorably perceive the current situation in their city or town, increasing the chances that they would vote for their current politician. In contrast, a recent loss might make them perceive times as bad, giving them more reason to vote for change.[33]

These researchers obtained some striking results. They found that when local football teams won about ten days before an election, it increased votes for incumbent politicians by about 1.5 percentage points on average.[34] This boost was about 3.4 percentage points in counties where football games had high attendance rates.[35] In other words, in a county where the football stadium is usually filled, an incumbent politician who received 48 percent of the vote after the local football team lost probably would have received about 51.4 percent of the vote had they won. The reason the game ten days before the election matters is that many undecided voters decide whom they will vote for about a week before the election, so the emotions from a win or loss ten days before are likely to have a meaningful impact on their voting choice.

Exploring this effect further, Healy, Malhotra, and Mo examined how March Madness games from the 2009 NCAA Tournament affected presidential approval ratings. Focusing specifically on Sweet Sixteen, Elite Eight, and Final Four games, they found that each win that a team achieved (above that team's expected number of wins) increased Barack Obama's approval rating by an average of about 2.3 percentage points in the area where the college team was from.[36] For intense fans, the estimated effect registered at about 5.0 percentage points, whereas it was only about 1.1 percentage points for less passionate fans.[37]

Northwestern political scientists Ethan Busby, James Druckman, and Alexandra Fredendall found a similar result for the 2015 College Football Playoff National Championship game.[38] The game ended with Ohio State defeating Oregon by a score of 42–20. The researchers found that the game caused a major spike in presidential approval ratings among Ohio State students and a major drop among Oregon students. Specifically, Obama's job performance ratings increased for the Ohio State students from 4.18 to 4.63 out of 7 (or roughly from 60 to 66 out of 100), and they went down for Oregon students from 4.56 to 4.12 out of 7 (or roughly 65 to 59 out of 100).[39] This study contributed to previous research by confirming that an important sports victory can increase feelings of goodwill between citizens and their political leaders whereas a major loss can have the opposite effect.

The upshot of this research is that victories in sports can impact how citizens feel about their leaders, even when those leaders play no role in the sports competition. After all, Obama did not help Ohio State win the 2015 national championship, but he still became more popular among Ohio State fans and experienced a drop in approval ratings among Oregon fans. When victories make sports fans excited or defeats make them depressed, these emotions get tangled up with the fans' feelings about life in general. Thus, sports can affect people's attitudes toward politics in a surprising, indirect way.

Another study published in 2023 supported this finding in the African context.[40] In Africa, major European soccer club teams like Arsenal and Liverpool have attracted large fan bases that often surpass the popularity of local teams. Rather than showing up to the stadium to cheer for the local team, many African soccer fans now prefer to go to cinemas and watch the European teams play.[41] Researchers Kyosuke Kikuta and Mamoru Uesugi conducted a study looking at 15,102 close soccer games from 2005 to 2019.[42] They found that losses of European club teams with African players increased peaceful political protests and lowered leader trust and approval ratings in the African players' home countries.[43]

Substantively, the study found that a close loss tended to roughly double the number of peaceful protests in the country in the following one to three days while decreasing leader trust and approval ratings by about 23 percent.[44] There was no detectable increase in leader approval ratings following close wins, but there was an increase in peaceful political protests, similar to what the researchers observed following a close loss.[45] Therefore, politicians in Africa appear to suffer when players from their countries on popular European teams lose, but they do not gain much when these players win.

What about other sports contexts? In the spring of 2024, I suggested to an IE University student named Jason Massouh, who was looking for a topic for his senior thesis, that he test how American professional sports championships affect U.S. presidential voting. A few weeks later, he came back to me with results that were truly remarkable. I have since redone and expanded the analysis, and I will offer my own take on the data here. I will start with the World Series, which begins in October every year and, in presidential election years, usually ends about a week or two before Election Day in early November.

We can look at how who won the World Series affected the vote share for presidential candidates who were either incumbents or who came from the same party as the incumbent (like John McCain in 2008 when George W. Bush was in the White House). Relative to their parties' performance in the previous presidential election, these candidates performed about 2 percentage points better in states that had won the World Series compared to states that came in second place (1976–2024).[46] This difference is statistically significant and very close to the estimate found by Healy, Malhotra, and Mo about college football games. Note that in this analysis, I chose to start at 1976 for two reasons: first, George Wallace ran as a third-party candidate in 1968 and received significant support in southern states, which muddled the sample data for both 1968 and 1972 (since 1972 uses 1968 as its baseline); second, by 1976, it was much easier for fans to watch the World Series on television.

If we look at the Super Bowl, the results are even more surprising. Although it is played about nine months before the U.S. presidential election, candidates whose party controlled the White House did about 3 percentage points better in states that won the Super Bowl compared to states that came in second place (again relative to their parties' performance in the previous presidential election). The results here are again statistically significant. This larger estimated effect may be explained by football being the most popular sport in the United States going back to at least 1972, and possibly earlier.[47] Therefore, winning the Super Bowl likely has a lasting impact on some fans' happiness that still impacts their decision-making about nine months after their team brings home the Lombardi Trophy.

Given these results, it is natural to wonder if there was ever a sports outcome that might have influenced who won a U.S. presidential election and thereby changed the course of history. In 2000, Vice President Al Gore ran against the challenger George W. Bush in an extremely tight election. The final electoral count vote was 271–266. In the Super Bowl that year, the St. Louis Rams defeated the Tennessee Titans in a close game that ended with a Titans' wide receiver being tackled on the Rams' one-yard line, preventing a potential game-tying score. If Tennessee had won the game and Gore had subsequently done about 2.25 percentage points better in his home state of Tennessee, then he could have won the election instead of George W. Bush.

Alternatively, we can look at the state of Florida, where Bush's margin of victory was razor-thin (0.01 percentage points). Although the Miami Dolphins, Jacksonville Jaguars, and Tampa Bay Buccaneers all won their games about a week before the election, the three teams all lost their prior games that were played fifteen to nineteen days before the election. Given that some voters in Florida likely decided who they would vote for about two weeks before the election (in the wake of these defeats), Gore might have won in Florida and subsequently become president if any of the three Florida NFL teams had won. It is worth wondering how different history would have been if Gore had become president instead of Bush, and in particular if the 2003 invasion of Iraq would have occurred under his leadership.

International Sports and Leader Approval

When it comes to international sports, we should expect games to exert an even greater influence on leader approval ratings because in many countries people draw a clear link between high-ranking politicians and their national sports teams. In other words, fans should be more likely to associate the success of their national teams as a sign that their governments are working well, while viewing struggles in international sports as an indicator of poor government performance.

In a widely publicized paper published in 2020, economists Emilio Depetris-Chauvin, Ruben Durante, and Filipe Campante tested how national team victories affected government popularity in sub-Saharan Africa. The researchers found that countries that barely qualified for the African Cup of Nations had 8.6 percent fewer cases of civil unrest in the following six months compared to countries that barely missed qualification (1997–2015).[48] In contrast to the study about Africa and European soccer, this finding suggests that politicians in Africa may receive a benefit from having their national teams qualify for the African Cup of Nations. However, the researchers did not find much evidence that victories in international soccer increase leader approval ratings. At most, the survey data that the researchers examined suggest that if there is a boost from a typical victory on the soccer field, it is probably not much more than 5 percentage points.[49]

Building on these results, we can test how the countries that barely qualified and barely missed the World Cup (examined in Chapter 1) compared in terms of cases of civil unrest. This test allows us to expand beyond sub-Saharan Africa, because about 90 percent of the 142 countries in the study from Chapter 1 come from outside sub-Saharan Africa. I repeat the same test we did before, except this time looking at a measure of the number of incidents of civil unrest per capita in each country rather than military disputes.[50]

Figure 2.1 presents the results from this analysis. As the figure shows, the qualifiers experienced about a 19 percent drop in their per capita cases of civil unrest, whereas the non-qualifiers experienced about a 19 percent increase. This difference is statistically significant, so it is very unlikely to have occurred by chance. Further, the gap was slightly larger for countries where soccer was the most popular sport. Importantly, the database of cases of civil unrest that I am using here includes a wide range of conflict events, not just anti-government protests.

In short, success in international sports has the potential to increase government popularity and decrease incidents of civil unrest. However, the opposite might be true when national teams come up short on the international stage.

FIGURE 2.1. Effect of the World Cup on cases of civil unrest for countries that barely qualified and barely missed qualification. The data show a statistically significant difference in the incidents of civil unrest. This difference is more pronounced when we focus on countries where soccer is the most popular sport.

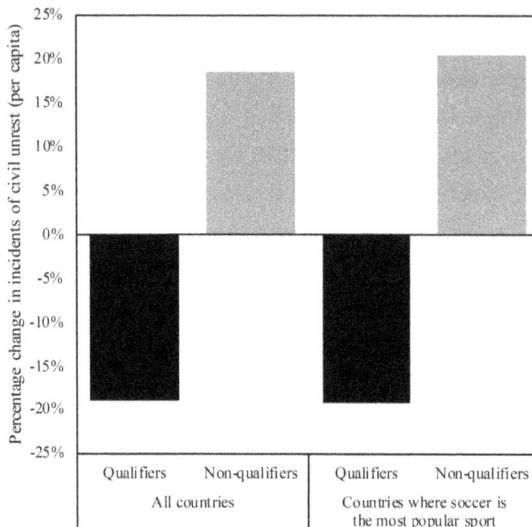

SUBNATIONAL FACTIONS

Two major quantitative studies have examined how international sports impact relations among different ethnic groups within a country. The first was the famous study from economics that looked at the African Cup of Nations and civil unrest. The authors of that study also examined survey data from the Afrobarometer project, which regularly asks African residents a wide range of questions about their beliefs and attitudes. The authors found that in the days following national team victories, people were about 30 percent more likely to trust other ethnicities (2002–2015).[51] In addition, barely qualifying for the African Cup of Nations reduced civil conflict related to ethnicity in the following six months (1997–2015).[52]

The second study was carried out by political scientists Leah R. Rosenzweig and Yang-Yang Zhou. These researchers looked at a single 2019 African Cup soccer game between Kenya and Tanzania and focused on a short two-week time period after the game. They found that winning (compared to losing) strengthened bonds between co-nationals.[53] They also found that the game improved respondents' attitudes toward refugees when the victory was framed as the result of cooperation amongst a diverse group of players.[54]

These studies provide evidence that success in international sports can reduce ethnic divisions within countries, as many proponents of international sports claim. Unfortunately, though, the duration of the effect appears to be quite short. Depetris-Chauvin, Durante, and Campante estimate that the long-term effect of qualifying for the tournament decreased the intensity of ethnic conflict only by about 3 percent. Therefore, the quantitative research suggests that sports success can bring ethnic groups within a country together in the short run but not necessarily in the long run.[55]

What can we learn from looking at the main cases from history where international sports supposedly helped unify competing subnational factions? Proponents of international sports frequently point to three examples: South Africa, the Ivory Coast, and Yemen. The case that is probably most often brought up is Nelson Mandela's use of the national rugby team to unite South Africa in 1995.[56] Up until the early 1990s, the country had been racially segregated, much like the United States before the civil rights movement. Ongoing racial tensions threatened to plunge South Africa into a civil war. In this heated political environment, South Africa was scheduled to host the 1995 Rugby World Cup.

Fears arose that the tournament could make the situation worse, because rugby was an almost exclusively White sport in South Africa. However, the country's first Black president, Nelson Mandela, used this sporting event to bring the country together. Under his leadership, the entire team was required to learn all the words to the country's new national anthem. The government also publicized the message that the players wanted to support the Black community and found a Black rugby player to join the otherwise all-White team.[57] After the team won the tournament, Mandela presented the trophy to the team's captain, Francois Pienaar, in one of the most famous moments in the country's history. It signified that the victory was an achievement for all of South Africa.

While this example does seem to show that international sports can unite different ethnic groups within a country, there are several reasons to be hesitant about drawing lessons from this specific case. First, South Africa was in a unique political situation in the mid-1990s.[58] The country had only recently been welcomed back into the international system after decades of isolation caused by its government's racist policies. South Africa was no longer a pariah in the international community. The public needed a national celebration.[59]

Second, the new government leaders were trying to win over domestic and foreign backers and needed to ensure that they conveyed a strong sense of national unity during the tournament. Therefore, they had good reason to brush grievances aside for the moment and make the situation in South Africa look as good as possible. As historian Albert Grundlingh explains:

> [The government leaders had] just moved into office and still had to demonstrate that they had effectively made the transition from a liberation movement to a responsible government committed to order and reconciliation. . . . At the time of the World Cup then, there was every reason for the [government] to conduct itself in an exemplary fashion.[60]

Illustrating this point, the South African minister for sport stressed that the Rugby World Cup offered "a wonderful opportunity and also sets a considerable test. If we pass this test, there could be important benefits for our country and people as a whole."[61]

Third, the unity created by the event was short-lived. The political and economic disparities between racial groups continued to cause resentment and conflict. Some members of the rugby team also lost face among the country's Black population soon after the tournament because they appeared less interested in bridging the divide than the government had made it seem. As South African social scientists Lynette Steenveld and Larry Strelitz explain, the national unity on display at the 1995 Rugby World Cup "was a temporary phenomenon and in no way laid the foundation—as the media and the government politicians would have us believe—for the creation of a collective self-identity."[62] As Christopher Hitchens put it, "no clear-eyed observer of the South African scene thinks that the *Invictus* moment was any more than a brief pause in the steady decline of friendship between the country's ethnic groups."[63]

Another much-publicized example is the Ivory Coast's qualification for the 2006 World Cup. The country had been fighting a civil war since 2002 between the Muslims in the north and the Christians in the south. However, the successful run of the soccer team brought the country together. The players took on a very active role in facilitating peace, especially their star player Didier Drogba. Diplomat Kari Jaksa explains:

> Following the match, as Ivoirian soccer fans danced and celebrated throughout the nation, Drogba, via a live television feed, beseeched his countrymen to lay down their arms and work toward peace. The warring factions heeded his plea, initiating a peace process that culminated in the 2007 Ouagadougou Accords and a tenuous coalition between the opposing groups.[64]

However, the power of international sports to promote domestic unity again proved limited. The elections were delayed six times, eventually taking place in 2010. The candidate from the predominantly Muslim north won, but the southern Christian regions refused to accept this outcome. They accused the North of election fraud and inaugurated the candidate from the South instead. This move reignited the civil war in 2011. The peace brought about by the national soccer team therefore proved to be unsustainable.

International sports are also credited with playing a key role in the unification of North and South Yemen in 1990. The two regions had major economic and ideological differences that made it difficult for them to come together as one country.[65] However, the government leaders saw the national soccer team as a key vehicle to encourage a united Yemeni identity. They chose players so that the North and South were equally represented, and they appointed one assistant coach from each state (along with a Brazilian head coach). During the games, the team captaincy alternated between northern and southern players.[66]

Much like in the cases of South Africa and the Ivory Coast, however, the ability of international sports to strengthen national unity was limited at best. Tensions between the North and South persisted through the early 1990s. In 1994, the country descended into a civil war. Although the nation held together, the divisions that led to this conflict did not go away. In fact, ongoing disputes between the northern and southern regions played a central role in reigniting a civil war in Yemen in 2015.

The main reason that international sports typically fail to create long-term domestic peace between competing subnational factions may be that they merely lead to *feelings* of national unity without resolving the complicated political problems that underlie the conflict. In post-apartheid South Africa, questions remained about how much power and wealth Whites would give up to the historically marginalized and repressed Black population. The 1995 Rugby World Cup temporarily brought the country together, but it provided no answer to that question. The story was very similar in the Ivory Coast. The national soccer team helped unify a country that was weary of civil war, but it provided no solution to the power-sharing disagreement between the Muslims in the North and the Christians in the South. In Yemen, international sports also proved incapable of resolving the country's complex political problems. Sports encouraged a new Yemeni identity, but they fell far short of creating a lasting peace.

THE OTHER SIDE OF NATIONAL UNITY

In 2013, British Prime Minister David Cameron agreed that, if re-elected, he would hold a referendum on his country's membership in the European Union before the end of 2017. Although he opposed the idea of Britain leaving the EU (along with most other British politicians), his government held the referendum on June 23, 2016. The electorate narrowly voted to leave (51.89%) over remain (48.11%), triggering Brexit and prompting Prime Minister Cameron to resign. The outcome, which surprised many, reshaped Europe both politically and economically. It plunged the continent into a series of controversial economic negotiations in the following years and raised concerning questions about the future of both Britain and the EU.

What does Brexit have to do with international sports, and specifically their relationship to national unity? In what might have amounted to a historic mistake, the British government scheduled the Brexit referendum during the 2016 UEFA European Championship (Euro), which ran from June 10 to July 10. The day before the Brexit vote, I published an article in the *Washington Post* arguing that the timing of the referendum made little sense.[67] Given that Prime Minister Cameron and most other British politicians hoped that voters would choose to remain, why would they hold the vote during the Euro? Many voters would be feeling more nationalistic than usual, and they were in large part choosing between their national and European identities.

Since we are focusing on one specific case here, it is hard to conclude how much the Euro really may have affected voting in the Brexit referendum. In particular, it is probably impossible to know with certainty that it had a decisive impact in swinging the narrow referendum outcome. That being said, this case provides a cautionary tale in two respects. First, it reminds us that even when international sports increase national unity, in doing so they can deepen divisions at the international level. Second, it underscores the importance of thinking carefully about the social and political consequences of sports. When people dismiss sports as a mere distraction from politics, as Prime Minister Cameron may have done in this case, they run the risk of being blindsided by the powerful and surprising effects that sports sometimes bring.

CONCLUSION

"Sport has the power to change the world," Nelson Mandela famously claimed in 2000.[68] "It has the power to inspire, it has the power to unite people in a way that little else does. . . . It is more powerful than governments in breaking down racial barriers. It laughs in the face of all types of discrimination."[69] Mandela was certainly right that sports can change the world, but unfortunately they often do so for the worse. In the last chapter, we saw that international sports can spark conflict, even war. In this chapter, we have seen that in some ways sports can increase national unity, but the story can be quite complicated. The outcome of the sporting event can matter greatly, as can what we mean by the term "national unity."

It is particularly unfortunate that winning seems to play such an important role in determining how much national unity an international sporting event can build. Sporting events tend to create more losers than winners. Of course, success is always relative. For some countries, making it to the knockout stage at the World Cup might be viewed as a great achievement. However, for many others, anything short of first place is a disappointment. This attitude may lead to only a very small number of countries enjoying a unifying effect from major sporting events.

Nonetheless, many important lessons can be taken away from the findings discussed in this chapter. Hospitals and women's shelters could be better prepared on the nights of important sports competitions, even if the sporting event is taking place in a different city. In addition, major sports organizations could try to sever the strong link between alcohol and sports, possibly looking for a healthier alternative beverage that fans could enjoy. Furthermore, during and after major international competitions, the diversity of successful teams could be highlighted and framed in such a way as to encourage fan appreciation of athletes from different backgrounds. Even though the relationship between international sports and national unity is complex, there are some straightforward ways that the potential for sports to bring people together might be improved.

Importantly, in this chapter we have largely focused on the unintended consequences of sports. However, sometimes politicians deliberately use sports for political purposes, including nefarious ones. When malign actors actually try to bring about bad outcomes, the impact of international sports can be far worse, and often in unexpected ways.

3

DICTATORS AND SPORTS

Imagine that humanity could choose one person to be our galactic ambassador and visit alien civilizations in our galaxy and beyond. Suppose that we could even bring someone back from the dead for this important mission. Who would we choose? Plato or Aristotle perhaps? Or how about Isaac Newton or Albert Einstein? Or Shakespeare or Jane Austen? Winston Churchill?

Surprisingly, this decision has already been made, and it happened about ninety years ago. When television broadcasting was first invented, it gave humans the ability to transmit television signals to nearby cities. Eventually, these signals became strong enough that they could escape Earth's atmosphere. This meant that they could go out into space. With little in outer space to stop them, any radio or television transmissions that escaped Earth's atmosphere traveled through our galaxy at the speed of light.

This means that any alien civilizations that have the technology to pick up our radio and television transmissions can watch and listen to what we broadcast. Disconcerting as it may be, somewhere out there aliens might be watching the Super Bowl, our political shows, and our children's cartoons. Further, the very first television broadcast that was strong enough to reach outer space would likely be the very first time that such alien civilizations ever saw human beings. It would be their first glimpse at who we are and what our species is like.

So who ended up being our galactic ambassador? The answer involves the Olympics. In fact, it involves the 1936 Berlin Olympics. Now commonly known as the Nazi Olympics, Adolf Hitler and his regime turned the Games into a huge publicity stunt. They began with the world's first-ever television broadcast that was powerful enough to reach outer space.[1] The broadcast featured Hitler announcing that the Games were officially open. This phantom transmission of Hitler is still traveling across the Milky Way Galaxy at about 186,000 miles per second, and it will continue to do so for roughly the next 75,000 years.[2]

The fact that the first television transmission that we sent into outer space included the opening ceremony of the Olympics exemplifies the importance of sports to humanity, including world leaders and dictators in particular. In fact, Hitler stands out as one of the greatest proponents of the Olympic Games. Under his leadership, iconic Olympic traditions like the torch relay were started, as we will discuss later in this chapter.[3] He was also the first person to have ever opened two Olympic Games, as his country hosted both the Winter and Summer Olympics in 1936.

Hitler's fascination with the Olympics also reflects a broad pattern in world politics: that dictators tend to care much more about international sporting events than democratic leaders.[4] Mussolini, Stalin, and Kim Jong Un are other famous examples of dictators truly taking sports seriously. Dictators also have a history of doping their athletes, intervening to sway the outcomes of important contests, and torturing athletes for poor performances.[5]

What is it about international sports that interests dictators so much? The answer can be found by examining history.

BEFORE WORLD WAR II

In the 1920s, dictators in Europe realized that sports could serve as a valuable tool for advancing their political ambitions. This movement was spearheaded by Joseph Stalin. Stalin's perspective was somewhat narrow.[6] He primarily saw sports as a way to prepare the Soviet population for war by making Soviet citizens stronger and healthier.[7] No doubt, the idea of using sports as preparation for war was nothing new. The ancient Egyptians and Greeks, imperial Romans, and Native Americans used sports to prepare their men for battle.[8] So did democracies prior to World War I. A common saying in Britain, going back as far as 1855, was that "the battle of Waterloo was won on the playing fields of Eton."[9] Similarly, the U.S. military used baseball to train soldiers, and many Americans believed that football prepared young men for war by making them tougher and braver.[10] In a centralized state with a dictator like Stalin, however, the use of sports was taken to an entirely different level.[11]

Given his goals, Stalin's vision was centered around mass sports rather than elite sports.[12] In fact, from his perspective, the elite sports model could be detrimental because it could lead to spectators becoming less fit. While elite sports did gain a foothold in the Soviet Union, Stalin did little to promote them. Likewise, to Stalin, major international sporting events like the World Cup and the Olympics were essentially pointless, and he showed very little interest in these competitions during most of his rule.[13] Therefore, the Soviet approach to sport was relatively isolationist compared to most other countries, and it would remain so until the 1950s.

Stalin's regime took control of sports in the country. His government encouraged a vast number of young people to participate in sports. The regime offered a "P.T.D." certificate that tested athletic abilities like running and jumping. It also included many skills that would be useful in warfare, such as throwing a grenade, shooting, and walking a kilometer while wearing a gas mask.[14] Interestingly, men were not the only ones who were expected to play sports. Women, who would have to contribute to the war effort, were also openly encouraged to become athletes, mainly so that they would be healthier and more productive workers.[15] This approach to promoting women in sports differed greatly from what happened in many Western democracies during this period, where women had far fewer opportunities in sports. In short, Stalin closely linked sports to war. Their value lied in helping to turn the Soviet population into a war machine.

Another reason Stalin tried to stay out of international sports competitions involved his fear that the Soviet teams would perform poorly, making his country look weak.[16] While Russia did participate in the Olympics before World War I, the Soviet Union that emerged following the 1917 Russian revolution adopted an insular sports policy. It did not enter the Olympics again until 1952, and only after Soviet leaders were convinced that the team would perform well, as we will discuss more in the next section.[17] Therefore, the Soviet Union's approach to sports under Stalin's rule was somewhat limited. It focused on the link between mass sports participation and the physical preparation of the Soviet population for military conflict.

Similar to Stalin, Mussolini took interest in sports as a means to strengthen his population physically, but he also viewed sports as a tool to keep ordinary Italians preoccupied so that they would not engage in anti-government protests.[18] This approach too can be traced back to Western democracies prior to World War I. In particular, imperial authorities encouraged their colonial subjects to play sports as a way to distract them from their poor working conditions and reduce the chances of uprisings, as well as for other reasons.[19] However, Mussolini took more interest in using elite sports as a diversionary tool. As the political scientist Eleonora Belloni explains, "The regime understood right away that the sport-spectacle, even more so than that practiced in free time, worked at distracting Italians from political interests, keeping them far from every possible idea of opposing the regime."[20] In this way, Mussolini's approach more closely fit the bread and circuses theory of sports, whereby sporting spectacles keep people from causing unwanted trouble.

As elite sports became an obsession across Italy, Mussolini's regime realized that they could also be utilized for propaganda.[21] In particular, he discovered that they could promote Italian national identity and strengthen the legitimacy of the fascist government. As the historian Xavier Pujadas describes, "The National Fascist Party not only institutionalized football as a 'fascist game,' but also tried to use football wins to control public opinion, infiltrate the daily life of citizens and obtain advantages in international diplomacy."[22]

In the 1920s, the Italian government took control of the national sports institutions.[23] The regime tried replacing foreign words in soccer with Italian words, and it pushed some Italian clubs to adopt more Italian-sounding names.[24] Football Club Internazionale Milano became Associazione Sportiva Ambrosiana, after Saint Ambrose of Milan, and Foot-Ball Club Internazionale-Naples became Associazione Calcio Napoli. The regime also forced foreign players out of the Italian league, since these players could not compete for the Italian national team in international competition and were thus limiting the development of Italian players. Many of their spots were taken by talented South American players of Italian descent, who could play for the Italian national team against other countries.[25]

The regime's strategy proved very successful. Italy climbed the ranks of international soccer to win both the 1934 and 1938 World Cups. It also claimed first place in the soccer tournament at the 1936 Berlin Olympics. Mussolini saw great political value in these achievements. As he explained, "You, athletes of all Italy, are charged with specific duties. You must be tenacious, chivalrous, brave. Remember that, when you compete beyond our borders, the honor and the prestige of the Nation is entrusted to your muscles and, mainly, to your spirit."[26] As the prolific writer John Tunis explained in 1936, "To Mussolini's mind, games are useful if they result in international victories and so reveal fascist superiority. The results are watched, collected, catalogued and exploited, at home and abroad."[27]

A notable game between England and Italy in 1933 demonstrated Mussolini's nationalistic approach to sports. The game, which took place in Rome, was highly politicized by the Italian government. Mussolini himself even attended, receiving lavish applause from the crowd.[28] This blatant use of sports for fascist leader-worship offended the English so much that they refused to travel to Italy for the World Cup the following year.[29]

The 1932 Los Angeles Olympics demonstrated another way that Mussolini tried to use sports for political gain. He wanted his athletes to succeed as much as possible to win the hearts and minds of Italian Americans, who might be able to sway American foreign policy in his favor.[30] Italy performed very well in Los Angeles, winning twelve gold medals and finishing second overall. The regime viewed the Olympic team's performance as a major success from a propaganda standpoint.[31]

The 1934 Italian World Cup showcased Mussolini's obsession with politicizing sports. His regime devoted enormous resources to the event. It paid 75 percent of the travel expenses of foreign visitors, provided free transportation for the competition within Italy, created a plethora of commemorative memorabilia, and displayed 100,000 World Cup posters throughout the country.[32] Italy's first-place finish at the tournament raised much speculation that the Italian government had bribed the referees. Regardless, Mussolini took the occasion to spread his fascist propaganda. Historian and sociologist David Goldblatt explains that the event "became an explicitly political as well as a sporting exercise."[33] Historian Simon Martin describes that it "was more like a fascist rally than a sporting contest."[34]

Since England refused to attend the 1934 World Cup, many still questioned which country was the best in Europe. This question would be settled when the two teams met to play a game in London in 1934.[35] The game, remembered as the Battle of Highbury, turned into a violent struggle, with one newspaper editor describing it as a "[t]heatre of international war."[36] Although the game took place in England, it was broadcast widely over Italian radio and listened to throughout the country.[37]

Hitler's approach to sports would build on what he saw Stalin and Mussolini do. However, he was particularly interested in using sports to discriminate against minority groups and regime critics. Starting in 1933, the Nazis began banning Jews from many sports organizations.[38] This type of discrimination was certainly not new. In fact, excluding individuals based on race or ethnicity, as well as class and gender, had long been present in sports, including in democracies.[39] However, the Nazis also made being an outspoken supporter of the regime a requirement to win important sports competitions.[40] Thus, Hitler used sports as a tool to both further stigmatize minorities and to incentivize public support for his government, especially among the country's top athletes.

Hitler also took much longer than Mussolini to realize that international sports competitions could be exploited to disseminate propaganda. The Germans had secured the 1936 Olympics for Berlin in 1931, before Hitler came to power. When Hitler took control of the country in 1933, he actually thought that the Olympics would be a waste of money.[41] At the time, his primary interest in sports lay in using them to make soldiers more fit and athletic.[42] However, he soon realized that the 1936 Olympics provided a platform for advancing the Nazis' fascist and militaristic goals.[43] As the political scientist Jules Boykoff explains, Hitler's "propaganda minister Joseph Goebbels convinced him that the Games were a prime opportunity to bathe the swastika in the Olympic glow on the world stage."[44]

At home, the Olympics could bolster Hitler's legitimacy and make German citizens feel more connected to the state. Abroad, the Olympics offered Hitler a chance to improve Germany's international reputation by fooling foreigners into thinking that the country was more liberal and democratic than many Nazi critics claimed at the time. In fact, Hitler skillfully used the 1936 Olympics to launch a charm offensive that left a positive impression on many people living abroad. This strategy of deception, which has recently become known as *sportswashing*, was on full display at the 1936 Nazi Olympics.[45]

Initially, the Games were a lightning rod for controversy. Jewish organizations and other critics of the Nazi regime called for a boycott. In the United States, the opposition movement was taken very seriously.[46] Hitler responded by inviting the head of the U.S. Olympic Committee, Avery Brundage, to visit Berlin in 1934. The Nazis gave Brundage VIP treatment and presented him with a highly sanitized image of Germany.[47] Although Brundage had been aware of Nazi anti-Semitism prior to his visit, he returned to the United States and assured the American public that Jews would not face discrimination at the Olympics.[48] The United States thus went on to participate in one of the darkest moments in international sports history.

Spain turned out to be the only country to boycott the Nazi Olympics.[49] Led by the Republican government (shortly before Franco's takeover), the Spaniards organized the People's Olympiad in Barcelona.[50] This alternative event was meant to resemble a less competitive version of the Olympics, more focused on popular participation in sports. However, the organizers had to cancel the event because the Spanish Civil War started just before it was supposed to begin. In fact, some foreign athletes stayed in the country to fight against Franco's military forces. This short-lived attempt to replace the Olympics ended up being a casualty to the Spanish Civil War, which would also claim the lives of an estimated 500,000 people.

Despite Spain's protest, the Nazi Olympics served as a huge propaganda win for Hitler. Foreign visitors were treated to extravagant receptions in Berlin, the anti-Semitic signs were taken down, and the regime instructed storm troopers not to harass Jews while the Games were taking place.[51] As the German historian Hans Joachim Teichler put it, Hitler "was thus able to perfectly camouflage his real intentions to rearm Germany."[52] The Games also provided an opportunity to promote Nazi propaganda within Germany.[53] The country dominated in the medal count, allowing Hitler to boast about the supposed superiority of the Aryan race.

Hitler was not merely content to host the Olympics in 1936. He actually believed that all future Olympics would take place in Berlin, as they once did at the ancient Greek religious site of Olympia. He therefore invested heavily in building the infrastructure for the 1936 Berlin Games. When an advisor informed him that the design of the Olympic track did not actually follow international standards, he brushed the issue aside, since in his mind the Olympic technical rules would eventually conform to the stadium of its new permanent host.[54]

The Nazis also started the tradition of the Olympic torch relay, which at the time resonated with the notion that German Aryans were the rightful heirs of the ancient Greeks.[55] Therefore, the torch relay that we are familiar with today was a tradition started by the Nazis. Even more disturbingly, it was linked to Hitler's delusional and sociopathic desire to dominate Europe. The 1936 torch relay allowed Hitler to spread pro-Nazi propaganda along the relay's route through southeastern and central Europe, regions that Nazi Germany would attempt to subjugate in the coming years.[56]

Along with the torch relay, the Nazis started other Olympic traditions.[57] These include the live television broadcast of the opening ceremony and live video transmissions of many of the athletic events. They also played one of Coubertin's favorite songs, Beethoven's "Ode to Joy," at the opening ceremony, which has been featured in many subsequent Olympics.[58] As the British historian Guy Walters describes:

> Every modern Olympics has elements of the Berlin games in it. If the '36 Olympics had happened in another country, the Olympics today might not be the same thing. But what the Nazis showed was that this event could be globalized, and nationalized, and politicized in a way that's always taken place since. There is no doubt that Berlin is at the root of the modern Olympics.[59]

Another striking part of the story was how the IOC responded to Hitler's actions. As the American historian David Clay Large explains, "[T]he IOC would go on in later years to favor many authoritarian governments. The IOC was not bothered by the fact that this regime was discriminatory, that it abused human rights."[60] The American historian John Hoberman describes, "What the IOC learned from putting on an Olympiad with a dictatorial regime was that the world at large would accept it. If the show is good enough, if the public relations maneuvering of the dictatorship is clever enough, then you can get away with it."[61]

Therefore, despite Hitler's obvious exploitation of the Olympics for political purposes, similar to what Mussolini had done with the World Cup, the IOC and FIFA proved more than willing to allow dictatorships to host their events after 1936. Both the Summer and Winter Olympics were scheduled for Japan in 1940, and the Winter Olympics were to take place in Italy in 1944. However, these events did not happen due to the Second World War. Meanwhile, the location of the 1942 World Cup had not been decided before the war broke out, but Nazi Germany had a good chance of being selected as the host.

For their part, the Nazi regime nominated Pierre de Coubertin for the Nobel Peace Prize.[62] The imperial Japanese government also nominated him, although he never received the award. As for Avery Brundage, the president of the U.S. National Olympic Committee who so adamantly supported the Nazi Olympics, he became the IOC president from 1952–1972.[63] During his time at the IOC, he was perhaps most famous for defending the racist, minority-rule regimes in Rhodesia and South Africa.[64]

THE COLD WAR ERA

The Cold War featured a military and nuclear standoff between the two great-est superpowers the world had ever seen. On one side, the United States cham-pioned capitalism and individual freedoms. In contrast, the Soviet Union stood for central planning and the idea of individual sacrifice for the collective good. Along with engaging in a heated arms race, the two sides competed to win allies abroad. Building strong bridges with other nations could tilt the balance of power in their favor and further spread their political ideologies. In this struggle for foreign allies, both sides wanted to convince the world that their political system was superior. Yet without actually going to war, how could either side persuade the world that its system was better at producing a strong and healthy population?

For the Soviets, the answer was sports.[65] While Stalin mostly avoided in-ternational sports in the 1930s, the Soviet government started to take them more seriously after World War II. In particular, Soviet leaders were intrigued by the Olympics, viewing them as an opportunity to challenge the United States in a highly visible arena of international relations. If they could beat the Americans, they could make their system appear superior to free-market capitalism.[66]

The Olympics also provided the Soviets with several important advan-tages. First, a medal for a woman at the Olympics counted just as much as a medal for a man, and the United States lagged in terms of competitive wom-en's sports.[67] The Soviets could make women's sports a priority and thereby gain an edge over their American rivals. Second, the Soviets could focus on some of the more obscure sports in which few Americans competed, such as speed skating, shooting, and weightlifting.[68] They established sports institutes throughout the country to identify children who excelled at such lesser-known sports and to help them become world-class athletes.[69] Third, the Soviets took advantage of an Olympic requirement that all athletes be amateurs by giving promising Soviet athletes sham government jobs that allowed them to train full-time while receiving a government paycheck.[70] This gave the Soviets a major advantage over the Americans, whose professional athletes could not participate in the Olympics. Fourth, the Soviets could give their athletes (in-cluding women) steroids, which would be unthinkable for the Americans, given the traditional gender expectations in the United States at the time.[71]

Despite the competitive advantages that the Soviets wielded over the

Americans, they were still reluctant to send a team to the Olympics because they feared that even a second-place finish would be an embarrassing failure.[72] They passed on the 1952 Winter Olympics, but opted to participate in the 1952 Summer Olympics under the firm belief that they would beat the Americans and finish first overall.[73] Despite their confidence, they narrowly lost to the American team based on the scoring system at the time. However, an erroneous tally led to the conclusion that they tied the United States, allowing them to claim that they had performed impressively at their first Olympic outing. The miscalculation was not discovered and corrected until 2002.[74]

Meanwhile, the Soviets excelled at the Olympics in the following decades. From 1956 until the collapse of the Soviet Union in 1991, the Soviets only lost the Summer Olympic medal count twice, both times coming in second. Over this same period, they lost the Winter Olympic medal count also just twice, again finishing second in those years. The Soviets had in fact created an Olympic machine. However, rather than proving the superiority of their political ideology, the Olympic success merely masked inefficiencies, corruption, and popular discontent. The Soviet state collapsed in the early 1990s, unable to keep pace with the American economy.

The Soviet-American Olympic rivalry peaked in 1979, when politics disrupted sports in a very direct way. The Soviets were scheduled to host the 1980 Summer Olympics in Moscow. The Americans would follow four years later by holding the 1984 Summer Olympics in Los Angeles. The IOC hoped that letting each superpower host the Olympics would help build a bridge between the two sides and encourage international understanding. However, controversy erupted when the Soviets invaded Afghanistan in 1979. President Carter subsequently announced that the United States would protest by not sending its team to Moscow in 1980. Sixty-five other countries joined in the boycott. With these nations absent, the Soviets dominated the 1980 Summer Olympics, winning 195 medals. Moreover, not one of the roughly 5,000 athletes at the 1980 Moscow Olympics was banned for performance enhancing drugs, likely due to the Soviet interest in protecting cheating athletes.[75]

The Soviets went on to skip the 1984 Los Angeles Olympics, claiming that their athletes would be unsafe in the United States because of anti-Soviet protests. The Soviets' true motives for staying home remain debated by historians. Some believe that they wanted to come to Los Angeles and beat the Americans on U.S. soil, but they feared many of their athletes could defect.[76] Others argue that the Soviet boycott was simply a retaliation for the American boycott of their Olympics in 1980.[77] Either way, the IOC's effort to reduce Cold War tensions through international sports backfired.

The modern Olympics has no doubt attracted much criticism and disdain throughout its history, and as such it has faced several attempts to replace it. The 1936 People's Olympiad in Barcelona, discussed in the previous section, might have reshaped history if not for the Spanish Civil War. Another major anti-Olympic movement arose in the 1960s. Like the People's Olympiad, it posed a potentially serious threat to the IOC. However, it had much different objectives, and it was spearheaded by a surprising nation—Indonesia.

Indonesia's idea of creating an alternative Olympics began as early as September 1962. The plan may have originally come from the Chinese government, which criticized the Olympics for being run by "imperialist" countries.[78] However, Indonesia moved forward with the idea in 1963 because of a diplomatic dispute involving the Asian Games, which were hosted in Indonesia's capital, Jakarta, in 1962.[79] The Indonesian government angered the IOC and much of the developed world by refusing to allow athletes from Taiwan and Israel to enter the country.[80] In reaction, the IOC expelled Indonesia from the Olympic Movement, effectively banning it from future Olympics.

The IOC intended this ban to be very brief. It simply wanted Indonesia to apologize and agree not to do something similar in the future. However, Indonesia's leader, Sukarno, responded by escalating the dispute even further. He accused the Olympics of being inherently political and biased toward developed nations, and he announced that Indonesia was launching an alternative Olympics called the Games of the New Emerging Forces (GANEFO). As he put it, "Sports cannot be separated from politics. Therefore, let us now work for a sports association on the basis of politics."[81]

GANEFO was meant to counterbalance the Olympics while at the same time mimicking it in many ways.[82] For example, it featured a torch relay, as well as opening and closing ceremonies.[83] The event also sought to take on a broader political significance by including a rally, an art exhibition from the participating nations, and other cultural events.[84] While the Olympics claimed to be impartial and apolitical, GANEFO intentionally sought to be political, but in ways that favored developing nations.

The first GANEFO event took place in Indonesia in November 1963. Athletes from about fifty nations participated. Some countries fully supported GANEFO, such as communist China, which was not a member of the Olympic Movement at the time. Other nations, like the Soviet Union, tried to strike a more neutral position to avoid siding strongly with Indonesia over the IOC.[85] Also, many countries chose not to send their best athletes because the IOC had made clear that any athlete who competed in GANEFO would be barred from the Olympics.[86]

With the Soviet Union and many other countries sending only their back-ups, China dominated the competition, garnering a boost in international prestige. In fact, China was so focused on using GANEFO to improve its international reputation that it avoided entering athletes into violent sports events like judo and boxing, fearing that these events could spark nationalistic tensions.[87] Chinese officials also instructed one of their badminton players to intentionally lose in the final match to his opponent from Indonesia, given the popularity of badminton in Indonesia.[88]

While the first GANEFO competition might be deemed a success, the movement died out in the years following the event, partly because most of the participating countries prioritized their relationships with the IOC.[89] Another key factor was that Sukarno, the Indonesian leader, faced domestic turmoil in the mid-1960s that led to his downfall.[90] Further, the Chinese began to lose interest in the movement.[91] The country declined to fund the construction of a new stadium in Cairo for GANEFO II, which was scheduled for 1967. This decision led the government in Egypt to withdraw their offer to host the second round of the competition. The event was moved to Beijing. However, China canceled the event in 1966 due to the Cultural Revolution, effectively ending the GANEFO movement. The only follow-up event that happened was the 1966 Asian GANEFO in Cambodia. The event featured under twenty countries, and Indonesia only sent fifty-seven athletes. Thus, the IOC survived another countermovement that might have fragmented the international sports world had it proved successful.

While GANEFO stood out as an unusual development in the history of international sports, the 1978 World Cup in Argentina echoed 1936. Similar to the Nazi Olympics case, Argentina had been granted the right to host the World Cup before the military junta took control of the country following a coup in 1976. The change in government had major consequences for the Argentinian population. The military regime carried out human rights abuses on tens of thousands of Argentinians. Like in the case of the 1936 Olympics, many activists and international actors criticized the authoritarian regime for its atrocities. Some even proposed a World Cup boycott using the slogan, "No football amidst concentration camps."[92]

Foreshadowed by Hitler's example, the Argentinian military dictatorship saw the World Cup as an opportunity to sanitize their international image. It was another classic case of sportswashing. A few months after the coup, they established a committee with roughly $700 million in resources to organize the event and provide hospitality to visitors.[93] When faced with internal criticism over the costs of the World Cup, the committee's president claimed that it was "a political event" and that its importance could not be captured by "the optic of a field such as economy or finances."[94] They also bulldozed Buenos Aires's worst ghettos and relocated their inhabitants to the Catamarca Desert.[95] In addition, they hired an American public relations company to help them project a progressive and peaceful image.[96] A major concern for the regime was the possibility that political opposition groups would protest during the tournament, which could cast a major shadow on the event.

In a recent article published in *American Political Science Review*, researchers Adam Scharpf, Christian Gläßel, and Pearce Edwards use fine-grained data on the Argentinian military junta's repression efforts to analyze how the dictatorship strategically cracked down on dissidents around the time of the 1978 World Cup.[97] The scholars explain that high-profile events like the World Cup offer dictatorships a "scrutiny-publicity dilemma." The media attention around such events can give dictators an opportunity to sanitize their image. At the same time, however, the events can also give regime opponents a platform to protest and call attention to the government's repressive policies. Dictatorships, therefore, try to maximize the positive publicity they receive from such events while also minimizing the likelihood that protests will draw negative attention to their regimes.

According to the study's findings, the military junta in Argentina ramped up repression in the lead-up to the 1978 World Cup, specifically in the five cities that would host World Cup games. Their goal was to lock up possible dissidents who might protest during the games as well as intimidate others who might cause trouble for them during the tournament. However, just before the tournament began, as reporters from other countries flocked to Argentina, the regime drastically reduced its repressive activities. Again, this change only occurred in the five cities that were hosting World Cup games. However, the government's repressive actions did not entirely dissipate in those cities during the tournament. Repression still took place, but mainly far away from hotels where reporters were staying and at times when the reporters were busy covering games.

The researchers also document how the Argentinian dictatorship courted foreign journalists with social events such as lavish meals, vineyard trips, and fashion shows. According to one journalist covering the 1978 World Cup, the press centers were staffed by "extremely charming, beautiful, 'outgoing' hostesses. . . . [T]he boys were relaxed, you know what I mean."[98] Further, the regime told journalists that they might receive propaganda from a subversive Argentinian domestic group attempting to delegitimize the government, pre-empting any potential concerns that might be raised by dissident statements or protests. Many visitors came away with the impression that the government in Argentina was running the country effectively and that the rumors of human rights abuses were overstated.

In many ways, the Argentinian military dictatorship's use of the 1978 World Cup was unsurprising given Hitler's example, but the 1980s featured a strange occurrence in the international sports world. In fact, the final Olympic results from 1980, 1984, and 1988 pose an intriguing puzzle. The country that per-formed second best, only slightly behind the Soviet Union, was East Germany. That country had a population that was about one fourth the size of West Ger-many and roughly 6 percent the size of the Soviet Union.[99] In 1985, it ranked forty-third in the world in total population.[100] East Germany's economic prob-lems also made it an unlikely nation to excel in international sports. It lagged well behind West Germany and many other developed countries throughout the Cold War, and by 1991 it only had about 31 percent the per capita national income of its western neighbor.[101] Yet on the Olympic stage, East Germany was a titan.[102] Its per capita success in winning medals was about fifteen times higher than the United States.[103] It claimed first or second in every Olympics in the 1980s except the 1984 Los Angeles Games, which, like the Soviet Union, it refused to attend.

How did the East German authoritarian regime achieve this seemingly extraordinary feat? The answer is both disappointing and disturbing, and it reveals how far some governments are willing to go to succeed in the inter-national sports realm. Starting in 1974, the East German government imple-mented a massive doping program.[104] While many athletes in East Germany were already doping, the government undertook a systematic effort to ad-minister performance enhancing drugs to aspiring Olympians, including children.[105] In total, over 10,000 athletes were given drugs, often without their knowledge.[106]

While East German athletes performed exceptionally well in international competitions, they also experienced harmful medical effects. These included heart and liver damage, and many of the female athletes developed facial hair and deeper voices.[107] Moreover, about one third of the female athletes showed signs of gynecological damage from steroid use.[108] Despite these health consequences, the regime continued to administer many of these athletes drugs for the sake of national glory.[109] When the program was exposed following the fall of the Berlin Wall in 1989, national glory turned to shame. Many remember the doping program as a human rights atrocity, similar to the experiments carried out by Nazi doctors in World War II.[110]

As the journalist Lucas Aykroyd explains about the state-sponsored doping program:

> The objectives were multi-dimensional. East Germany treated sports as a vehicle to show the superiority of socialism over capitalism, divert attention from its underperforming economy, and provide an independent source of national pride without jeopardizing its security in the Warsaw Pact military alliance.[111]

In the short run, the program partially achieved these goals. However, sporting success proved inadequate in curbing the rise of popular discontent in East Germany that led to the collapse of the regime in 1989.[112] Following German reunification, revelations about the doping program exposed the depravity of the East German government. It also proved costly for the well-being of many athletes and saw some of the doctors and officials who participated in the program face criminal charges after the Cold War ended.[113]

AFTER THE COLD WAR

While the appalling crimes committed by the East German regime shocked and outraged much of the world, Vladimir Putin took them as a source of inspiration. Putin had in fact worked in East Germany as a KGB officer in the 1980s in coordination with the East German secret police, who played a major role in the East German doping scandal. Putin would create a more sophisticated doping system in Russia about three decades later that would allow the fledgling Russian Olympic team to triumph on the world stage, as the East Germans had in the 1980s.

Russia's state-sponsored doping program appears to have started around 2010, but it ramped up in 2011, largely out of desperation. Russia was scheduled to host the 2014 Winter Olympics in Sochi. However, the team performed poorly at the 2010 Vancouver Winter Olympics, ranking sixth in total number of medals won and eleventh in gold medals won. The prospects of hosting a costly Winter Games in Sochi, accompanied by another underwhelming performance, seemed to have been a major concern for Putin's government. Facing this embarrassing scenario, Putin opted to implement a massive and complex doping program with the help of his security apparatus that allowed Russia to finish first in total number of medals and second in gold medals won.[114]

Early on, the plan involved having the Moscow Anti-Doping Laboratory, which was tasked with monitoring Russian athletes, change the positive test results to negative for the tests it ran in between international competitions. When international competitions came around, the athletes would simply pause their drug use so that they could test negative at the event. However, to achieve the most impressive results at the Sochi Olympics, the government wanted to continue doping Russian athletes throughout the event rather than pausing their drug use. This meant that many of the Russian athletes would not be able to pass a urine test. The solution was for Russian security officials to swap out their contaminated urine for clean urine after the athletes were tested. This process involved an elaborate scheme of passing the supposedly tamper-proof bottles of urine through a "mouse hole" in the Sochi Laboratory and replacing their contents with clean urine.[115]

The World Anti-Doping Agency exposed Russia's doping scandal in 2015.[116] However, Russia largely evaded punishment until its invasion of Ukraine in 2022.[117] For example, Russian athletes were allowed to compete at the Olympics from 2016 until February 2022 with the identification "Olympic Athletes from Russia" (OARs) and later "Russian Olympic Committee athletes" (ROC athletes). Russia's lenient punishment may partly be explained by Putin's influence in the world of international sports.[118] In addition, many believe that a number of elite Russian athletes continued doping throughout this period, thus calling into question the legitimacy of many of the competitions.[119] Whatever the reason for letting Russia off easy, the cost may have been the integrity of international sports over a six-year period.

Despite the international blowback, Russia's success in international sports did provide Putin with several benefits. First, it increased his domestic popularity. Putin enjoyed a boost in his approval ratings during and after the 2014 Sochi Olympics.[120] According to *The Guardian*, 67.8 percent of Russians approved of Putin's performance about a week after the Olympics ended, which marked Putin's highest approval rating since May 2012.[121] Part of this change in public opinion came from Putin's invasion of Crimea that occurred just days after the Olympics ended, but Sochi still undoubtedly played an important role.

The story was somewhat different with the 2018 World Cup. On one hand, Russia did not succeed on the soccer field like it did at the Sochi Olympics, and in fact it was knocked out by Croatia in the quarterfinals. In addition, on the first day of the 2018 World Cup, the Russian government announced that it would raise the national pension age in the country by about five years, as mentioned in the Introduction of this book. Roughly 90 percent of Russian citizens opposed this reform.[122] The fact that Putin chose to make this announcement on the first day of the 2018 World Cup illustrates how he sees international sports as a political tool.[123]

Second, the construction of stadiums and other facilities for the 2014 Sochi Olympics and 2018 World Cup provided Putin with opportunities to funnel billions of dollars to his oligarch supporters.[124] Rather than create a fair and transparent process through which companies could bid for different projects, Putin gave oligarchs lucrative deals without real free-market competition. This cronyism caused the Sochi Olympics to cost about four times the initial projection. The 2018 World Cup faced similar issues. In the end, Putin was able to channel billions of taxpayer dollars to some of his most important political supporters, thereby gaining tighter control of the Russian government.

Third, the luxury resorts built for the 2014 Sochi Olympics have mitigated the costs of Western sanctions by providing wealthy Russians with an alternative vacation destination when it is difficult for them to travel abroad. Following the 2014 invasion of Ukraine, for instance, Sochi offered an appealing vacation destination for many Russians who were banned from traveling to Europe. Even many non-sanctioned Russians turned to Sochi as an alternative because of the declining value of the ruble, as well as fears that Russians traveling abroad would be ostracized by opponents of Putin's war in Ukraine.[125] In short, Putin was able to use the Olympics to create a travel alternative for the Russian elite that could mitigate the costs of the sanctions.

Fourth, Putin used sports to shift international attention away from his anti-democratic policies and military aggression. As we saw earlier, this type of sportswashing is nothing new, as it underpinned Hitler's strategy to use the 1936 Berlin Olympics to transform Germany's image on the world stage. In Putin's case, the 2014 Sochi Olympics and 2018 World Cup provided opportunities to present the Russian government as well-run, legitimate, and successful.[126]

Steve Rosenberg of the BBC described after the 2018 World Cup, "Russia has come across as friendly and hospitable: a stark contrast with the country's authoritarian image. All the foreign fans I have spoken to are pleasantly surprised."[127] As one English fan visiting Moscow in 2018 described, "Everything the British government has said about Russia is a lie. It's propaganda. Fair play to Putin. He's done a brilliant job with the World Cup."[128]

China's use of sport in the last several decades shares similarities with the Russia case, but it evolved in a much different sociopolitical context. During the Cold War, China primarily focused on using sports to develop healthier, stronger citizens, as well as engaging in bilateral sports exchanges to strengthen its relations with communist and non-aligned states.[129] However, China boycotted many high-profile sporting events during the Cold War to protest Taiwan's participation.[130]

When the Chinese Civil War ended in 1949, the Chinese Communist Party had assumed control of mainland China, while the Nationalist forces had retreated to Taipei. Nevertheless, the Nationalist government in Taiwan continued to hold China's seat at the United Nations until 1971 and participated in international sports under the name "Republic of China." The Chinese Communist Party was angered that the Nationalists were allowed to compete and refused to participate in any events that they attended, including the Olympics. As relations between mainland China and the West improved in the 1970s, however, the Chinese Communist Party relaxed its stance on Taiwan's participation, insisting only that they no longer compete as Republic of China. The IOC made Taiwan change its name to "Chinese Taipei" in 1979, and China finally ended its boycott and participated in the 1980 Winter Olympics.[131]

Once China rejoined the world of international sports, its government set out to use success on the playing field to project an image of a strong, thriving nation to the world while also boosting national pride at home.[132] However, its strategy for achieving sports success was quite disconcerting. It has been described by scholars as China's "human ladder."[133] Specifically, the government set up sports academies for children who demonstrated talent for certain sports, in particular those that could bring the country Olympic glory. These children began by practicing for three hours a day, four or five days a week. The most successful children increased their practice time to four to five hours a day, five or six days a week. The top performers were eventually promoted to professional or provincial teams, and then the best of them advanced to the national teams.[134]

According to a 2007 study, China's "human ladder" resulted in about 95 percent of the athletes failing out of the program. With little or no primary or secondary education, many of these children had few fallback options once their improbable sports dreams came to an end.[135] This system might seem appalling by ethical standards in the West and many other parts of the world. However, the poor outcomes for so many young athletes fit with China's ideology of individual sacrifice for the collective good.[136] In this case, the collective good was Chinese national pride and glory.[137]

By providing a platform to showcase top athletes on the world stage, the Olympics facilitated the creation of this sports system in China. The Chinese government's plan came with great humanitarian costs, especially for children. Even within China, many experts in the 1980s and 1990s warned about the dangers of the elite sports model, arguing that the government should instead invest in grassroots sports programs that would provide the public with opportunities for recreation and exercise.[138] However, the allure of Olympic prestige proved too much for the Chinese Communist Party, which prioritized obtaining medals over the well-being of young Chinese athletes.

China's efforts to exploit international sports culminated in the 2008 Beijing Olympics. The event was widely viewed as the coming out party for the rising great power.[139] In particular, the opening ceremony featured an elaborate program intended to showcase the country's economic rise and win respect and favor abroad.[140] The government also used the event to present China as an appealing country for potential business partners and investors.[141] At home, the government utilized the event to distract Chinese citizens from the country's inflation, unemployment, and political corruption while also uniting them around a common goal.[142] China finished atop the medal table with 48 gold medals, although the United States had more total medals (112 to 100).

China also hosted the Winter Olympics in 2022, again using the event for propaganda purposes. However, in 2022 China faced significant criticism for its human rights record, including a diplomatic boycott from the United States, Britain, Australia, and several other countries.[143] We will discuss their hosting of the 2022 Olympics more in Chapter 6.

Similar to Russia and China, North Korean leader Kim Jong Un has used sports for various political ends, and in fact seems to be a genuine fan of sports. He grew up rooting for Michael Jordan and the Chicago Bulls, who were the premier team in the NBA in the 1990s. After Kim Jong Un came to power in 2011, former Chicago Bulls legend Dennis Rodman was one of the first Westerners to gain access to the country. He was accompanied by the Harlem Globetrotters and a *Vice* film crew. The thirty-minute video that came out of the visit, published by *Vice* on YouTube, reveals a number of ways that Kim Jong Un uses sports for political ends.[144]

This video provides a rare glimpse into a country that is very challenging for academics to study. It is clear from the documentary that Kim Jong Un used the sports trip to project a falsely positive image of North Korea to the visiting players and film crew. In addition, it seems that he used the presence of Dennis Rodman and the other players to bolster his legitimacy and reputation in the eyes of the North Korean public. For instance, he sat next to Dennis Rodman during the game and later held a dinner with Rodman and the other players that was publicized on North Korean television. Rodman took several more trips to North Korea in the following years, sparking controversy in the U.S. media given the potential undesirable political impact that his presence might have had in North Korea.[145]

Kim Jong Un also exploited the 2018 Winter Olympics in South Korea to improve his international image abroad. At the time, his country desperately needed relief from the United Nations sanctions, which were taking a serious toll on the regime and its supporters. Kim Jong Un saw the Games as an opportunity to soften North Korea's international image and potentially convince some countries to lift the sanctions.

The IOC was also eager to have North Korea participate in the Olympics. As discussed earlier, the IOC claims that sports can build bridges between countries and reduce the chances of interstate war. IOC officials therefore viewed the 2018 Olympics as an opportunity to bring the North and South Korean governments together and, of course, to take lots of credit for doing so. The statements of self-congratulations coming from the IOC for including North Korea continued long after the competition ended.[146]

Many South Korean government officials also wanted North Korea to participate in the Games, in part because they worried that Kim Jong Un might disrupt the event with missile threats if the North Korean Olympic team stayed home.[147] When South Korea hosted the Olympics in 1988, North Korea refused to attend and instead called for an international boycott. Given the regime's propensity for missile testing and saber rattling, leaving North Korea out of the event was a potentially risky move for the South Korean government.

With this convergence of interests between North Korea, South Korea, and the IOC, it is not surprising that the North Koreans ended up participating in the Olympics. Despite some initial uncertainty, North Korea announced that it would send a team in January of 2018, a month before the Olympics started. The North Korean athletes marched with the South Koreans in the opening ceremony, and they also organized a joint hockey team with the South Koreans that received a great deal of attention.[148]

Kim Jong Un's sister (Kim Yo Jong) also played a prominent role in the Olympics, traveling to South Korea to attend the Games and meet with South Korea's president. At the time, Kim Yo Jong was the head of North Korea's Department of Propaganda and Agitation, the main organization in charge of censorship in the country. Internationally, she is well-known for her record of human rights abuses and support for her brother.[149]

Although this was a blatant example of a vile dictatorship using sports to project a false image to the world, the North Korean regime received a lot of positive publicity and goodwill from the event. In fact, many major media outlets fell short of clearly framing North Korea's participation as a charm offensive. The New York Times published an article called, "Kim Jong-un's Sister Turns on the Charm, Taking Pence's Spotlight."[150] ABC News announced that "North Korea's 200-plus cheerleaders steal spotlight at 2018 Winter Olympics with matching outfits, synchronized chants."[151] Reuters posted an article titled, "North Korea Judged Winner of Diplomatic Gold at Olympics."[152] Many of these pieces did note the brutal nature of Kim Jong Un's regime and warned readers not to be fooled. However, readers could have benefited from clearer and more direct condemnations of the sportswashing campaign that included comparisons to past cases such as the 1936 Olympics.

Some reporters and policymakers did put the focus on how North Korea's publicity stunt was misleading propaganda.[153] U.S. Vice President Mike Pence called out Kim Jong Un's charm offensive, taking the occasion to remind the world of North Korea's atrocities. "As we speak, an estimated 100,000 North Korean citizens labor in modern-day gulags," he explained.[154] "Those who dare raise their voices in dissent are imprisoned, tortured, and even murdered; their children and grandchildren routinely punished for their family's sins against the state."[155] As one of his aides added, "everything the North Koreans do at the Olympics is a charade to cover up the fact that they are the most tyrannical and oppressive regime on the planet."[156]

These statements brought much-needed clarity to the situation, as did an important and insightful essay by the political scientist Timothy Bynion. After discussing several articles from prominent media outlets, Bynion described the positive press coverage as "problematic and potentially dangerous for a number of reasons, the most important of which is the brutality of the government that Kim represents."[157] Therefore, Kim Jong Un's charm offensive certainly drew harsh critics. However, it was alarming how many people missed the opportunity to clearly and directly denounce the North Korean regime for engaging in sportswashing, especially given past examples of dictators using international sports to get positive publicity.

Saudi Arabia illustrates another recent case of a nation trying to use sports to remake its image, and it involves a wide range of sports, from golf to auto racing. As Karim Zidan of *The Guardian* explains, the Saudi government has recently been trying to "transform a controversial kingdom marred with human rights abuses into a tantalizing hub for global sports and entertainment events."[158] In 2018, Saudi Arabia signed a ten-year contract to host WWE events. Since then, the country has hosted important Formula 1 events, horse races, and boxing and tennis matches. Further, Saudi Arabia's sovereign wealth fund purchased a majority stake in the English Premier League team Newcastle United in 2021 and stocked it with talent, rocketing its position in the Premier League standings from twelfth to fourth.[159] Meanwhile, the Saudi domestic league has spent billions to acquire some of the world's foremost players, including Cristiano Ronaldo and Karim Benzema.

The Saudis have also made major inroads into the world of professional golf, most notably their LIV Golf League, which has recently competed against the PGA for many of the world's top golfers. This fight has hardly been fair given that the Saudi sovereign wealth fund has more than $500 billion, compared to the PGA that has about $1.5 billion, and the Saudis are not necessarily interested in making a profit.[160] Rather, the goal is national rebranding, and Saudi Arabia may be willing to lose a great deal of money in the process of achieving it, which could result in the PGA having no fair chance to compete. The objective behind Saudi Arabia's decision-making is well described by Steven A. Cook, a senior fellow at the Council on Foreign Relations. As he describes, "There's something to the fact that Saudi Arabia wants to be known for something other than oil, religious extremism, and the past in which women couldn't drive."[161]

Saudi Arabia has been just one of several Middle Eastern countries to recently try to use sports to improve its international image. Another notable example is Qatar, which hosted the World Cup in 2022 and Formula 1 Grand

Prix races in 2021 and 2023. We will examine the Qatari case in more detail in Chapter 6. Another example is the UAE's Sheikh Mansour's purchase of a controlling share of the Manchester City soccer club in 2008. As political scientist Sean L. Yom explains:

> Over the past decade, the leading Gulf kingdoms have kicked their sportswashing campaigns into overdrive. . . . [T]hese regimes were eager to rebrand themselves from what they were—illiberal ruling monarchies lucky to have survived that regional wave of revolutionary uprisings. Instead, they sought to remake themselves as international sites of progressive, cosmopolitan knowledge.[162]

Is Saudi Arabia's sportswashing strategy really all that similar to Hitler's use of the 1936 Olympics or the Argentinian military's use of the 1978 World Cup? There is a strong argument that it is not. Such classic examples of sportswashing centered around single events, whereas the Saudi strategy seems to be more broadly focused. This distinction matters because it is easier to deceive the world when the sportswashing campaign is trained on a single event such as the Olympics. The government just needs to control the media narrative around that event while the spotlight is on them, and many dictatorships have proven successful at doing this. However, the Saudi government's approach to sports invites long-term scrutiny, which may signal its intention to make significant reforms.

These reforms are explained in the Saudi Vision 2030 Agenda, which aims to boost foreign investment, create jobs, increase tourism, and encourage fitness.[163] Whether Saudi Arabia will modernize to the point that its human rights record and foreign policy become accepted around the world remains an open question. Nonetheless, it does appear that this case differs notably from many past examples of sportswashing and that Saudi Arabia's presence in the world of sports is likely here to stay.

Will the Saudis make inroads into other traditional Western sports leagues? The NFL seems unlikely because it has a hard salary cap, meaning that if the Saudis acquired an NFL team, they could not simply buy their way to success by signing the top players on the market.[164] On the other hand, leagues with softer salary caps, like the NBA and MLB, could allow a Saudi-financed team to accumulate a massive amount of talent. How would a fan base in a traditional American sport react to Saudi ownership, even if the Saudi money led to multiple championships? Further, how would the fans of other teams respond?

These questions may get answered in the coming years. If the examples of LIV Golf and Newcastle United provide any indications, the situation could get contentious.

CONCLUSION

As the cases discussed in this chapter show, dictators have used sports for a variety of political purposes, including preparing their populations for war, distracting their citizens, signaling national strength through sports victories, projecting a (false) positive image to the world, discriminating against minorities and political opponents, and funneling money to corrupt political cronies. As authoritarian leaders often learn from and copy each other, many of these strategies have appeared across different cases.

In their efforts to leverage sports for political gain, dictators have also left their fingerprints on international sports. Hitler stands out as probably the most influential in this regard. If you know the history, watching the opening ceremony of the Olympics is simply a much different experience. More broadly, dictators have been partly responsible for solidifying the close ties between international sporting events and nationalism, as well as elevating the status and importance of international sports around the world. Had it not been for dictators, international sporting events may never have grown into such powerful global spectacles that capture so much of the world's attention.

Some dictators have also shown a strong willingness to cheat at sports, which raises questions about whether events like the Olympics and World Cup are even worth watching.[165] If some athletes have an entirely unfair advantage because their governments are helping them get away with using performance enhancing drugs, then international sports competitions cease to be legitimate sporting events.[166] They instead serve as propaganda tools for cheating authoritarian governments.

It is within the realm of possibility that some major international sports competitions will lose the interest of the democratic world unless sports officials take a stronger stance against state-sponsored doping, even when very powerful countries do it. Further, from an ethical standpoint, examples like Russia's doping system and China's "human ladder" raise the question of whether including such countries in international sports is inherently unethical. Could the only morally defensible approach to international sports be one that largely limits competition to democracies, or maybe one that breaks from the nation-centric format entirely?

In this chapter, we have also seen that the IOC and FIFA have historically been willing to have close ties with notorious dictatorships. From the dictators' perspective, it is unsurprising that they would want to have such close relationships with major sports organizations. From the perspective of the organizations, there are several factors that may explain their keen interest in working with dictators. First, many institutions like the IOC and FIFA champion sports as a powerful force for good in the world.[167] From this viewpoint, allowing despots like Hitler, Putin, and Kim Jong Un to participate in international sports should encourage these leaders to become more responsible members of the international community.[168] Second, dictators are often willing to take international sports much more seriously than democratic leaders, which can bring more prestige to organizations like the IOC and FIFA. Third, dictators may be more likely to crack down on critics who oppose the sporting event. As one sports administrator put it, "less democracy is sometimes better for organizing a [sports mega-event]. . . . When you have a very strong head of state who can decide, as maybe Putin can . . . that is easier for us organizers."[169] Another possible factor is that dictators might be willing to bribe international sports officials to host events. However, bribery seems to be at most only part of the story, as we have seen many examples of international sports organizations working with dictators in the apparent absence of bribes.

Recently, the fact that the IOC and FIFA banned Russia after Putin's 2022 invasion of Ukraine suggests that the tide may be turning. Notably, Putin not only violated international human rights norms, but he also broke the rules of the international sports world by doping his athletes and violating the Olympic Truce three times. The willingness of the IOC and FIFA to ban Russia appears to be a clear indication that these organizations do have red lines that, if crossed, will get a dictator banned. Where exactly that line lies remains unclear, but the strong stance taken by FIFA and the IOC is an important development.

Lastly, a surprising finding that emerged from this chapter was the role that authoritarian regimes played in promoting women's sports. When the Soviet government did so after World War I to improve women's health, the strategy likely provided important societal benefits. However, as the Soviet Union and other authoritarian regimes placed greater emphasis on using women's sports to attain international prestige, the impact on women became more compli-cated. Indeed, the elite sports model can pose many challenges for athletes regardless of gender. A century ago, a group of female physical educators un-derstood this point well. In fact, they opposed the idea of elite women's sports that is so widely applauded today. While these women may have lost the battle of history, their voices have not been forgotten.

4

SPORTS AND WOMEN'S EMPOWERMENT

Exhibition games normally receive little attention. However, on September 20, 1973, around 50 million people tuned in to watch an exhibition tennis match played in the Astrodome in Houston, Texas.[1] This exhibition game stood out for much more than its Super Bowl–sized audience. It was played between the twenty-nine-year-old women's superstar Billie Jean King and the fifty-five-year-old former men's tennis standout Bobby Riggs. Riggs had spent the months in the lead-up to the event making chauvinistic statements about the supposed superiority of men over women.[2] King had kept a much lower profile, focusing on preparing herself for the contest. The match represented much more than entertainment: it was a moment when female athletes had the chance to stand up to the intolerance and bigotry that had held them back in the world of sports for so long.

The place of women in sports had been marginalized from the beginning of the modern sports movement. In the early 1900s, prominent sports officials argued that women should be excluded from many sports.[3] These male leaders claimed that women lacked the strength and athletic ability of men. They also asserted that it was unhealthy for women to compete, except in less strenuous sports like tennis and golf.[4] Another concern was that spectators would not be interested in watching women's sports (except possibly for deviant reasons).[5]

As Pierre de Coubertin, the founder of the modern Olympics, wrote in 1912:

There remains the other possibility, that of adding women's competitions alongside men's competitions in the sports declared open to women, a little female Olympiad alongside the great male Olympiad. What is the appeal of that? ... In our view, this feminine semi-Olympiad is impractical, uninteresting, ungainly, and, I do not hesitate to add, improper. It is not in keeping with my concept of the Olympic Games, ... the solemn and periodic exaltation of male athleticism, based on internationalism, by means of fairness, in an artistic setting, with the applause of women as a reward.[6]

Coubertin maintained this prejudice into his old age, at least as late as 1934.[7] In comparison, the experience for women in ancient Greece was even worse. Women were not even allowed to watch the Olympics, and the punishment for breaking this rule was death.[8]

Nevertheless, women in many past societies did participate in organized sports. Perhaps most common was foot racing, but other sports practiced by women historically include wrestling, boxing, stickball, folk football, cricket, and archery.[9] Even in ancient Greece, females had their own event that paralleled the Olympics called the Heraean Games, intended to honor the goddess Hera.[10] Plato even endorsed female sports.[11] In various forms, women's sports survived in Europe from the time of the Romans, who for a period had female gladiators and chariot racers, through the Middle Ages, Renaissance, and Industrial Age.[12] In the late 1800s, women competed in various types of sports, sometimes even winning coed competitions (for instance, in long-distance walking).[13] However, attitudes in the upper-class male-dominated sports establishment around the turn of the century were quite hostile to the notion of women engaging in sports, particularly at the elite level. This opposition meant that aspiring female athletes faced an uphill battle just as modern sports were rising in prominence around the globe.

By the time that Billie Jean King faced Bobby Riggs in the Battle of the Sexes, the situation had improved, but not by much. The percentage of female athletes at the Olympics had only risen to about 15 percent in 1972 (compared to 0 percent in 1896). There was no Women's World Cup, which would not emerge until 1991. In most countries, women still faced significant barriers to participation in sports. In Brazil, for example, it was illegal for women to play soccer. The English Football Association's ban on women's soccer had only been lifted in 1970. In the United States, Title IX had just been passed in 1972, and its implications for college athletics had yet to be appreciated or understood.

Riggs entered the Astrodome in a chariot pulled by attractive young women wearing t-shirts that read "Sugar Daddy." King, in turn, entered on a chariot pulled by scantily clad men. The match lived up to the hype. King won three straight sets to defeat Riggs in decisive fashion. Many onlookers viewed her victory as a major triumph in the struggle for gender equality and an inspiration for women around the world.[14] An editorial published in the *New York Times* claimed that "In a single tennis match, Billie Jean King was able to do more for the cause of women than most feminists can achieve in a lifetime."[15] A *Seventeen* magazine poll conducted in 1975 found the magazine's readers viewed King as the most admired woman in the world.[16] As the scholars Eileen McDonagh and Laura Pappano explain, "To our eyes today, the match proved little about male and female athletic ability. . . . However, in 1973, when virtually any male was deemed superior to any female at virtually anything not domestic in nature, it was a symbolic event."[17]

The fact that women have gained more freedom and opportunity to engage in sports no doubt constitutes a positive development and reflects improved gender equality more broadly. A much deeper question lurks here, though, which will be the subject of this chapter. Should we credit sports with advancing women's rights outside the sporting realm, such as by improving public attitudes toward women, teaching girls and women important life lessons, and providing female athletes with a platform to champion social and political causes? As we discussed in Chapter 2, major sports competitions have been linked to spikes in domestic violence, which should give us pause when considering the role of sports in improving women's welfare. Likewise, the experiences of elite athletes in authoritarian countries discussed in Chapter 3 raise serious questions about whether sports really empower women. To take a more systematic approach to answering this question, we will begin by briefly examining the history of women in sports and some of the misconceptions, challenges, and debates that have arisen along the way.

THE HISTORY OF WOMEN IN MODERN SPORTS

As modern sports spread across the world in the nineteenth and early twentieth centuries, women remained largely excluded from intense athletic competition, due in part to opposition from male sports leaders. Coubertin's condescending dismissal of the notion of holding more events for women at the Olympics exemplifies the chauvinistic attitude held by many men at the time. In fact, throughout much of the 1900s, female participation at the Olympics paled in comparison to men. Parity in participation rates has only occurred recently. Figures 4.1 and 4.2 show the gender balance at the Summer and Winter Olympics throughout history.[18]

This aversion to women's sports extended far beyond the Olympics. As the social scientist Jennifer Hargreaves explains, "The particular difficulties of Olympic sports for women have tended to be exaggerated examples of problems and complexities intrinsic to women's sports in general."[19] The Victorian era (1837–1901) had emphasized the importance of women avoiding strenuous physical activities, and medical scientists also raised concerns that intense physical exercise could make it impossible for women to have children.[20] In particular, many resisted the notion of women participating in more "mas-

FIGURE 4.1. Gender balance at the Summer Olympics: 1896–2024

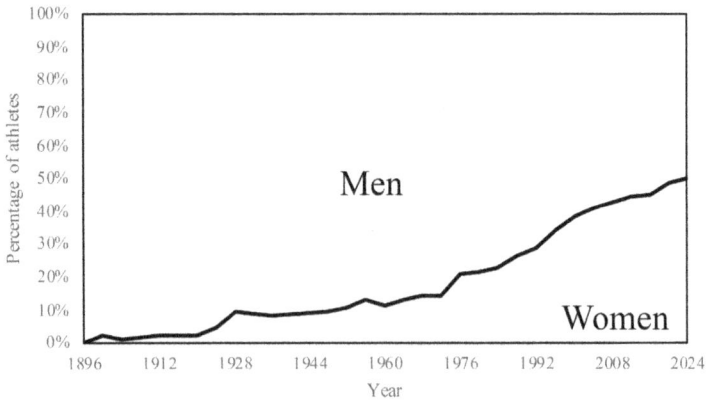

FIGURE 4.2. Gender balance at the Winter Olympics: 1924–2022

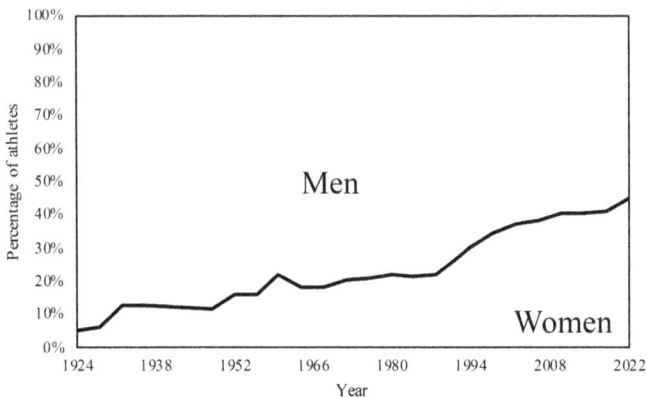

culine" sports like soccer and running, which require physical strength and stamina.

The implications of women's near absence from competitive sports during this critical period of modern history were profound and long-lasting. In fact, they continue to have a major impact on sports today. To understand why, it is first necessary to realize that there is no "natural" or "obvious" sport. Rather, sports are human inventions.[21] The traditional sports we take for granted—such as soccer, football, and basketball—were products of their cultural and political contexts.[22] These social contexts were controlled by and heavily biased toward men. Therefore, it is unsurprising that the most popular modern sports today favor traditionally masculine qualities like strength, power, speed, and height.[23]

Had gender equality prevailed 200 years ago, the world might have developed a different set of highly popular sports that did not favor such masculine traits. These sports might have included bowling, archery, fencing, rock climbing, ultra distance running, distance swimming, sailing, and equestrianism. In some of these sports, women would have clear physiological advantages over men, such as long-distance swimming, and in others there would be very little in the way of a gender gap.[24] Early sports leaders might have also developed other more complicated sports that either favored women's natural strengths or were gender neutral. Therefore, the key point is that this early period did not just feature rampant gender discrimination in sports, but it also resulted in the rise of a particular set of modern sports that favored traditionally masculine skills over traditionally feminine ones.[25]

As such, the most popular sports in the world today, in which the top male athletes outperform the top women, perpetuate the myth that men are physically superior to women. In other words, they suggest women's weakness in comparison to men, rather than their strength. This perceived athletic gap is so large that elite male and female athletes rarely even compete against each other, with many people just taking for granted that female athletes are physically inferior.[26] In this respect, the modern sports system may actually be an impediment to women's equality by perpetuating a false stereotype.[27]

Despite the structural disadvantages confronting aspiring female athletes and the disdain they face from many men, there were early examples of women taking up competitive "masculine" sports. One of the most famous examples occurred in Britain during World War I. As many men left the country to fight on the Western Front, women needed to take over the factories. These women were encouraged to engage in sports to stay healthy and fit for their jobs.[28] They formed teams and named their teams after the factories where they worked. The most successful soccer team—Dick, Kerr Ladies—became famous and played about 800 games, including against some male teams.[29] After the war, however, the English Football Association banned women because it worried that the women's game would divert resources from the men's game.[30] As mentioned earlier, the ban was not lifted until 1970.

Some women interested in competitive sports set up their own sporting events in the 1920s.[31] These sports events included disciplines like track and gymnastics that were not offered to women at the Olympics. The International Women's Sports Federation (FSFI) was founded in 1921. Spearheaded by French women, this organization set up its own "Olympic" games to be held every four years.[32] It first took place in Paris in 1922 and attracted an audience of about 20,000 spectators. Fearful that this new movement would become a competitor, the IOC reached a deal with FSFI to include women's track and field at the 1928 Olympics, although the IOC ultimately offered women a very limited program that only included five events.[33]

FSFI continued until the Great Depression forced it to shut down in the 1930s. It succeeded in getting women's sports expanded in the real Olympics, but female track and field would henceforth be controlled by the IOC. Under their leadership, the development of women's sports would take many decades. For instance, following the 1928 Olympics, the IOC did not include individual track events for women beyond the 200-meter race until 1960, and it did not introduce women's soccer until 1996.[34]

In the United States, some women had opportunities to participate in competitive sports, in particular in the industrial leagues and at historically Black women's colleges.[35] There was even a women's basketball team founded in 1936 called the All-American Red Heads that competed against men's teams for more than fifty years and won around 90 percent of their games.[36] Unlike most women's basketball teams before the 1970s, which played under a less strenuous version of the rules, the All-American Red Heads achieved their success under men's rules. In addition, the All-American Girls Baseball League was founded in 1943 to fill the gap left by male players during World War II.[37] However, for many girls and women, particularly those in the middle and upper classes, there was not much opportunity or encouragement to engage in competitive sports.[38]

The Women Who Challenged Elite Sports

Modern-day observers might be tempted to view this era as merely reflecting male oppression. That is, it might seem that women simply wanted to compete, and misogynistic men stopped them. Such a narrow reading of history, however, misses the full story. Surprisingly, many important female sports leaders also opposed the idea of having women compete at the Olympics and other high-profile sporting events.[39] For instance, when the IOC considered adding more women's events in the early 1900s and later after World War II, many women's sports leaders in the United States strongly *opposed* such reforms. In fact, many of these activists did not want women competing in the Olympics at all.[40]

What motivated this seemingly puzzling stance by many of these early sportswomen? The answer is remarkably straightforward. Similar to the organizers of the People's Olympiad in Barcelona, these women opposed the elite sports model, believing that it had many adverse effects on both athletes and society more broadly.[41] As the scholars Jean O'Reilly and Susan Cahn describe, these sportswomen believed "that highly competitive sport damaged the few skilled female athletes while neglecting the many, whereas higher participation rates in less competitive events benefited all."[42]

In particular, these early female sports leaders feared that the elite sports model could harm the mental and physical health of star athletes.[43] Their resistance to highly competitive sports became a major issue in the 1950s when the United States government wanted to gain more medals in women's events to counter the Soviet advances.[44] The women's sports leaders believed that the primary goal of women's sports should be to benefit women, not to enhance U.S. prestige. Describing the attitudes of these female sports leaders on this point, historian Mary Jo Festle explains that "Both a win-at-all-costs philosophy and a desire to please the fans shifted the focus away from the participants' best interests. Females should not be exposed to coaches who lost perspective, allowing their best players to compete even if they were injured, or pushing athletes beyond what they were capable of."[45]

The alternative model that these women developed involved using sports for fun, exercise, and to make social connections.[46] It often took the form of intramural games within colleges or high schools, without any spectators.[47] Higher-level competitions between the best athletes from different schools or colleges were rare. However, these physical educators sometimes organized "play days" where one group of female students would visit another campus for games. In such cases, the teams were usually mixed so that there was little chance for interscholastic rivalry.[48] The goal was to encourage women to continue engaging in sports in a healthy way after they graduated and thus enjoy the social and physical benefits of sports throughout their adult lives.

There were certainly advantages with this less competitive approach, but it also came with a number of drawbacks. First, it left men to dominate high-profile spectator sports, which attracted much more societal attention than female intramural games and play days. Second, it essentially provided a justification for a massive financial disparity between "serious" men's sports and "unserious" women's sports. For instance, in the early 1970s, only about 1 percent of U.S. college sports budgets went to women.[49] Third, not all girls and women were satisfied with this philosophy. Some female athletes wanted the same rights as men to compete in high-level competitions, yet they had little opportunity to do so under this system.[50]

To a critic of the elite sports model, discouraging women from taking such a competitive attitude toward sports might have seemed like the correct approach. However, there was much disagreement in the early 1970s over which approach to sports was better, including among women.[51] Further, a more fundamental issue regarding gender equality colored this debate: in a free society, it seemed like men and women should have similar opportunities in competitive sports.[52] Yet if elite sports came with serious downsides, as many female sports leaders had long argued, then would increasing gender equality in elite sports negatively impact women? Would it not make more sense for men to move closer to the female model of sports?

The Controversial Rise of Elite Women's Sports

A major turning point occurred with the passage of Title IX in 1972, the year before Billie Jean King would meet Bobby Riggs on the tennis court.[53] Title IX required any college receiving federal aid to take important steps to increase female students' opportunities in competitive sports.[54] The legislation is widely credited with leading to a massive rise in women's participation in sports, as it gave talented female athletes much more opportunity and incentive to become serious competitors.[55] Female high school participation in sports in the United States jumped about a thousand percent in the 1970s, from about one in twenty-seven in 1971 to about one in three in 1979.[56] The extent to which Title IX actually explains this increase is contested, as the law did not have much of a direct impact on most college programs until the 1980s.[57]

The rise in female participation, therefore, is also likely explained by broader societal changes in addition to Title IX.[58]

Since its adoption, some scholars have argued that by integrating women into the male sports system, Title IX actually had negative effects on many female athletes despite increasing women's participation in sports.[59] In particular, it led many sportswomen to accept the norms and rules of the male sports system.[60] Indeed, by the early 1980s, the NCAA had taken over women's college sports, pushing out the Association for Intercollegiate Athletics for Women (AIAW), which had been run by women.[61] Most colleges integrated their men's and women's sports programs into one department, almost always run by a man.[62] Another serious issue was that as more money and attention poured into women's sports, many men took jobs coaching female sports.[63] Therefore, Title IX was arguably both a triumph for women in sports while also a victory for the elite sports system developed and run by men.

The perpetuation of the elite sports system also raised the important question of whether female athletes should compete against men or only against other women athletes.[64] Some scholars and sportswomen believed that keeping men's and women's sports separate would feed notions that women were genetically inferior to men and essentially make women second-class citizens in the world of sports.[65] Importantly here, this debate emerged shortly after the civil rights movement in the United States, when many people realized that "separate but equal" could never really mean equal.[66] Many female sportswomen feared a similar fate for women if they were kept separate from men in sports. Nevertheless, concerns that elite women would simply not be able to compete with elite men prevailed, and organized competitive sports remained sex-segregated at nearly all levels.[67] As such, sports remain one of the few realms of modern society that is largely segregated by sex.[68]

Further, recent questions about where transgender athletes fit into this binary sports model have sparked an intense debate between many traditional women's rights advocates and LGBTQ+ rights advocates.[69] It should be noted that the roots of this disagreement lie in three important legacies. The first is the emphasis that so many former sports leaders, particularly men, placed on elite sports and winning. If they had instead emphasized the participatory model of sports, there would be little to debate regarding transgender athletes. Second, the advantages that our most popular sports give to traditionally "masculine" qualities raise important questions about fairness when it comes to LGBTQ+ rights in women's sports. If modern sports had arisen in a world with greater gender equality, then our most popular sports might not favor traits like strength and speed that give elite transgender women such a competitive edge. Third, the decision to keep sports segregated by sex rather than adopt a coed elite sports model made women's sports exclusive by definition. This choice was an understandable and practical response to the first and second legacies. However, the fact that sports remain one of the only highly visible areas of social life that is segregated by gender has made it a lightning rod for debate about LGBTQ+ rights.

Beyond the controversy surrounding transgender athletes, another significant issue involves difference in sexual development (DSD) athletes. Many of these individuals are born female and have always considered themselves to be female, but gender testing by elite sports organizations has revealed that they have at least one biological feature typically associated with males (for example, a Y chromosome).[70] Had it not been for sex testing, many or all of these individuals may have gone their entire lives without ever knowing that they fell into the DSD category. However, when elite sport organizations become determined to find out which athletes really do and do not count as "women," many complications can arise.

Sex testing in Olympic sports began as early as the 1930s and typically involved physical examinations of female athletes.[71] In 1968, the IOC ramped up its operation by requiring that all female competitors take a chromosome test that effectively showed whether or not they had two X chromosomes.[72] The problem was that, as mentioned, not all women match this description, and the IOC quickly found itself in the uncomfortable position of essentially telling some women that they were not actually "biological women." This "revelation" (and the stigma that came with it) upended the lives of a number of women.[73] It was not until 2000 that the IOC finally abandoned the chromosome test.[74] The focus has now shifted to whether female athletes have abnormally high levels of testosterone.[75] This condition, known as hyperandrogenism, prevents female athletes from competing in certain events at the Olympics unless they take measures to suppress their testosterone levels.[76] Predictably, it has proved about as controversial as the chromosome tests.[77]

Is sex segregation in sports even justified to begin with? Is it a mistake to have men and women compete separately? First, it is crucial to emphasize that men are not better at sports than women, because there is no such thing as a "natural" sport. As already discussed, sports are products of the cultural and political environments that give rise to them. Currently, the most popular

sports in the world favor traditionally masculine traits, because they were pro-
duced in a world where men dominated and women were marginalized. Most
traditional sports, therefore, celebrate traditionally masculine skills. It is thus
very difficult for elite female athletes to compete with their male counterparts
when it comes to soccer, football, rugby, basketball, and so on. It is not proof
that men are better at sports than women, but rather lingering evidence of
the harsh societal discrimination faced by women throughout modern history. Given the current situation, some scholars of women's sports argue that
it makes sense to allow women to maintain their own female-only leagues, as
they have been the historically underprivileged gender throughout history.[78]
However, it might also make sense to encourage female athletes to participate
in male leagues when they want to do so and can make the cut.[79]

In a thought-provoking book, Eileen McDonagh and Laura Pappano discuss
how sports are frequently segregated based on sex when there is little competitive reason for doing so.[80] For instance, shooting was not sex-segregated at the
Olympics but eventually became so. Top male athletes also lack a clear competitive advantage in sports like bowling, billiards, and long-distance swimming. Moreover, paired figure skating at the Olympics is forced to be coed, and
the man must lift the woman, even if the woman is stronger. But why institute
such a rule, and why require the pairs to be one man and one woman? Even in
a sport like football, the position of field goal kicking, depending much on an
athlete's focus and composure, presents an opportunity for women to become
heroes and role models in a traditionally male-dominated sport. Moreover,
before children reach puberty, there is little average difference between boys
and girls when it comes to strength, speed, and height. Yet many children's
leagues are segregated by gender, more for social reasons than for any competitive rationale.[81]

In the realm of elite sports, an interesting innovation could be to create
high-profile swimming events in which elite male and female swimmers would
be about evenly matched. In the swimming pool, female swimmers tend to be
more buoyant than their male counterparts, which gives them a major advantage in long-distance swimming. In fact, a race that lasted about an hour could
be sufficient for a close contest between the top male and female swimmers in
the world.[82] If an organization like the Olympics included such a coed event, it
could provide a captivating competition while simultaneously challenging the
myth that men are superior to women at all sports.

Along with the debates over whether women should follow the competitive model and remain segregated from male athletes, another controversy within women's sports centers on the fact that perceived attractiveness often gets female athletes more media attention, more money in sponsorships, and possibly even higher salaries on teams.[83] Since sports are supposed to be a meritocracy, this type of discrimination seems highly unfair.[84] However, this issue is not as simple as it might at first appear.

Spectator sports are an entertainment business, like cinema and the music industry. If an actress gets a role not just because of her acting but also because she is widely perceived as attractive and will therefore greatly increase box office revenue, many people would not find her getting the role as ethically problematic. Similarly, many people would not object if a very attractive singer secured a better record deal in part because of his popularity with the public. Even if a singer obtained better scores at Eurovision (Europe's annual song contest) because large numbers of fans voting from home perceived him to be physically attractive, most people would not object. This is despite the fact that Eurovision resembles a large sporting event in many respects, including that it involves physical skill and coordination (in the form of dancing).

Yet when it comes to sports, such discrimination seems highly unfair. No doubt, the purpose of sports teams is not just to win but also to put fans in seats so that the franchise remains financially sustainable. Would it really be wrong to pay an athlete a higher salary because of her or his attractiveness? Similarly, is it wrong for sponsors to pay such athletes more if they will help sell more of their products, or for media outlets to cover them more if they will increase their TV ratings?

In fact, this issue arises in both men's and women's sports, but it has caused more controversy in women's sports, where fans and commentators have taken much more interest in the perceived attractiveness of athletes.[85] Some critics of this tendency have not only directed their anger against men for "objectifying" women, but also against female athletes who pose as models. These women, according to their critics, play along with sexist male attitudes in an effort to gain money and attention. A major factor exacerbating this controversy is that both men and women involved in women's sports have often felt compelled to highlight women's beauty simply in order to sell enough tickets to stay financially stable.[86] In fact, the history of sports is rife with failed women's teams and leagues that did not generate enough revenue to survive. Historically women's teams have even held beauty pageants at games to attract larger audiences.[87]

The academic literature largely sides against privileging female athletes for being conventionally attractive, but the views on this subject are more nuanced than one might expect.[88] For instance, scholars have pointed out that many male athletes have capitalized on their attractiveness, and telling women that they cannot do the same could be considered sexist.[89] However, indulging viewers' biases regarding attractiveness might be little better than indulging the racial biases of a racist fan base.[90] Certainly racial discrimination would be unethical. Even here, however, leagues have sometimes sought players from certain countries to try to attract fans from those markets. The phenomenon is known as the "Yao Ming effect," after the Chinese basketball player who propelled the NBA's popularity in China.[91]

The dual expectations—that sports should be a meritocracy and that teams and leagues have the right and responsibility to do what makes sense economically—at times create ethical predicaments. Some academic research has also cast doubt on the extent to which sexualizing women athletes actually increases interest in women's sports, suggesting that it might instead turn off fans.[92] Thus, whether female attractiveness should play a role in sports remains controversial; it is a question that is fundamentally rooted in the function of sports as both a meritocracy and as entertainment.

In sum, the increased presence of women in the elite sports model presents important challenges. On one hand, it requires sports organizations to take on the controversial task of distinguishing between who is and is not a woman. In addition, the attention that athletes draw from fans, and the financial implications of such attention, create further controversy regarding the role that female attractiveness should or should not play in the seemingly meritocratic world of sports.

The Global Perspective

The United States has been a leader when it comes to competitive women's sports, but it only constitutes a small part of the global picture. Like the United States, Europe has seen a rise in female sports participation. However, this change has been much more recent, mainly occurring over the last decade.[93] The primary drivers have been grassroots efforts to increase interest in women's sports and much greater commitment from sports institutions to develop and promote female athletes.[94] Fan interest has also risen notably in some countries over the last few years.[95] Nevertheless, as in the United States, women's sports in Europe still lag behind men's sports in terms of the interest they generate, athlete salaries, and coaching opportunities for women.[96] With respect to the continent's most popular sport, soccer, men coach the majority of women's soccer teams in Europe, around 90 percent in many countries.[97] At the same time, there have been hardly any examples of women coaching men's teams.[98]

While Europe and the United States offer examples of notable yet incomplete progress for women in sports, many countries in other parts of the world have achieved far less in the last hundred years. For instance, the state of women's sports in much of South America has been abysmal. In the world of soccer, professional female players have earned just a fraction of what their male counterparts make, in some cases around 1/200th of the wages of male players.[99] Further, administrative positions in the soccer governance institutions of the continent have been overwhelmingly dominated by men.[100] Many of the national governments of South America have also seemed indifferent to women's sports. Chile disbanded its women's national soccer team in 2014, resulting in the team going more than two-and-a-half years without playing a game. The next year, Argentina's team suffered a similar fate.[101] In fact, most of South America's women's national teams were removed from the FIFA rankings in 2015 because they had simply stopped playing games.[102] While the situation has improved recently, it is still far behind the men's game.

Many countries in Asia and Africa have experienced similar problems. There are some notable exceptions such as Australia and New Zealand where women have done better. Meanwhile, in authoritarian countries like China and North Korea, where elite sports are primarily used for sportswashing and other political purposes, female athletes are developed in ways that in many cases are detrimental to their long-term health and well-being.[103] For most of the other countries on these continents, women's sports have been marginalized or actively repressed. The first Saudi Arabian women's national soccer team game took place in February of 2022. The Saudia Arabian government's interest in rebranding itself through international sports and hosting the Olympics may lead it to continue supporting women's rights in the sporting realm. In Afghanistan, where women were banned from playing sports by the Taliban before 2001, the situation changed drastically after the U.S. invasion. Nonetheless, the Taliban reinstated its ban on women's sports following the U.S. withdrawal from the country in 2021.

Women still face significant barriers in the world of sports, with a large range of variation across countries. However, the question remains whether sports actually empower women outside the sporting realm. We will turn to this question in the next section.

DO SPORTS EMPOWER WOMEN IN OTHER AREAS?

Social science theories involving causality consist of two parts. The first is a causal statement, like X causes Y. The second is a causal logic about how X leads to Y. In other words, X causes Y because it does A, B, and C. Importantly, when evaluating any theory, we need to consider the causal logic carefully. If a theory has a faulty causal logic, then that makes it a problematic theory.[104]

The theory that we are considering in this chapter is that sports empower women beyond the playing field. As far as the causal logic goes, there are several ways that sports might improve gender equality. First, watching female athletes might improve attitudes toward women in the general public.[105] Furthermore, sports could promote female athletes' personal development, such as by teaching them important skills and lessons that are useful in other areas of life.[106] Sports could also create economic opportunities for female athletes, and they could provide superstar female athletes with a platform to promote gender equality or other causes.[107] Finally, great female athletes could serve as an inspiration for other women to accomplish their own goals.[108] These are not the only ways that sports could impact gender equality off the playing field, but they are some of the most common that are advanced by proponents of competitive women's sports. In this section, we will go through each of them in detail to evaluate whether they do in fact provide compelling reason to believe that sports empower women in other areas of life.

Spectators' Perceptions of Female Athletes

Regarding whether watching female athletes improves spectator attitudes toward women, academic research suggests that sports may often have the opposite effect. First, a large body of research has found a substantial gender gap in terms of media coverage between male and female athletes.[109] As the scholar Jaime Schultz described in her 2018 book on women's sports, "Studies conducted in North America, Europe, Australasia, Canada, Africa, and parts of Asia have all yielded similar results: Women are significantly underrepresented in sport media. Dependent on the culture, sportswomen receive between 1.8 and 10 percent of coverage across all media platforms. . . . Scholars call this inattention 'symbolic annihilation.'"[110] Such disparities in sports media coverage can send the message that the accomplishments of women deserve far less attention than those of men.[111]

Studies have also found that the attention that female athletes do receive often focuses on their physical appearance.[112] In addition, female athletes who conform to existing gender stereotypes (e.g., look "feminine" while playing "feminine" sports) can be more likely to get press coverage.[113] Also, media attention often seems to portray female athletes as less qualified than their male counterparts, as well as describing male sports competitions in an enthusiastic tone while describing women's sporting events matter-of-factly.[114] Further, after elite female athletes perform well, journalists sometimes credit a husband or male coach for their accomplishment.[115] The problem is that sports are embedded within a world where gender biases are pervasive. As such, sports may serve more as another arena where gender stereotypes are perpetuated.

Media portrayals of sportswomen have also tended to be impacted by both race and religion. In the twentieth century, the U.S. mainstream media often ignored the accomplishments of non-White female athletes and instead focused on less talented White female athletes who behaved in conventionally feminine ways.[116] Although non-White athletes have received much more media coverage in recent decades, some of this attention has reinforced racial stereotypes.[117] In addition, sports broadcasters often comment when Muslim sportswomen wear headscarves, although they rarely do so when Christian athletes wear crosses or when members of various other religions have tattoos with religious symbols.[118]

The scholars Cheryl Cooky, LaToya Council, Maria Mears, and Michael Messner carried out one of the most extensive research projects on media coverage of female athletes.[119] This project began by analyzing U.S. sports media shows in 1989, with follow-up analyses carried out in 1993, 1999, 2004, 2009, 2014, and 2019. The scholars examined both *SportsCenter* and local sports media coverage at three different times of the year. The researchers found no notable increase in women's sports coverage in 2019 compared to 1989.[120] Across all the years, women's sports stories never received even 10 percent of the airtime on these sports television shows, and they often garnered far less.[121] In 2019, 80 percent of the sports news and highlight shows covered no women's sports stories at all.[122] The scholars also found this dearth of women's sports coverage reflected in the official online newsletters and Twitter accounts of CBS Sports, NBC Sports, and ESPN (although espnW did cover women's sports more extensively).[123] In addition, when female athletes were covered on television, their stories were often presented in what the scholars describe as a "boring, inflection-free manner."[124] The researchers concluded their study by blaming daily sports news and highlight shows for "shoring up stubbornly persistent ideologies of male superiority."[125]

Personal Development of Female Athletes

What about the notion that sports could teach girls and women important lessons that prove valuable in other areas of life? No doubt, sports can teach athletes important lessons like the value of goal setting, time management, and hard work.[126] However, this fact alone does not mean that sports are generally positive for personal development. In an insightful essay published by *Forbes*, former youth sports coach Bob Cook suggested that sports are not actually that beneficial for teaching athletes important life lessons.[127] After all, people can learn similar lessons through other more productive endeavors. Examples might include learning a foreign language, engaging in a reading group, participating in community service projects, or joining clubs that teach science, business, or writing. There is no lack of alternatives to sports, and the list likely includes at least a few things that would capture the interest of any individual, were they encouraged to go in that direction. In addition, while sports do teach some useful life lessons, they can also teach people the wrong lessons, like viewing experiences with an overly competitive mindset and overvaluing symbolic accomplishments like throwing a ball in a hoop.[128]

Research on how sports impact the personal development of athletes largely focuses on adolescents, and it suggests that sports have both benefits and drawbacks. In two review articles that covered close to 100 academic studies on the effects of youth extracurricular activities, researchers Amy Feldman Farb and Jennifer Matjasko come to a number of interesting conclusions about how sports affect young people.[129] Regarding the benefits, participation in youth sports seems to be associated with positive self-esteem, feelings of well-being, and academic aspiration and achievement, although the findings are somewhat inconsistent across studies. Participation in sports also seems to have little relationship or possibly even a negative association with smoking, drug use, sexual activity (for girls), and certain types of delinquency (like shoplifting). Further, participation in sports is linked with youth alcohol use (particularly for girls), other types of delinquency (like drunk driving), sexual activity (for boys), and homophobia.

There are several important issues to consider when it comes to this research. First, the findings come from observational studies, not experiments. The treatment variable (sports participation) was not randomized. Therefore, we need to be careful about concluding that the observed associations are explained by the causal impact of sports participation rather than other differences between athletes and non-athletes.[130] Second, these studies look mainly at youth sports in the United States, and the results might look different in other contexts. In addition, the research suggests that whether sports participation has a positive or negative impact depends a lot on what the alternative would be. For example, if a person does not participate in sports, is the alternative more participation in academic clubs, more time volunteering in the community, or more TV? If playing a sport gets someone with a sedentary lifestyle off the couch, it could have a very beneficial impact for that person.[131]

Regarding the TV example, one of the most important factors to consider is an individual's baseline levels of physical activity. If someone already engages in a lot of exercise, then sports do not stand to provide as much benefit. However, for people with otherwise inactive lifestyles, sports could prove extremely beneficial. This is because moderate levels of exercise can have tremendous physical and mental health benefits. As one of my graduate school statistics professors told me, exercise is so healthy that if pharmaceutical companies could put it into a pill, it would be a wonder drug that would revolutionize the medical industry overnight.

Importantly, not all sports are equal in terms of their health benefits. For instance, research has found that activities like swimming and cycling may not provide much benefit when it comes to increasing bone density.[132] On the other hand, athletes can develop stronger bones by playing impact sports, which include almost any sport with a ball.[133] Sports involving balls are also often stimulating for the mind, which can lead to important cognitive benefits.[134]

In addition, many sports can cause negative health consequences.[135] For example, sports that involve repetitive motions can lead to overuse injuries.[136] Furthermore, engaging in any one sport too often could be a risky endeavor. There is likely more health benefit in playing a variety of different sports than one sport all the time.[137] Additionally, cold weather sports like skiing and ice skating can lead to lung problems from breathing in cold air, and swimming presents similar risks due to breathing in chlorine.[138] There are also individual medical factors to consider. For instance, some people with preexisting heart conditions may be putting themselves in great danger if they push themselves to their limit.[139] Whatever sports a person chooses to engage in, it is important to understand the benefits and downsides of those specific sports, as well as any individual factors that play into the story.

Beyond physical considerations, the academic literature suggests that the impact of sports participation on individuals seems to vary based on the associated sports culture.[140] If the culture surrounding the sport is rife with drinking, for example, then increased alcohol consumption might diminish the positive health benefits of sports. In addition, female athletes competing in aesthetic sports like gymnastics, figure skating, and cheerleading have been prone to develop eating disorders.[141] The same problem emerges in sports where being thin is viewed by some athletes and coaches as conferring a competitive advantage. These sports include running, cycling, diving, rock climbing, and ski jumping.[142] Moreover, sports like rowing and wrestling sometimes require athletes to be under a certain weight in order to compete in specific weight classes, which could also encourage disordered eating habits.[143] Sports cultures in which athletes frequently take performance enhancing drugs can also pose a threat to participants, as the long-term consequences of using such drugs can be severe.[144]

We cannot simply conclude that sports participation always brings more benefits than drawbacks. It can vary greatly on a case-by-case basis. Especially important are the person's baseline levels of activity, what other activities they might do instead of the sport, and the specific sport and its associated sports culture. Further, many of the potential downsides to sports participation—including eating disorders, overuse injuries, lung problems, and the opportunity costs that come when one dedicates a significant amount of time to training—can be more likely to arise when individuals follow the elite sports model. These issues should be much less pronounced when people use sports for fun, exercise, and to make social connections, as many of the early leaders in women's sports advocated.

Economic Opportunities for Female Athletes

What about the third possibility—that sports could create economic opportunities for female athletes? Unfortunately, women are unlikely to make significant money from sports except in the rarest of cases. Those cases are often the ones that receive the most attention, which can distort public perceptions about the prospects of becoming a career female athlete. Several serious impediments make it very unlikely that sports can empower (most) women through this mechanism.

To begin with, the chances of becoming a professional athlete are extremely small for both men and women.[145] According to one set of estimates, the chance that a U.S. female high school basketball player will make it to the professional leagues is about 1 in 13,015.[146] For men, the estimate is about 1 in 11,771. The chances of becoming a professional football player are extremely slim as well, estimated at about 1 in 4,233. For soccer, they are about 1 in 5,768. The bottom line is that becoming a professional athlete is an exceedingly rare feat. For every professional player in sports like basketball, soccer, and football, there are many other athletes who never make it to that level despite their hard work and sacrifice.[147]

In the United States, some top athletes do receive athletic scholarships and occasionally even significant money from name, image, and likeness (NIL) deals.[148] However, relatively few college athletes make large amounts of money through NIL.[149] Further, there are several reasons why athletic scholarships provide only a very limited economic benefit. First, universities usually only give them to exceptional athletes. About 1 percent of college students receive athletic scholarships.[150] Further, many athletic scholarships only partially cover the costs of going to college. In fact, only about 1 in 100 college athletic scholarships are "full ride" scholarships, leaving many college athletes to foot much of the bill even if they are on scholarship.[151] Finally, athletic scholarships require student athletes to devote a substantial amount of their time and energy to training and competing rather than studying. From this perspective, a pure academic scholarship is often much more valuable than an athletic one, because it provides a student with a better opportunity to take advantage of the educational benefits of college.[152]

Activism of Female Athletes

What about the possibility of sports providing a valuable platform for female athletes to promote political and social causes? The cause could be greater gender equality, as was the case with Billie Jean King. However, sports could also empower women to take on other causes, like we saw with the efforts of Naomi Osaka and Simone Biles to raise awareness about anxiety and mental health.[153] Similarly, the soccer superstar Megan Rapinoe has used her platform to advocate for LGBTQ+ rights and other causes, for which she received the Presidential Medal of Freedom in 2022.[154] In addition, the Chinese American skier Eileen Gu used the 2022 Beijing Olympics to try to promote international friendship and understanding. In fact, athlete activism has become increasingly common in the world of sports, and much research has examined whether or not it can change public attitudes regarding important issues.[155]

Regarding activist female athletes specifically, research suggests that efforts to promote traditional feminist causes like equal pay tend to receive a better public reception than activism that centers on more controversial issues such as police brutality and racial bias in the criminal justice system.[156] For example, while the U.S. National Women's Soccer Team recently secured a great deal of support in their fight for equal pay, a large and racially diverse group of players from the Women's National Basketball Association (WNBA) faced a more mixed reaction in their advocacy of the Black Lives Matter movement.[157] In particular, when the superstar Maya Moore stepped away from basketball to take on social justice causes, she received a surprisingly limited amount of media attention given her elite status within women's basketball.[158]

We should also be cautious about the idea that athlete activism is a force for women's empowerment given that men's sports tend to receive much more attention. No doubt, sports have given important platforms to some influential activist female athletes. However, the issue remains that male athletes tend to receive far more attention than female ones.[159] For example, according to ESPN's 2019 rankings of the top 100 most famous athletes in the world, only three of the athletes were women: Serena Williams (17), Maria Sharapova (37), and Sania Mirza (93).[160] In an overcrowded information economy that gives people information overload, this means that the overall impact of athlete activism is giving a much larger voice to men than to women.

The recently published study by Cooky and colleagues underscores the concern that athlete activism amplifies the voices of men more than women. After analyzing an extensive amount of U.S. sports coverage from 2019, the researchers concluded that "men athletes and teams are frequently elevated in news and highlights shows due to their community and charitable contributions. Women athletes' community contributions, including their social justice activism, almost never make it into the frame of women's sports stories."[161] Given that the United States is in many ways ahead of the curve globally when it comes to women's sports, the challenges are likely greater for activist female athletes in many other countries.

Noteworthy activist female athletes certainly stand out, but whether this mechanism empowers women (relative to men) is questionable. Further, the example of Maya Moore suggests that the problem may be particularly challenging for non-White women.[162] Therefore, the overall impact of athlete activism is quite problematic from a gender equality perspective. We will examine the topic of athlete activism more in the next chapter when we look at sports and racial equality.

Women Being Inspired by Female Athletes

What about the possibility that great female athletes could serve as an inspiration for women, as we saw with the Billie Jean King example at the beginning of this chapter? This possibility would probably be most beneficial if such athletes inspired women to participate in sports for fun, exercise, and to make friends. Alternatively, it might also benefit women if it encouraged them to pursue other important life goals outside of sports, rather than leading them to try to become professional athletes themselves. As we have seen in this chapter, pursuing a career as a professional athlete is not a realistic goal for the vast majority of people. Therefore, it is somewhat troubling, for example, that following the boom of women's tennis in the 1970s, many girls devoted substantial time and energy trying to become the next elite tennis star. Such ambitions often proved very costly to their families and prevented the girls from pursuing other beneficial opportunities.[163] Similar concerns also arise when it comes to the increased seriousness of girls' soccer and basketball that has followed the success of the U.S. national teams in more recent decades.

In sum, there are serious reasons to question the extent to which sports actually empower women beyond the playing field, because they often have the opposite effect. Thus, the widespread belief that girls and young women should generally be encouraged to devote their time and energy to competitive sports might be harmful. The best approach for the vast majority of young people, regardless of gender, might be to enjoy a variety of sports and not take them too seriously, especially if they might be a distraction from more beneficial activities.

What About True Athletic Superstars?

It may be rare, but can we at least conclude that elite sports benefit the few women who reach the top? Surprisingly, history suggests that we should be very cautious about assuming that this type of success typically benefits female athletes, or their male counterparts, all that much. In fact, even for the extremely small percentage of people who make it to the top of the sports world, success often fails to prove as rewarding as it might appear.[164] For example, there are many stories of gold medal winners, both male and female, going through periods of extreme depression after the Olympics. Michael Phelps estimates that about 90 percent of American Olympic athletes suffer some kind of post-Olympic depression that, in his case, led him to contemplate suicide.[165] Dealing with success might be even harder than dealing with failure, especially in individual sports where athletes do not have teammates to lean on.[166]

There are several reasons why elite athletes might struggle after achieving their sports goals. First, no matter how much an athlete accomplishes, they could always do more. Even an athlete who becomes the best in the world is unlikely to remain at the top for long—no one can sustain success permanently. In this way, sports can make elite athletes feel like they come up short, no matter how much they actually achieve. Also, the opposite problem can arise, in that becoming a champion at a young age might leave a person with a sudden loss of direction regarding what to do next with their life.[167] Chasing an ambitious goal can give an individual purpose, and when that goal is achieved, the person might feel lost, without direction. Another reason for these struggles is that increased media scrutiny puts pressure on athletes, especially when they make mistakes. Many people look for heroes and role models in the world of sports, and this can put a tremendous amount of pressure on athletes to live perfect lives. Phelps describes media scrutiny as one of the greatest challenges of being a sports superstar.[168] Social media has likely increased the pressure on athletes in recent years, since it can turn their private lives public and also make it easier for ordinary people to criticize them.

There is another important reason that athletic stardom might prove hollow. Athletic achievements may simply not be the type of thing that makes a person happy in the long run. Research suggests that only about 10 percent of a person's level of happiness is explained by events and circumstances.[169] These might include positive developments like getting a raise or winning a sports competition, or negative events like failing to achieve a certain goal. In contrast, two other factors appear to be much more important: genetics, which accounts for about 50 percent of a person's happiness, and daily activities and practices, which is the remaining 40 percent.[170] Therefore, both genetics and daily habits tend to have a much larger impact on happiness than merely accomplishing goals.

What types of activities and habits are the most likely to lead to a happy and rewarding life? Research suggests that people should engage in a variety of activities that they enjoy, switching between them and not doing any one of them too often, as well as adding a social component if possible.[171] This can keep the activities exciting, fresh, and new—otherwise the mind adjusts and the boost in happiness diminishes. Likewise, people seeking happiness should work toward a variety of goals and switch between them often.[172] It is important for people to make sure that their goals and activities fit their personality and interests, and that they are what they value (not what others value).[173] Happiness can also be boosted in the long term by engaging in a variety of gratitude activities, like recalling past positive experiences, and also by performing acts of kindness.[174]

Therefore, chasing sports success is not a promising approach for reaching a happy and fulfilled life. However, engaging in a variety of sports might be one component of a balanced lifestyle that does lead to sustained happiness in the long run. In the end, twenty-first century research backs the philosophy of the early women's sports leaders who resisted the elite sports model.

CONCLUSION

Before ending this chapter, it is worth considering one final way that sports may empower women. It is an idea that very few people would think of, but it may in fact be the single most powerful way that sports contribute to gender equality. The idea emerges from a 2012 working paper about the legal profession in South Korea, which was written by the political scientists Jong Hee Park and Andrew Martin. Examining data on who passed the South Korean (second) bar exam to become a lawyer, judge, or prosecutor from 1996 to 2011, the authors uncovered an intriguing pattern. Every four years, there were jumps in the proportion of women (compared to men) who passed the exam—specifically in 1998, 2002, 2006, and 2010.[175] In fact, over the entire time period, four of the five largest increases in the proportion of women passing the exam came in those years.[176] The pattern likely has to do with the fact that the test is held in June, and when the World Cup takes place, many men study less compared to women.[177]

No doubt, watching sports can be an enjoyable experience that provides people with the opportunity to bond over their favorite teams. However, it can also distract people from achieving their life goals. Because far more men watch sports than women, spectator sports could be holding back many of these men, creating more opportunities for women. This may not be what most people have in mind when they say that sports empower women, but this example shows one way they actually can in the real world.

5

SPORTS AND RACIAL EQUALITY

We began the last chapter by discussing the 1973 Battle of the Sexes tennis match between Billie Jean King and Bobby Riggs, which attracted a television audience of around 50 million people. This case illustrates a broader lesson in the history of sports: athletic competition tends to draw more attention if the opposing sides are seen as representing different societal groups.[1] In the Battle of the Sexes, the defining difference was gender. Far more often it is race, nationality, ideology, religion, or some combination of these identities. Furthermore, it seems that the greater the antipathy is between the opposing sides, the more compelling the sporting event is to spectators.[2]

Throughout history, many sports promoters have been keenly aware of the capacity of social cleavages, particularly race, to draw attention to sports.[3] Thus, sporting events very often came to feature symbolic battles between racial groups that had histories of conflict. These contests would sometimes spark real-world racial violence, as occurred following the 1910 boxing match in the United States between Jim Jeffries and Jack Johnson. After the Black boxer Johnson won a decisive victory over his White opponent, racial violence broke out in many U.S. cities, with hundreds of Black Americans being attacked by angry White Americans and at least twenty people being killed.[4] It was the most widespread instance of racial uprising in the United States until the assassination of Dr. Martin Luther King Jr. in 1968.[5]

Despite the link between sports and racial conflict, there are reasons to think that sports have contributed to racial equality in a variety of ways. While sports remain one of the last spheres of public life to be largely segregated by gender, they were actually often at the forefront of racial desegregation.[6] Levels of racial equality in sports have varied greatly based on sport and location, moving at different speeds in different contexts and unfortunately still having a long way to go in many places.[7] However, sports were frequently ahead of the times in the movement to end racial discrimination in the twentieth century. Some of this credit goes to the IOC, which banned racial discrimination in its charter. Although this ideal was not always upheld in practice, it nevertheless led to iconic moments like the African American sprinter Jesse Owens upending Hitler's myth of Aryan supremacy at the 1936 Nazi Olympics.[8]

The role of international sports in shaping domestic politics was exemplified in the international sports bans of apartheid South Africa beginning in 1957. At the time, South African society was structured around formal racial segregation in nearly all areas of life. This system drew international attention because South Africa sent all-White sports teams to international competitions despite being a majority non-White country. This blatant racial discrimination outraged many nations, particularly in Africa. South Africa soon found itself banned from nearly all international sports, an outcome that was partly driven by the threat of a major international boycott of the 1968 Mexico City Olympics if South Africa were allowed to attend.[9]

The 1968 Olympics also featured the famous Human Rights Salute by African American athletes Tommie Smith and John Carlos after they won gold and bronze in the 200-meter dash. Their actions sparked outrage in the United States and led to the two runners being kicked out of the Olympics.[10] However, their protest lives on as one of the most memorable moments in the history of sports. It has also inspired many other athletes to speak out against social injustice.[11]

Sports have been deeply connected to questions of racial equality throughout their history, for better or for worse. In its purest form, sports have no racial biases, since the athletes with the most talent and determination should win no matter their background. However, sports do not happen in a vacuum. Many fans, referees, coaches, and team owners have held racial prejudices. Further, the societies that athletes grow up in can also advantage certain groups in ways that spill over into sports. Therefore, sports can both provide opportunities for people from underprivileged backgrounds to rise above their circumstances and at the same time perpetuate many racial injustices.

This chapter will explore whether we should really consider sports a vehicle for the advancement of civil rights. Similar to the last chapter, we will evaluate several popular notions about how sports could promote racial equality.

SPORTS AND BRIDGING SOCIAL CAPITAL

Can grassroots sports help break down racial barriers in society? Two examples already discussed in this book suggest that sports participation can build bridges between individuals from different racial groups. Social scientists call these types of connections *bridging* social capital because they connect people from different backgrounds who might otherwise not meet.[12] The first example that we saw in this book was Robert Putnam's story about the sixty-four-year-old Black man who received a kidney from a thirty-three-year-old White man from his bowling league. The second was the FIFA-sponsored games between Israeli and Palestinian children discussed in Chapter 1, in which the players are split up so that the Israeli and Palestinian children play with each other rather than against each other. Both of these examples suggest the potential for the popular participation model of sports to generate bridging social capital and help break down racial barriers.

Interestingly, the literature on sports and social capital suggests that grassroots sports may often be a powerful source of bonding social capital, in which bonds are strengthened *within* different societal groups but not *between* them.[13] In fact, bonding social capital can have the undesirable impact of hardening the divides between different social cleavages. The reason is that when people play sports, they often do so with others like them. Throughout much of history, community sports have often been largely segregated because of formal rules, geographical constraints, the preferences of participants to play with people like themselves, and variation between different racial groups in terms of the sports that they play.[14]

The sports world has always been a realm of exclusion. This overt discrimination is obvious in the long history of wealthy people playing certain sports that working-class people are not allowed or cannot afford to play. The wealthy often play these sports in specific locations, such as country clubs or expensive private schools, where working-class people cannot typically go. Wealth is just one example of how people who play sports often segregate, with gender, age, and race all being other key factors.[15] In this sense, Putnam's example of an older Black man and younger White man meeting through bowling stands out as an atypical case in the history of grassroots sports. In fact, Putnam chose bowling rather than sports like football, baseball, and basketball because bowling has a broad and diverse membership and those other sports do not.[16]

Importantly, a key limitation of the distinction between bonding and bridging social capital is that people typically belong to many different social groups.[17] For example, a Black player on a high school basketball team might develop a strong friendship with one of his White teammates. This example might seem like a clear case of bridging social capital. However, the two players could be from similar economic backgrounds and in fact even live in the same neighborhood, in which case their friendship would resemble bonding social capital from the perspective of class. Therefore, when we think about the potential of sport to break down racial barriers by generating social capital, we have to think about whether it helps build valuable relationships across racial lines, regardless of whether the social capital generated is best thought of as bonding or bridging (or something in between).

Thus, in cases where teams consist of players from different racial groups, as is common in many sports over the last few decades, the resulting social capital between teammates could be very beneficial for improving racial equality in society. However, there are still many examples of teams and even entire sports that are largely racially homogeneous, and historically such racial sorting has often been the norm. In such cases, we should expect sports to generate bonding social capital within different racial groups, which might in fact deepen the racial divides in society.

What about cases where organizations bring together people from different backgrounds to play with each other, like FIFA's soccer games involving mixed teams of Israeli and Palestinian children? Do such grassroots sports have the power to generate bridging social capital between the members of the different groups? In 2020, the political scientist Salma Mousa published a study in the journal *Science* that investigated this question.[18] Mousa conducted a field experiment in Iraq involving Christians and Muslims who had been displaced by ISIS. Working in a predominantly Christian area, she invited Christian teams to play in a two-month soccer league. She then randomized the participating teams to receive either three additional Christian players or three additional

Muslim players. Thus, her research design randomized Christian players to play on either all-Christian teams or mixed teams.

After the season ended, Mousa found that the Christian players who had Muslim teammates were more open to play on a mixed team the next season, much more likely to vote for a Muslim (who was not on their team) to win a sportsmanship award, and much more likely to train with Muslims six months later.[19] However, when it came to life outside sports, playing with Muslims appeared to have little impact on the Christians' behavior and attitudes. They were only slightly more likely to attend a mixed social event for Christians and Muslims after the season ended, and they appeared only moderately more likely to visit a restaurant in a nearby Muslim-majority city.[20] Further, they were not any more likely to donate money to a mixed NGO.[21] These results suggest that bridging social capital generated from sports participation may have limited relevance off the playing field.[22]

Sports participation appears to have limited ability to generate bridging social capital, but there are two important caveats to keep in mind. First, watching sports might offer spectators a promising avenue to build bridges across racial lines, at least when they congregate with other people from different racial groups. In other contexts, sports can even provide strangers with something to talk about, a way to break the ice, that can get a conversation going.[23] Nonetheless, we should expect these types of interactions to occur much more often among men than women.[24] Further, given the rise of smartphones, people may interact with strangers much less than they used to, whether at sporting events or elsewhere.

The second caveat is that sports might improve racial equality when they build social capital within minority racial communities.[25] For example, after the color line was drawn in American professional baseball in the late 1800s, Black players formed the Negro Leagues, which provided opportunities for many Black people to meet and build valuable social connections. No doubt, the notion that sports might advance racial equality without necessarily breaking down racial barriers is controversial, especially when it occurs in the context of forced segregation and significant economic disparities between racial groups.[26] We will return to consider this possibility in more depth later in the chapter.

Changing Spectator Racial Biases

What about the potential for elite sports to reduce racial biases, particularly among spectators. In the last chapter, we saw that media portrayals of female athletes often reinforce gender stereotypes rather than reduce them. The story seems to be different for racial biases. Rooting for players from different racial/ethnic backgrounds does in fact appear capable of making people more racially tolerant.[27] A classic example is Jackie Robinson, who was the first Black person to play in Major League Baseball when he joined the Brooklyn Dodgers in 1947. Despite facing racist abuse from fans and other players, Robinson is now considered by many to be a hero of the civil rights movement for breaking the color barrier in U.S. baseball and for shifting public attitudes toward Black people in the United States.[28] As Martin Luther King Jr. described, Robinson was "a pilgrim that walked in the lonesome byways toward the high road of Freedom. He was a sit-inner before sit-ins, a freedom rider before freedom rides."[29]

Two other classic examples are Michael Jordan and Tiger Woods. In the 1990s, Jordan became one of the most famous people in the world, as well as possibly the first elite Black athlete to be recognized primarily for his skill rather than his race.[30] Similarly, Woods became a superstar in a sport with a long history of racial discrimination and injustice. In fact, Woods's unprecedented twelve-stroke victory in the 1997 Masters came less than a decade after Augusta National Golf Club, where Tiger won the Masters, accepted its first Black member in 1990.[31] Therefore, the rise of a multiracial American like Tiger Woods to the very top of the world of golf could be celebrated by many as a powerful sign of racial progress. Some have even gone as far as to argue that for many White fans, looking up to Michael Jordan and Tiger Woods was a necessary step for them to be open to electing America's first Black president in 2008.[32] From this point of view, Obama's talent in sports may partly explain his widespread popularity in the lead-up to the 2008 U.S. presidential election.[33]

The power of sport to reduce racial biases among fans was also documented in a 2021 study about Liverpool's superstar player Mohamed Salah, written by political scientists Ala' Alrababa'h, William Marble, Salma Mousa, and Alexandra A. Siegel.[34] Salah, who is a practicing Muslim, joined the team in 2017. He celebrates goals by doing the sujud, the Islamic act of prostration that involves bowing down in the direction of Mecca, which has become a trademark of his game. Using statistical analysis, the researchers found that hate crimes dropped by about 16 percent in the Liverpool area from June 2017 to April 2018 because of Salah's performance on the playing field.[35] The researchers also found that Salah's move to Liverpool led to about a 50 percent drop in anti-Muslim tweets from Liverpool fans.[36]

Unfortunately, counterexamples demonstrate that sports stars from minority backgrounds do not always achieve this level of success in reducing racial biases. In fact, they can be unfairly put in the challenging position of being goodwill racial ambassadors to the wider public. For example, when the star African American tennis player Althea Gibson rose to prominence in the 1950s, many expected her to be the Jackie Robinson of tennis.[37] However, she struggled with the enormous pressure of this role, which Robinson had also found very difficult during his career.[38] Gibson faced high levels of media scrutiny and eventually developed a reputation of being unfriendly toward reporters.[39] Frustrated by the situation, she nearly quit tennis altogether. However, in the mid-1950s the U.S. government decided that it wanted Gibson to represent the United States in international competitions to counter Soviet criticisms over racial discrimination in America.[40] The U.S. government frequently promoted Black American athletes during the Cold War in this way, hoping to win hearts and minds abroad, particularly in Africa.[41] Thus, Cold War politics revitalized Gibson's game. She went on to an accomplished career, including eleven Grand Slam titles.

In addition to the pressure of being goodwill racial ambassadors, athletes from minority backgrounds can be criticized or scapegoated by fans and the media when they fall short.[42] This type of backlash arose when three Black players for England—Marcus Rashford, Jadon Sancho, and Bukayo Saka—missed penalties in the decisive shootout of the Euro 2020 final.[43] However, many fans came to the defense of the three Black players, denouncing the racism against them.[44] Therefore, when high-profile players lose, it seems likely that it would increase racial prejudices, but in the process it might also result in some people becoming more aware of racism in their societies. For this reason, such ugly incidents might sometimes improve racial equality in the long run.

Along with racist scapegoating, another possible concern is that some fans might become more intolerant from rooting against minority players from other teams.[45] For instance, it has not been uncommon for Black players in European soccer to face racial abuse by heckling fans, including monkey chants.[46] For this reason, sports stars differ from other celebrities, such as musicians and actors, because they frequently face fans who are actively rooting against them. These potentially negative effects might be reduced or eliminated in leagues where every team has many players from minority backgrounds, such as the NBA and NFL. Likewise, in cases where truly transcendent athletes emerge, like Michael Jordan and Tiger Woods, they may attract their own very large fan bases who root for them. Such superior athletes, however, are much more the exception than the rule.

Another concern is that seeing athletes from underprivileged minority backgrounds succeed could give spectators the false impression that racial challenges in their societies are overstated or do not exist at all.[47] In other words, when elite players succeed at the highest level, sign huge contracts, and gain admiration from the public, it could cause many observers to think that the racial prejudices in their societies are not that serious a problem. Further, seeing successful Black athletes can reinforce certain racial prejudices, like that Black people are innately more inclined to athletic achievements rather than intellectual ones.[48]

Another important consideration is the tendency that we discussed at the beginning of this chapter for sports rivalries to take on racial, ethnic, or national dimensions that can make a game feel like a type of proxy battle between two different identity groups. Examples of this phenomenon in sports are wide-ranging. At international competitions like the Olympics and World Cup, teams consisting mostly or entirely of White Europeans sometimes compete against teams of Africans.

Subnational competitions can also take on racial and ethnic dimensions, whether intentionally driven or inadvertent. For instance, the Los Angeles Lakers' rivalry with the Boston Celtics came to be linked with racial tensions in the United States, with some Black fans choosing to root for Magic Johnson and the Lakers and many White fans choosing to root for Larry Bird and the Celtics.[49] Bird, who in 1978 was drafted into a league full of mostly Black star players, was called by many the "Great White Hope."[50] It is particularly interesting that the rivalry took on some of these dimensions because the Boston Celtics had been at the forefront of hiring Black players and coaches in the 1950s and 1960s. This example illustrates that broader social forces can shape collective perceptions of sports teams and rivalries, even when those perceptions do not accord with reality.

In sum, players from minority backgrounds can reduce racial biases in certain contexts, but it often greatly depends on how they perform and whether fans are rooting for their team or the other team. In fact, there are various reasons to think that sports might actually tend to worsen racial prejudices. Contextual factors seem to be of utmost importance in this discussion.

Personal Development of Minority Athletes

Could sports improve racial equality by teaching people from minority backgrounds important life lessons? For the reasons discussed in the last chapter, the answer is possibly yes. Sports can teach valuable lessons like the importance of hard work, time management, and teamwork. However, other more productive activities can teach those same lessons, and sports can also teach some harmful lessons, like constantly thinking with a win-lose mindset.[51] As discussed in the last chapter, research on extracurricular activities suggests that youth sports participation can have both benefits and drawbacks.[52] Much depends on the culture surrounding the sport and individual-level factors, like a person's baseline level of activity and the alternatives the person would engage in if they chose not to participate in competitive sports. Therefore, it would be a mistake to take an overly positive or overly negative view of how sports affect participants. There is not a single formula that applies to everyone.

It is important to note here, however, that many young people from underprivileged backgrounds lack the types of alternative options that are often available to people who come from more economically prosperous communities. The choice might not be between sports and Science Club, for example, but between sports and activities that could get a young person into trouble. It is not rare at all for professional athletes to mention that when they were growing up their involvement with sports helped them avoid drugs or other forms of crime. On this point, Harry Edwards recently shifted his views about young Black people playing sports. His previous long-held opinion was that sports garnered too much of their attention, preventing them from learning more constructive skills. He has more recently argued that sports can offer youngsters a path to help them avoid making life-altering mistakes.[53]

Economic Opportunities for Minority Athletes

As we saw in the last chapter, relatively few people obtain full-ride college athletic scholarships, and the chances of becoming a professional athlete are also remote. Of course, many people understand these realities. However, an astonishingly large number of people greatly overestimate their chances of making it in sports.[54] A study carried out in 2021 found that about 60 percent of American men and 22 percent of American women thought that they could be Olympic athletes, with the figure reaching almost 70 percent for people under the age of thirty-five.[55] Basketball, soccer, and swimming were particularly common choices, despite the fact that these sports are some of the most difficult in which to qualify due to their popularity.

While these numbers may sound hard to believe, other surveys have also found striking results. According to a report published in 2016, about one in five men and one in three women in Britain thought that they could have been a professional athlete if not for an injury, bad luck, or their loss of interest in the sport.[56] Similarly, many American college athletes greatly misjudge their chances of going pro.[57] For instance, a 2015 *Inside Higher Ed* article reported that more than 60 percent of Division I hockey players thought they would make it to the NHL, even though less than 1 percent actually do.[58] The numbers look similar among Division I basketball and football players.[59]

In addition, many children and teenagers greatly overestimate their chances of making it big in sports, and they spend a significant amount of their time and energy chasing that dream.[60] The sociologists Scott Brooks and Dexter Blackman suggest that this tendency is particularly strong for children from minority backgrounds, many of whom grow up in communities where sports may be seen as the only legal way to achieve economic success.[61] Historian John Hoberman makes a similar argument, suggesting that societal stereotypes about Black people possessing superior athletic skills encourage youngsters to overcommit to sports.[62] Sociologist Earl Smith has also written on this topic, emphasizing the lack of opportunities for many young Black people outside of sports.[63]

Even for the tiny percentage of athletes who do make a significant amount of money from sports, it is not always easy for them to keep it. In fact, many elite athletes who become very wealthy at young ages lose their money quickly. For instance, in a 2015 study that looked at more than 2,000 former NFL players, economists Kyle Carlson, Joshua Kim, Annamaria Lusardi, and Colin Camerer estimated that between 15 percent and 40 percent of players declare bankruptcy in the twenty-five years after they retire from the league.[64] The researchers suggest that many young athletes may overestimate how long their careers will last or lack the knowledge and experience to save money so that it will support them long into their retirements.[65] In this way, athletics differ from many other career paths, in which people typically start with relatively low salaries and slowly make more money as they grow older and more experienced.

The Strengths and Limitations of Athlete Activism

What about the idea that sports could provide elite athletes with the opportunity to champion racial equality and other social causes, especially male athletes who are more likely to capture public attention? Without question, athletes from minority backgrounds have a long history of using their platforms to make political statements.[66] One of the earliest cases of athlete activism was Paul Robeson, who was the most famous Black football player in the United States before World War II.[67] Beyond his exceptional football accomplishments, he was also a talented scholar and lawyer, and in fact was studying at Columbia Law School when he was recruited to play in the newly formed NFL in 1921.[68]

After his playing career ended, Robeson was an outspoken critic of racist policies in the United States.[69] In the early stages of the Cold War, he stated, "It would be unthinkable that American Negros would go to war on behalf of those who have oppressed us for generations against the Soviet Union."[70] In this sense, Paul Robeson contrasted with Jackie Robinson, who tried advancing civil rights by working within the rules and constraints of American society.[71] While the two were at odds in the early Cold War, Robinson came to side with Robeson later in his life as he grew frustrated with the lack of meaningful racial progress in U.S. society.[72]

In a similar spirit, Muhammad Ali refused to be drafted into the military in 1967 during the Vietnam War. As he explained, "Why should they ask me to put on a uniform and go 10,000 miles from home and drop bombs and bullets on brown people in Vietnam while so-called Negro people in Louisville are treated like dogs and denied simple human rights?"[73] Ali was sentenced to prison for five years for draft evasion and stripped of his titles, although the Supreme Court eventually overturned his conviction. In the coming years, Ali became a major voice in the anti-war movement, speaking at protests around the country. As former U.S. Attorney General Eric Holder put it, "His biggest win came not in the ring but in our courts in his fight for his beliefs."[74]

A year later at the 1968 Olympics in Mexico City, American track stars Tommie Smith and John Carlos raised their fists in the air on the podium as the national anthem played.[75] Smith claimed that they were giving a Human

Rights Salute, but many in the American media interpreted it as the Black Power Salute. Both athletes were dismissed from the Games after the incident. While they initially faced a great deal of backlash in the United States, they each continued to succeed in sports and therefore stayed in the public spotlight. Their protest during the medal ceremony has come to be considered by many as a great moment not just in the history of the Olympics but also in the civil rights movement.

Some of the most prominent recent cases of athlete activism have been the statements against police brutality made by U.S. athletes. After Eric Garner's death in 2014, NBA and NFL stars like LeBron James, Kobe Bryant, and Reggie Bush began wearing "I Can't Breathe" shirts before games. American swimmer Simone Manuel also spoke out about this issue after she became the first African American woman to win an individual gold medal in swimming at the 2016 Rio Olympics. "It means a lot, especially with what is going on in the world today, some of the issues of police brutality," she explained. "This win hopefully brings hope and change to some of the issues that are going on. My color just comes with the territory."[76] Colin Kaepernick drew even more attention to this cause when he refused to stand during the U.S. national anthem before his NFL games. Many other players joined in on the protest, even outside the United States, making the politics of the pregame ceremonies nearly as confrontational as the games themselves. The protests of these athletes sparked major debates in the sports and news media about the problems of police brutality and whether the players were being un-American.

Athlete activism fits into the broader category of celebrity activism, whereby celebrities—such as famous musicians, movie stars, and entrepreneurs—take up social or political causes.[77] However, athlete activists differ from other types of celebrity activists in several respects. First, they are more likely to come from minority backgrounds, as a quick survey of the NBA or NFL illustrates. Second, they are much more likely to be male, as mentioned in the previous chapter. Third, sports celebrities have different fan bases than other types of celebrities. Specifically, they perform for sports fans, who can vary by sport but often come from a different ethnic and racial background than the athletes themselves. Fourth, sports stars have to deal with the large groups of fans from other teams who root against them out of loyalty to their own teams, an issue that musicians and actors do not have to face. Sometimes an actor might have to play the role of a villain, but the audience can still separate the character from the actor in a way that is not possible in sports. Fifth, athletes have to deal with strong societal expectations that sports and politics should be kept separate. Many people turn to sports because they want to be distracted from society's problems rather than reminded of them. When fans feel this way, they are unlikely to be very receptive to athletes who make political statements.

While the historical record might seem to suggest that athletes can play an important role in shaping political attitudes and discourse, there are actually several reasons to question whether sports stardom really provides a favorable platform for championing social and political causes. First, athlete activists often spark backlash from the other side of the political debate.[78] Academic research that looks at public responses to political statements made by athletes indicates that they commonly face a great deal of criticism.[79] While traditional media outlets often side with the athletes, this is not always the case.[80] For instance, when LeBron James spoke out on politics in 2018, one media show host responded, "It's always unwise to seek political advice from someone who gets paid $100 million a year to bounce a ball."[81] Muhammad Ali, Tommie Smith, and John Carlos also faced harsh criticism for their political stances, and it was only later, after public attitudes shifted, that their protests came to be widely viewed as courageous rather than subversive.[82]

It is not entirely clear whether the backlash that activist athletes face hurts or helps their cause. On one hand, it could harden the positions of people already opposed to their political views. Further, media personalities may distort or misrepresent the message that an athlete is trying to send in ways that make it seem illogical or extreme, as well as reframe issues in a way that is biased against the athlete.[83] On the other hand, backlash could also generate more attention for the sports stars and their causes.[84]

It also helps to distinguish here between politicized and non-politicized causes. An athlete who opposes a war, endorses a political candidate, or criticizes the government is likely to experience pushback. On the other hand, many athletes use their platforms to raise awareness about issues like fitness, mental health, and charitable causes.[85] For instance, Tiger Woods has worked to create educational opportunities for underserved youth while taking a more neutral stance when it comes to politics.[86] In such cases, athletes are much less likely to face resistance, and therefore may be better positioned to promote positive change.

A second concern regarding athlete activism is that athletes' potential conflicts of interest might discourage them from speaking out. Without question, the costs of athlete activism can be high. Muhammad Ali faced widespread backlash, had his title stripped, and lost some of the prime years of his boxing career due to his stance against the Vietnam War.[87] Tommie Smith and John Carlos were both kicked out of the 1968 Olympics and had to leave Mexico.[88] Colin Kaepernick may have lost his job as an NFL quarterback because of his protests against police brutality, which could have led many general managers and owners to conclude that he would be too much of a distraction if they signed him.[89] Therefore, it is not surprising that many athletes have chosen to stay out of politics given the potential economic and reputational costs of athlete activism. When Michael Jordan was asked why he was not more outspoken about politics, he famously responded, "Republicans buy sneakers, too."[90]

When athletes do decide to speak out, their stances can be undermined by potential conflicts of interest. For instance, Eileen Gu, the Chinese American skier who became famous when she competed for China in the 2022 Beijing Olympics, sought to promote mutual understanding between China and the United States. However, like many other athletes, actors, musicians, and international corporations, she had financial interests in China, which led many to question her integrity and motives.[91] For instance, some suggested that she was downplaying human rights abuses in China to make money.[92] Further, it can be difficult to decipher the true motivations of an activist athlete, and even if the athlete is being entirely authentic and not motivated by money or attention, the perception of a conflict of interest may greatly undermine their efforts.

Third, young athletes may be inexperienced and lack a deep understanding of the controversial issues into which they are wading. Sports are problematic in this respect because most superstar athletes reach their peak before the age of thirty. Moreover, the immense training that it takes to become a star athlete far from guarantees that a person will become well-informed about complex social and political issues.[93] A classic example is Muhammad Ali. In his early twenties, the young superstar athlete formally joined the Nation of Islam, an organization that favored racial segregation and claimed that White people were evil (Ali would disavow this organization later in his life).[94]

This concern may arise for some older athletes as well. For instance, Dennis Rodman's friendship with Kim Jong Un suggests that even much more experienced athletes might lack the necessary knowledge to be effective activists.[95] Remarkably, Rodman's trip to North Korea with the Globetrotters in 2013 may have been the first time that Americans visited the country since Kim Jong Un came to power. The *Vice* documentary covering his trip reveals how the dictatorship attempted to exploit this "goodwill" visit for domestic propaganda, in particular by portraying a respectful friendship between Rodman and Kim Jong Un.[96] In fact, Rodman, who became (in)famous in the NBA in part due to his provocative antics on and off the court, went to North Korea with little background in international relations. According to an ESPN documentary, at the time Rodman's trip to North Korea with the Globetrotters was initially being planned, Rodman's agent did not even understand the difference between North and South Korea.[97] After the visit, Rodman described his feelings toward Kim Jong Un by saying, "I love him. The guy's really awesome."[98]

Many other athlete activists have made very questionable, sometimes even outlandish, political statements. After returning from the 1936 Olympics, Jesse Owens called Hitler "a man of dignity."[99] Running back Jim Brown, arguably the greatest football player of all time, criticized the racial integration movement and Martin Luther King Jr.'s approach to advancing civil rights.[100] Another football legend, defensive end Reggie White, spoke out strongly against gay rights in the late 1990s, lending legitimacy to anti-gay activists at a critical moment in U.S. history.[101] No doubt, athletes like Jim Brown, Reggie White, and many others have made tremendous contributions to society through their charity work and advocacy of non-controversial social causes.[102] But when it comes to heated political debates, activist athletes sometimes find themselves on the wrong side of history.

In such cases, it is hard to entirely blame the athletes, who often demonstrate great courage in standing up for what they believe. In my view, the fault mainly lies with society for giving them so much attention and placing them in positions that they might not be prepared to handle. It is simply asking a lot to put such responsibility on people who are not experts and very often are quite young. If the media shifted the spotlight away from these star athletes and placed more attention on people who made important intellectual or practical contributions to society, it might lead to much more positive social and political change in the world.

Some activist athletes have benefited from having an older scholar who gave them advice and guided them through difficult situations. For example, during the civil rights movement, many activist athletes worked with Harry Edwards. At the time, Edwards taught at San Jose State College.[103] He played a leading role in founding the Olympic Project for Human Rights, which sought to use the participation of Black athletes in the Olympics to contribute to the civil rights movement.[104] Since the 1980s, he has provided guidance to many Black athletes in American professional sports, including in the NBA and NFL.

Therefore, the problem of the lack of knowledge and experience of young athletes can be overcome. However, activist athletes looking for guidance need to find the right people to advise them, and there is no guarantee that they will always be able to do so.

Further, the cases of Michael Jordan and Tiger Woods discussed earlier suggest that celebrity athletes who try to stay politically neutral might still have a large impact on politics, possibly even more so than athletes who get involved in politics more directly.[105] Although it is impossible to know whether Obama would have been elected in 2008 had it not been for Jordan and Woods, the theory is plausible given the immense popularity of both athletes and Obama's connections to sports. Had Jordan or Woods taken on controversial political causes that alienated many fans, they would likely not have remained so widely admired, and the United States may not have had its first Black president in 2008. From this perspective, it may be ironic that many people criticize Michael Jordan for trying to stay out of politics. His approach might have made him one of the most politically impactful athletes in history.

Therefore, when it comes to athlete activism, and particularly athletes weighing in on controversial political issues, there is reason to question whether such efforts are likely to lead to positive change. Some famous cases from history suggest that athletes can have an important voice. Nevertheless, the academic research and deeper consideration of the subject reveal many problems that could cause activist athletes to have a minimal or even counterproductive impact. In contrast, when it comes to less controversial issues, these athletes appear to be much better positioned to bring about positive change. In this way, sports stardom can help some individuals from underprivileged backgrounds change the world for the better.

THE ROLE OF SPORTS IN DECOLONIZATION MOVEMENTS

Despite the somewhat pessimistic conclusions reached in this chapter so far, there is actually another major way that sports have influenced racial equality. It is just not one that most people think about. It has to do with geopolitics—a topic that we did not explore in the previous chapter. The reason is that when it comes to gender, every country in the world has roughly the same ratio of men to women. Even within countries, the geographical distribution of gender across the world is fairly even. When it comes to race, however, variation is the norm. This is true between continents and within them. Moreover, there are pervasive power imbalances between different regions of the world, including in the world of sports. This geographical variation is very important to recognize when considering the relationship between sports and race, both historically and in the present.

The first step is to acknowledge the role that sports played in the independence movements of many countries.[106] As sports like soccer, rugby, cricket, and baseball spread around the world along the trade routes of the vast European and American empires, local populations picked up the games. The colonizers often promoted their national sports with the goals of encouraging cultural assimilation, increasing colonial control, and diverting attention from the often-harsh working conditions in the colonies.[107] The strategy was very much in line with the bread and circuses theory of sports—colonizers saw sports as a tool to distract the masses and prevent rebellion. However, sports were often a key institution that indigenous populations mobilized around independently of their colonial governments.[108] In this way, sports created important social and institutional networks that would play a significant role in future independence movements.

Competition on the playing field also gave local populations the capacity to challenge the imperial powers without having to resort to war.[109] In the process, it fostered national identities distinct and in fact opposed to the imperial powers. For example, after American expatriates began promoting baseball in Japan in the 1860s, the game soon became a symbolic arena in which Japanese teams could fight back against presumptions of American superiority.[110] Similar contestations played out with soccer in Africa and with cricket in India and parts of the Caribbean.[111] As the political scientist Robert Elias explains, "A sport can promote empire and social control but can also foment liberation and nationalism."[112]

Surprisingly, one reason that sports can play this role is their status as seemingly unserious activities. The political activist C. L. R. James made this observation in his memoir *Beyond a Boundary* about cricket in the West Indies. As he explained:

> [I]n those years social and political passions, denied normal outlets, expressed themselves so fiercely in cricket (and other games) precisely because they were games. . . . The class and racial rivalries were too intense. They could be fought out [in cricket] without violence or much lost except pride and honor. Thus the cricket field was a stage on which selected individuals played representative roles which were charged with social significance.[113]

In other words, it was the seemingly apolitical guise of sports that allowed athletic competitions to take on profound political meaning.

In many colonies, the teams and fan bases went on to take an active role in resisting the colonial governments.[114] For example, in the case of soccer, the historian and sociologist David Goldblatt describes that in many British colonies, "the colonists' game was turned against them. . . . [F]ootball was an instrument of social organization, cultural self-expression and a yardstick for demonstrating the limits and fragilities of the colonizing authorities."[115] In China, Japan, Central America, and the Caribbean, baseball functioned as a central institution wherein nationalists gathered, created their own rituals and traditions, and built social relationships and shared identities.[116] As one revolutionary described in Cuba, "[W]e couldn't meet in public, so we had to meet during our baseball games."[117]

After these new countries gained independence, their national teams provided focal points for the continued development and solidification of new national identities that transcended existing ethnic and religious loyalties.[118] Throughout much of Africa and the Middle East, rooting for national soccer teams became central to the construction of national pride and identity. In Japan, Taiwan, Korea, as well as in parts of Central America and the Caribbean, the American import of baseball became a preferred national sport and a venue whereby countries could compete against the United States and each other. Sports thus proved remarkably amenable to being both denationalized and renationalized by local actors to consolidate new collective identities in emerging power centers around the globe.[119]

Despite the role that sports played in the global decolonization movement, the story has been much different since the arrival of satellite television in the mid-1990s.[120] For instance, as discussed in Chapter 2, much of the African population has become obsessed with European soccer, thanks largely to the very successful efforts by European teams to expand their fan bases globally. A 2011 survey found that around 55 percent of the African population regularly watches the English Premier League, and it is no longer surprising to see people on the streets of African cities with jerseys and banners for Arsenal, Liverpool, or Chelsea.[121] This shift in attention to Europe has led to far fewer Africans following their own domestic leagues, which now see only a small fraction of the fan turnout that they did three decades ago.[122] Without fans buying tickets, many African clubs have failed to perform the necessary maintenance on their stadiums to keep them safe for spectators, which has led to a string of deaths from stampedes and other tragic accidents in recent years.[123]

As African club teams struggle to remain relevant, the vast majority of the continent's best soccer players have moved to Europe. Meanwhile, many less talented players have spent much of their money traveling to Europe for the chance to play for a less competitive club that might provide them with the launch point for a bigger career. Sadly, relatively few of them have managed to climb the European soccer ladder.[124]

When it comes to the players who do succeed in Europe, many of them return to their home countries to play for the World Cup, but it has not helped the continent achieve much success on the playing field. Only one African country has ever reached the semifinals of the World Cup: Morocco in 2022, which finished in fourth place. Only three other African countries have ever made it to the quarterfinals—Cameroon in 1990, Senegal in 2002, and Ghana in 2010. Likewise, no African club team has ever won the FIFA Club World Cup, played between the top club teams from each continent. As Goldblatt describes, "football has been linked to global economic, technological and cultural networks that have put the continent at a disadvantage, and accentuated rather than narrowed existing inequalities between Africa and the world."[125]

Like Africa, South America has lost much of its top soccer talent to Europe, lowering the quality of play in its national leagues.[126] South America also lags behind in terms of financial revenue and resources, with its soccer industry being worth about 10–15 percent of that of Europe.[127] However, South American national teams have continued to perform well in international competition. At the time of the writing of this book, South America has two men's national soccer teams, Argentina and Brazil, ranked first and fifth in the world, and two others in the top fifteen. Clubs from Brazil have also won the FIFA Club World Cup four times since 2000, although only European teams have won it since 2013.

Asia and the Middle East have followed paths more similar to Africa, with audiences often turning their attention to European soccer more so than their local leagues.[128] Match-fixing and corruption have also been a concern for some countries in the region, which has turned away fans.[129] Japan, South Korea, Australia, and New Zealand stand out for sustaining relatively strong domestic sports leagues, although Australia and New Zealand are predominantly White nations. Asian teams have also floundered at the World Cup, with only one country ever reaching the semifinals (South Korea in 2002) and only one other country ever reaching the quarterfinals (North Korea in 1966).

Some of the wealthiest Asian countries have achieved more success at the Olympics, in particular China and Japan. However, when it comes to soccer and basketball, the most popular sports in China, and baseball, the most popular in Japan, the domestic leagues in these countries lag far behind European soccer, the NBA, and MLB.[130] In terms of revenue, the ten most successful sports leagues are all in Europe or North America. Therefore, looking beyond Australia and New Zealand, Asia may offer a few partial success stories. However, there is a great deal of variation. Many countries are closer to the situation in Africa and South America than in Europe or North America.

CONCLUSION

Analyzing whether and how sports can advance racial equality is challenging, in part because different ethnic and racial groups face different circumstances, and the experiences of individuals within these groups can also vary greatly.[131] In this chapter, we have focused on several questions that should be broadly relevant across contexts, including whether sports participation tends to build social capital, whether seeing athletes of different ethnicities could reduce racial biases in the public, and whether athlete activism is likely to prove effective. As we have seen, racial politics interact with sports in a variety of complex ways. An athletic competition can turn into an arena of racial conflict, debate, and potential progress.

The 1968 Mexico City Olympics demonstrates this point well. Facing racial injustices at home, American Black athletes debated whether they would boycott the event or participate and support the United States in its ideological struggle against the Soviet Union. Meanwhile, many countries threatened their own boycott if apartheid South Africa was allowed to participate. When the international boycott movement succeeded, it represented a moment when countries shamed a racist government through sports. At the event itself, the protests of Tommie Smith and John Carlos caught the world's attention and sparked anger and debate in the United States.

The 1968 Mexico City Olympics also featured another serious controversy. About a week before they were set to begin, Mexican security forces gunned down a large number of student protestors in one of Mexico City's major plazas. The event is known as the Tlatelolco Massacre. The story behind it reveals some of the pitfalls that can arise when cities host major sporting events, as we will see in the next chapter.

6

HOSTING MAJOR
SPORTING EVENTS

To some proponents of spectator sports, hosting a major sporting event is one of the best ways that a city or country could spend its money.[1] To critics, major sporting events often constitute a large waste of time, energy, and resources.[2] Further, they might worsen government corruption, lead to environmental degradation, and cause a wide range of other problems.[3] Many point to the jobs and economic activity that major sporting events create for the local community. However, these jobs often pay low wages. People work part-time as food vendors, janitors, and garage attendants—the types of jobs that can exacerbate income inequality.[4] Further, governments could create jobs by funding many other types of projects, and they could attract tourists in other ways besides hosting a sporting event.[5] The question is whether a major sporting event, as a societal project, is worth it.

The first step in determining whether something is worth paying for is to understand exactly what it is. In the simplest sense, a major spectator sporting event is a gathering where a small number of elite athletes compete and many fans watch from the stands or on TV. For this gathering to be possible, the organizers first need infrastructure, which can include new or upgraded stadiums, ways for people to get to and from the event, hotels for the athletes and visitors, security to monitor the event, food options for everyone, and the list goes on. Maybe this infrastructure already exists or maybe it will need to be built. In return, the sporting event brings its own sources of revenue—ticket sales, TV rights, and sponsor endorsements.

However, a sporting event is not a mere economic calculation. It is a massive cultural spectacle. As such, it can have a variety of other social and political consequences.[6] Many of these effects have already been discussed in this book. In this chapter, we will mostly focus on topics that we have not yet explored.

FINANCIAL IMPLICATIONS

Given how much academics love to debate, the degree of scholarly agreement on the financial impact of major sporting events is striking.[7] Put simply, research suggests that hosting large sporting events usually does not provide a net economic benefit for cities or countries. In fact, such efforts often are prone to lose money. This lack of major economic benefit has been found for the Olympics,[8] the World Cup,[9] Formula 1 races (in Europe),[10] NCAA basketball tournaments,[11] and major league sports teams in the United States.[12] As the social scientists Rasmus Storm and Tor Georg Jakobsen explain, "the widely used (and popular) claim of economic benefits associated with hosting [major sports events] is misleading or—at best—overrated."[13] Regarding the Olympics specifically, the economists Robert A. Baade and Victor A. Matheson conclude, "the overwhelming conclusion is that in most cases the Olympics are a money-losing proposition for host cities."[14]

This assessment contrasts sharply with how many politicians frame major sporting events. In the leadup to the 1976 Montreal Olympics, Montreal's mayor famously claimed, "[T]he Olympics can no more have a deficit than a man can have a baby."[15] Unfortunately, the mayor did not live to see Montreal pay off the debts incurred from the event, which did not happen until 2006, more than seven years after his death. The mayor's prediction, considered foolish in hindsight, actually mirrors how many other people in government have championed the economic promise of sporting events in recent history.[16]

The first challenge that makes it hard to profit from major sporting events is that they usually cost a lot of money to host.[17] They can include not just sports-related expenses like stadiums, but also additional infrastructure like new airports and subways. It is hard to put exact numbers on the costs on any event, in part because of the difficulty of determining which types of expenses to include. However, estimates suggest that hosting events like the Olympics or World Cup can cost hundreds of millions of dollars to tens of billions of dollars.[18] Of particular note, economist Andrew Zimbalist puts the estimated costs of the 2014 Sochi Winter Olympics at somewhere between $51 billion and $70 billion, which illustrates how major sporting events can lead to astronomical spending.[19]

Of course, these events certainly can bring in tourists. However, research studies have come to contradictory conclusions about whether such tourists provide meaningful economic benefits.[20] On one hand, major sporting events only last for a short period of time. This makes the temporary spike in tourism more of a one-time shock than a long-term reality, unless the event is somehow successful enough to change long-term tourism patterns.[21] In addition, the influx of tourists from the sporting event might deter other people from visiting and could even encourage residents to leave while the event is taking place, which can reduce the economic benefits brought by the short-term tourism boost.[22]

One of the most systematic studies on the financial costs of the Olympics was carried out by the Oxford researchers Bent Flyvbjerg, Allison Stewart, and Alexander Budzier.[23] These researchers examined all Olympics from 1960 to 2016. Data availability allowed them to compare actual costs to the projected budgets for nineteen of the Games held over this period. The authors concluded that all nineteen of these Games had cost overruns.[24] As they described, "47 percent of Games have cost overruns above 100 percent. . . . [F]or a city and nation to decide to stage the Olympic Games is to decide to take on one of the most costly and financially most risky type of megaproject that exists, something that many cities and nations have learned to their peril."[25] The tendency of large events like the Olympics to greatly exceed their budgets and to fail to deliver their expected benefits has come to be known as "mega-event syndrome."[26] It appears to be a regular feature of large spectator sporting events like the Olympics and World Cup.[27]

What explains why mega-event syndrome is such a frequent problem in the world of sports? Research suggests that there are several explanations. First, organizers often underestimate the costs of hosting major sporting events.[28] A key issue is that sports events are scheduled to start on a particular date. Therefore, delays that would normally be an inconvenience for other types of large construction projects can pose a crisis for a sporting event and require the host to pay a large sum of money to resolve.[29] The rush to complete infrastructure can also result in workers facing long hours and dangerous working conditions, which can result in worker deaths.[30] In addition, preparations for major sporting events begin years in advance, and unforeseen issues like inflation, new security threats, and new regulations can elevate the costs of the project.[31] Furthermore, it can be difficult to project years in advance how many tourists will want to attend the event, which can lead organizers to over-build and overprepare to be on the safe side.[32]

These issues can lead to major sporting events having massive cost over-runs. The 1980 Lake Placid Olympics, the 1992 Barcelona Olympics, and the 2014 Sochi Olympics all ended up costing around 300 percent more than their projected budgets.[33] Yet cost overruns can turn out far worse. The 2007 Pan American Games in Rio cost about nine times more than their original budget.[34] Similarly, the stadiums for the 2010 World Cup in South Africa ended up costing about ten times more than projected.[35] Perhaps most egregiously, the 2010 Commonwealth Games in New Delhi were estimated to cost about $50 million, but they ended up costing around $4 billion, approximately eighty times as much as expected.[36]

Second, organizers also seem prone to overestimate the benefits of hosting a major sporting event.[37] For instance, they often claim that expensive new stadiums will be used regularly after the event is over, a hope that has proved naive in many cases.[38] Part of the reason is that the crowds needed to fill the stadium simply may not come after the event ends and tourists leave. Further-more, maintaining a stadium can be extremely costly, meaning that often no one has much financial incentive to take care of the stadium after the event has ended.[39] As a result, many expensive new stadiums fall into a desolate state of disuse.[40]

Another reason is that staging major sporting events often results in the use of public resources for private interests.[41] While the public sector com-monly pays for many of the preparations for the competition, private investors also sometimes get involved. The government typically has to bail out these actors if unexpected financial problems arise that require additional resources to make sure that the necessary infrastructure is ready on time. This means that the public sector allows private investors to make risky investments and then shifts the risk from the private investors to the public.

Furthermore, the needs of the event often end up getting prioritized over the host's needs.[42] In other words, the sporting event takes control of the host city or country instead of the other way around.[43] For instance, the social scientists Martin Müller and Christopher Gaffney explain that although the 2016 Rio Olympics did accelerate the city's infrastructure development plan, it led to the plan being altered in ways that were not helpful to the city. For instance, the development of the city's metro line was changed to accommodate the event at great expense.[44] The case of Rio is just one example. Similar stories played out in the lead-up to the 2010 World Cup in South Africa and the 2018 World Cup in Russia.[45]

Finally, government cronyism can lead to valuable building contracts being gifted to regime loyalists.[46] When this occurs, it not only enriches elites at the public's expense, but it can also strengthen the political support of corrupt governments, making them more entrenched. The 2014 Sochi Olympics and 2018 Russia World Cup demonstrated how this process can unfold. Many of Putin's oligarch political allies made fortunes off government contracts, which in turn helped solidify their support for Putin's authoritarian government. The 2014 World Cup and 2016 Olympics in Brazil exhibited similar cronyism. Regarding Brazil and the 2014 Sochi Olympics, Müller and Gaffney describe that "the events were used as opportunities for the redistribution of public resources [to] maintain a political economy of construction-associated graft and patronage."[47]

Importantly, some cities can host major sporting events at lower costs because they already have large, preexisting sports and hotel infrastructures. For example, Los Angeles found itself better positioned than most cities when it hosted the 1932 and 1984 Olympics, largely due to its established sports facilities, including those linked to the University of Southern California and UCLA.[48] In both cases, Los Angeles also benefited from having stingy organizing committees that focused on conserving money, minimizing waste, and maximizing revenue.[49] However, possessing substantial infrastructure by no means guarantees that a city will avoid the pathologies of mega-event syndrome. For instance, the economist Paul Oyer highlights the 2012 London Olympics as an example where a city paid far too much for a sporting event with far too little return on investment.[50]

Some have suggested creating two permanent host locations for the Winter and Summer Olympics, which could save a significant amount of money while also potentially making the Games much more environmentally friendly.[51] However, it could be very difficult to reach a consensus on which cities should be chosen as the permanent hosts. The problem is not only that politicians might fight over which two cities are the most deserving, but also because many citizens now oppose hosting major sporting events.[52] In short, there is significant misalignment of interests between many of the players involved.

Besides existing infrastructure, another important factor seems to be regime type. Specifically, democracies tend to be more insulated from the economic pitfalls of hosting major sporting events compared to non-democracies.[53] The reasons seem to be that democracies have stronger public accountability and are usually better suited to use the infrastructure after the event has concluded. However, this in no way implies that hosting major sporting events will be profitable for democracies, as the case of the 1976 Olympics in Montreal clearly demonstrated.

Research has also found that developed nations tend to be less susceptible than developing nations to the pitfalls of major sporting events.[54] This is because the costs of building the necessary infrastructure are likely to be more affordable for developed nations. Furthermore, the opportunity costs may be much lower compared to developing nations, and the likelihood that the facilities will be maintained and used in the future are also likely much higher. Major sporting events in developed countries would also be more likely to generate significant revenue from fans attending games. The local population, with higher income levels, would be more likely to attend the sporting event, and potential tourists may be less worried about crime. Therefore, some of the disastrous consequences of hosting major sporting events that have occurred in Brazil, South Africa, and Russia might be less pronounced in developed countries, but that by no means makes hosting such events a profitable enterprise.

NATIONAL BRANDING

Although major sporting events may cost much more money than they bring in, could cities or countries use them to project a positive image to their own population and to the rest of the world? We saw some examples of this in Chapter 3 when we discussed dictators and sports, such as Hitler's use of the 1936 Berlin Olympics to deceive the world about the nature and goals of his government. A more positive example was Barcelona's hosting of the 1992 Summer Olympics, which many people have argued helped establish the city as a major tourist destination.[55] In fact, many other cities and countries have attempted to rebrand themselves by hosting major sporting events. Prominent examples include Argentina with the 1978 World Cup (discussed in Chapter 3), South

Africa with the 1995 Rugby World Cup (discussed in Chapter 2), and Beijing with the 2008 Olympics (discussed in Chapter 3).

Academic studies on how major sporting events impact the reputation of host cities and countries come to several conclusions. First, hosting a major sporting event can improve the image of the host city or country, both in the short and long term.[56] For example, survey data from a number of countries suggest that Germany received a reputational boost from hosting the 2006 World Cup.[57] Similarly, researchers Eva Kassens-Noor, Joshua Vertalka, and Mark Wilson examined 21 million tweets from 2016 related to the Olympics and found that Rio received a boost in positive tweets during the Summer Olympics.[58] Likewise, researchers Dongfeng Liu and Chris Gratton found that the 2008 Shanghai F1 Grand Prix had a mostly positive impact on spectators' views of Shanghai.[59]

Also, the event can be remembered more positively than the host city/country. For instance, research has found that people had favorable memories of the 2012 London Olympics, but that these feelings did not clearly translate into more positive views of London.[60] Viewers therefore appear capable of distinguishing between the event and the location. This implies that host cities and countries may not enjoy a reputational bump even if they put on a successful event. Exactly how this happens is a question requiring further research. However, it seems that cities with well-established reputations are unlikely to improve their images much by hosting major sporting events.[61]

A successful sporting event in a lesser-known location may boost tourism even long after the competition ends. For example, researchers Yong-Soon Kang and Richard Perdue find evidence that the 1988 Seoul Olympics increased tourism to South Korea, although the effect appears to diminish over time. They estimate that South Korea brought in an estimated $1.3 billion in the three years following the Olympics.[62] However, it is usually hard to know how much of a long-term boost in tourism can be attributed to a sporting event as opposed to other factors, making such statistical analyses suggestive at best.

Sometimes the host's image can actually suffer a great deal because of an international sporting event.[63] One way this can happen is the scrutiny-publicity dilemma discussed in Chapter 3.[64] For instance, China's international reputation diminished during the 2022 Beijing Olympics. First, the country's human rights abuses, particularly against the Uyghurs, took center stage before, during, and after the event. Many critics argued that China should not be allowed to host the Games, and several democratic countries staged a diplomatic boycott.[65] China also received criticism for Beijing's dirty industrial cityscape, with a *Washington Post* headline describing the setting of the Big Air Venue as "Post-Apocalyptic."[66] In addition, complaints arose regarding the rules applying to the media, as well as the harsh treatment of athletes quarantined because of COVID-19.[67]

Qatar faced a similar problem when it hosted the 2022 World Cup. First, critics argued that the small, arid, oil-rich country acquired the rights to host the World Cup because its government had bribed FIFA officials.[68] Further, the spotlight of the World Cup caused many to question women's rights in Qatar, as well as those of LGBTQ+ individuals.[69] Regarding women's rights, a 2021 Human Rights Watch report highlighted how women in Qatar could not marry without the permission of their male "guardians," and in many cases they also needed permission to travel abroad or to receive certain types of reproductive health care.[70] Meanwhile, Qatari men could marry up to four women at a time without needing permission from their other wives.[71] Another major concern centered around the rights and safety of migrant workers in Qatar, especially those who were working on infrastructure projects related to the World Cup.[72] Because Qatar is a very small country, it needed to undertake major construction projects in the lead-up to the World Cup, including new stadiums, roads, and major airport upgrades.[73] This work was primarily carried out by migrant workers from poorer African and Asian countries, such as India, Kenya, and Bangladesh.[74]

Because the Qatari political system lacked the necessary laws to protect these workers, many faced terrible living conditions in Qatar and were required to work in the country's dangerous summer heat.[75] Concerns about potentially large numbers of migrant worker deaths arose in 2013.[76] According to an article published in *The Guardian* in 2021, more than 6,500 migrant workers died from 2010 to 2020, although admittedly it is difficult to estimate the number of these people who were working on World Cup–related projects.[77] Facing a potential boycott, both FIFA and Qatar took these concerns seriously, and Qatar made a number of reforms that improved the situation somewhat by 2021.[78]

Nevertheless, the increased scrutiny brought by the World Cup may have left a lasting negative image in the minds of many regarding corruption and human rights violations in Qatar. For instance, a YouGov survey carried out in Britain found that around 70 percent of the British population had a negative view of Qatar just before and after the tournament, compared to only about 10 percent who had a positive view of the country.[79] Another poll taken about a month before the tournament found similar levels of anti-Qatar sentiment in Spain, France, and Germany.[80] Attitudes toward Qatar may also have soured somewhat in the United States, with more people reporting opposition to Qatar's hosting of the 2022 World Cup during the tournament compared to before it.[81]

Even for democracies, a host's image can suffer due to poor hospitality or other factors. When England hosted the 1966 World Cup, its treatment of foreign teams and reporters was so abysmal that it damaged England's international reputation. For example, the training grounds reserved for Brazil and Argentina did not have goalposts. Accommodations for foreign visitors also left much to be desired, and transportation miscues caused a great deal of inconvenience and confusion.[82] The quarterfinal game between England and Argentina was particularly violent, with Hugh McIlvanney of *The Observer* describing it as "not so much a football match as an international incident."[83]

The foreign press coverage that England received was so negative that at one point the British Embassy in Rome was asked to look for an Italian reporter who would be willing to write a favorable article about England's hosting of the World Cup. The embassy replied, "Sportswriters in the Italian press were universally critical of the organisation of the World Cup. . . . and it is highly unlikely that anyone of the necessary stature could now be induced to defend Fifa and British organisation of the competition for any money."[84] On the day after England won the tournament, one of the largest newspapers in Bolivia wrote, "England has sold its hard-earned reputation for chivalry, for fair play and for correctness, for a football trophy. Today there are thousands of people who have always admired England who no longer admire England, because accomplishments that are dirty and fabricated can inspire only contempt."[85] Echoing Orwell, the British diplomat Sir Patrick Fairweather proclaimed after the tournament had finished, "[T]he World Cup in England has provided further proof, if proof were needed, that a very good way to damage international relations is to have a really big sporting competition."[86]

The impact of a major sporting event on the host's reputation can go in either direction. Poor planning, concerns over human rights, political controversies, and cultural differences can tarnish the reputation of a host city or country. On the other hand, some hosts have secured a reputational boost from hosting a major competition, so doing so is certainly possible under the right circumstances.

OTHER EFFECTS

Hosting a major sporting event can have many other important consequences beyond economics and reputational considerations. On a positive note, staging major sporting events can make some citizens happier, at least in the short run.[87] This potential boost in happiness could be one factor that explains why many politicians want to host major sporting events.[88] However, in cases where the event costs much more money than it brings in, some of this happiness might be unwarranted. As Heather Mitchell and Mark Fergusson Stewart point out, "Although people feel happy when hosting these events, this is probably because they are unaware of, and certainly do not feel personally responsible for, the cost of both acquiring and putting on the event."[89]

A more cynical view is that specific actors such as construction companies, executives in the hotel industry, and unethical politicians favor hosting major sporting events because doing so can benefit them economically or politically.[90] While hosting may not often make economic sense at the societal level, many elites and corporations have benefited personally from these events. The 2014 Sochi Olympics is a textbook example, as it brought major political gains to Putin, as well as economic benefits to his oligarch supporters.[91] However, perverse incentives can arise for politicians in democracies as well. As Mitchell and Stewart explain, "The lure of being photographed with a sports star is often too much for a politician to resist. Thus, regardless of whether hosting these events actually generates economic benefits, it seems that political motivation is the driving factor behind the decision to bid."[92]

The population displacement that often comes with these competitions also demonstrates how a major sporting event can run counter to the public interest.[93] This is especially true when governments want to clear the neighborhoods around sports venues so that foreign visitors will not see their impoverished citizens. Major population displacements took place in the lead-up to the 2008 Beijing Olympics, the 2010 South African World Cup, the 2014 Sochi Olympics, the 2014 Brazilian World Cup, and the 2016 Rio Olympics.[94] In democracies, the problem can arise from the sporting event driving up property values and thereby causing gentrification.[95] As social scientists Müller and Gaffney explained in 2018, "Since at least 1988, large-scale displacement of residents has been a persistent feature of the mega-events."[96] This citizen relocation is one way that a major sporting event can exacerbate economic inequality and harm some of the country's most vulnerable citizens.

It is not surprising, then, that despite some survey evidence indicating that hosting major sporting events can make people feel happier, the opposite can also be true. In particular, irresponsibly hosting an international sporting event can incite public outrage.[97] Brazil proved this point when it hosted the 2014 World Cup and 2016 Olympics. The country spent about $27 billion on these two events and forced roughly 75,000 people out of their homes during the preparations, causing millions to take to the streets in protest.[98] In fact, according to a poll conducted before the World Cup, about 61 percent of Brazilians were opposed to holding the tournament because it took money away from public services like schools and healthcare.[99] Similarly, a poll taken before the Olympics found that about 60 percent believed the event would bring more harm than good to the country.[100]

No doubt, these events partly explain why presidential approval ratings in Brazil tanked in the 2010s, dropping from about 85 percent in 2010 to about 20 percent in 2016.[101] As political scientists Pedro Santos Mundim and Gleice Meire Almeida da Silva explain regarding the 2014 World Cup, the event "transformed from a classic case of bread and circuses into a catalyst for popular dissatisfaction. Instead of a popularity boost and a smooth path to reelection in 2014, Brazilian political leaders found themselves scrambling to deal with the legacy of a World Cup own goal."[102]

Major sporting events can also lead to important changes in the law, often in the name of providing security for the event and accommodating visitors.[103] No doubt, security concerns constitute a key issue for major sporting events, as the global spotlight can attract nefarious actors seeking attention.[104] The brutal attack by the Black September terrorist organization on Israeli athletes and coaches at the 1972 Munich Olympics demonstrates the need for extensive security measures.[105] The shocking tragedy resulted in the deaths of eleven members of the Israeli delegation, along with a West German police officer, marking one of the darkest moments in Olympic history.

In fact, the organizers of the 1972 Munich Olympics had kept security relatively light out of fear of reminding people of another very dark moment in Olympic history—the militaristic 1936 Nazi Olympics.[106] They only spent about $2 million on security.[107] The catastrophe that ensued would make such a restrained approach unthinkable for all future Olympics.[108]

While it is easy to understand the need for extensive security measures at major sporting events, legal changes sometimes outlast the event and can have long-term effects on the host community. For example, critics of the Olympics have pointed out that the Games provide governments with a pretext to pass undemocratic laws.[109] The potential threat of terrorism at these major sporting events also gives law enforcement a justification to acquire high-tech military equipment.[110] While this equipment could be used to combat or deter terrorists at the Games, it might also be turned against citizens during or after the event.[111]

Security concerns related to major sporting events can also serve as catalysts for deadly government crackdowns. Chapter 3 described how the military regime in Argentina targeted its critics in the lead-up to the 1978 World Cup, characterizing them as a subversive domestic threat. Another famous case occurred before the 1968 Olympics in Mexico City, in which Mexican security forces gunned down a large number of anti-government protestors. Although the exact number of victims is not known, experts believe that around 200 people may have died, many of them students.[112] The protestors wanted to draw attention to the repressive and anti-democratic practices of the Mexican government.[113] However, the government's interest in having the Games run smoothly may have been key to its decision to quell the protests in brutal fashion.[114] Following the massacre, government forces rounded up and imprisoned thousands more individuals.[115]

Beyond what governments might do themselves, sports organizations sometimes pressure the host country to change its laws.[116] For example, FIFA demanded that Brazil allow fans to drink in stadiums for the 2014 World Cup, even though Brazil had banned alcohol at soccer games in 2003 in an effort to reduce fan violence.[117] Deadly fights between fans have been a major problem in South American soccer, including in Brazil.[118] However, FIFA was unwilling to respect the Brazilian law, possibly because Budweiser is one of its main sponsors.[119] FIFA also pressured Qatar to sell alcohol in stadiums during the 2022 World Cup. Qatar initially agreed, but the decision was reversed two days before the tournament started.[120]

Beyond these legal and security issues, sporting events can also have detrimental environmental effects, especially when host cities and countries need to build new infrastructure.[121] Although sports organizations often publicize their commitments to sustainability, it may be unrealistic to think that these competitions can be ecologically friendly given their energy, construction, and transportation requirements. In a 2017 book called *Greenwashing Sport*, social scientist Toby Miller argues that many major sports organizations try to win public goodwill by talking about sustainability when in fact their competitions are typically very harmful to the environment.[122] The idea that major sporting events create a lot of environmental fallout has in fact caused trouble for sports organizations in past decades. For instance, the public in Denver voted to turn down the opportunity to host the 1976 Olympics partly due to worries over environmental degradation.[123]

Beyond the obvious resource consumption, pollution, and energy costs of sports mega-events, there are also alarming examples of these competitions leading to clear and sometimes seemingly senseless environmental destruction. For the 2014 World Cup, the Brazilian government uprooted acres of the Amazon rainforest to make room for a FIFA-quality stadium, spending about $300 million in the process.[124] Similarly, preparations for the 2018 Pyeong-Chang Olympics involved large-scale forest destruction to create a ski run.[125] Another forest was partly cleared to make way for a ski run in the preparations for the 2022 Beijing Olympics, in this case through Yanqing Songshan National Forest Park, which is the home of numerous rare species.[126] Put simply, major international sporting events have been detrimental from an environmental perspective.

What about the possibility that hosting a major sporting event could encourage local populations to engage in sports more often, which might boost the health and well-being of the public in the long run? This could occur either because the sporting event inspires fans to participate more in sports or because the facilities continue to be used after the event by the local population. Unfortunately, a number of studies have concluded that major sporting events tend not to cause much of an increase in sports participation among the general public.[127] In fact, it is plausible that the population might actually become less healthy because sporting events often get sponsored by soda, fast food, and beer companies.[128]

CONCLUSION

As mentioned earlier, a logical takeaway from this chapter might be to give major sporting events permanent locations. Ideally, these host locations would be in economically developed democracies, and particularly in cities where there is broad public support to host major sporting events. More could also be done to encourage popular participation in sports through these events, like by creating fan zones where spectators can play the sports themselves, as well as organizing other sports opportunities for the public around the event.

Lastly, these events could do more to use their platforms to raise awareness about the importance of maintaining a healthy diet and lifestyle rather than selling advertising rights to the highest bidder. If some of these changes occurred, major sporting events might have a much more positive impact on host cities and countries than they currently do.

These ideas about improving sporting mega-events add to a long list of possible policy reforms already suggested in this book. Indeed, developing ideas for how sports could better serve humanity stands out as a key research topic moving forward.

CONCLUSION

THE FUTURE OF SPORTS

At a 2023 speech in Mumbai in front of Indian Prime Minister Narendra Modi, Thomas Bach, IOC president at the time, had some excellent news.[1] While acknowledging that the Olympics needed to adapt, Bach happily reported that artificial intelligence envisioned a bright future for the Olympic Movement. AI predicted that the Olympics would "likely become more inclusive, . . . promoting diversity and gender equality. The Olympic Movement may also adapt to changing societal values, addressing issues such as athlete mental health and social justice, and striving to be a force for positive change on a global scale."[2] Overall, AI gave the Olympics a glowing endorsement: "the future of the Olympic Games promises to be a compelling fusion of tradition and progress, maintaining its status as a unifying global event while adapting to the changing values and expectations of the modern world."[3] It seemed that the gospel of sports had found its next great proponent: AI.

A more sobering assessment came the next day, when sportswriter Alan Abrahamson reported what AI told him about the Olympics:

> The Olympics are a global celebration of athleticism, nationalism, and corporate sponsorship. They're a rare event that unites the world, showcasing the best athletes and their countries. However, they're also a massive financial burden on host cities, often leaving them with unused infrastructure and debt.[4]

There is no mention here of concerns about rampant doping, population displacement, or the glorification of dictators. However, AI still touched on an impressive range of problems. Regarding the future, AI suggested that "The Olympics should be reimagined as a rotating event between a few cities with existing infrastructure, reducing costs and increasing sustainability."[5] This approach would likely prove much more cost effective, but it would require the IOC to sacrifice its current model, which seems unlikely.[6]

The Olympics will certainly evolve in the coming years, as will sports in general. Much is at stake in how these developments unfold. Sports can reshape the world in both positive and negative ways. They can be a powerful source of social capital as well as a pernicious distraction from important social and political issues. Sports can worsen relations between countries, even leading to military conflict. They can also decrease suicide rates and incidents of civil unrest. Politicians' approval ratings have fluctuated based on sports outcomes. Various actors throughout history have tried to harness the power of sports to bring about social and political change, from Pierre de Coubertin to Adolf Hitler to Muhammad Ali. Sports have affected issues of gender and racial equality, sometimes in unexpected ways. They have reshaped host cities and countries for better and for worse, often leading to a range of social and economic problems.

For sports to play a more positive role in the future, we need to think more critically about them. We should abandon the simplistic bread and circuses view that sports merely distract people from politics. While sports certainly can be a distraction, thinking about them strictly in this narrow way can make us miss the broader social and political effects of sports. Likewise, putting our faith in the gospel of sports can impede future progress. Sports certainly can have many positive effects. They can bring people together, make them feel more connected to their communities, improve health, and provide many other benefits. However, they are most likely to do so when people think carefully about how they engage with sports. Without this critical thinking, the gospel of sports can devolve into an entirely unwarranted and harmful ideology, especially dangerous when blindly followed by influential actors. If we do not take the drawbacks of sports seriously, then promoting them could do more harm than good.

This book has also challenged the notion, held by some, that sports have almost exclusively negative effects.[7] Rather, it has shown that the pathologies of sports often arise when fans and athletes become too emotionally invested.

Such an approach can lead to harmful sports addictions and unwise community investments. The goal should therefore be to adopt a thoughtful and responsible approach to sports, analyzing them critically without being overly critical.

THE ELITE SPORTS MODEL

A critical evaluation of sports does suggest that the elite sports model has become overemphasized at the expense of popular participation in sports. An experience that I had as a graduate student illustrates this point well. When I was in graduate school, I would frequently go to the gym to play pick-up basketball. I understood the value of cardiovascular exercise for long-term health, but because I always disliked running, basketball was a great alternative. In this way, pick-up basketball provided me with a sustainable lifestyle habit that was fun, kept me healthy, likely reduced my future doctors' visits and medical bills, and made me some friends along the way.

Despite the social and physical benefits that pick-up basketball gave students like me, the basketballs that the university provided for our play were dismal. They were low quality and worn down through excessive use. Some were deformed. Others were coming apart at the seams. Providing students with adequate sports equipment for recreational play simply did not seem to be a priority at the school. The real priority was Division I athletics. The university spent huge sums of money on its Division I athletes, including their coaching, equipment, and travel expenses. Nevertheless, many of the programs attracted little interest from spectators. They also required significant training from the athletes. Of course, few of these athletes had any realistic chances of becoming serious professionals. They likely would have been better off studying and engaging with sports at a recreational level.

So why did the university and its donors place such importance on elite athletics? The answer, I believe, comes down to a pathological misalignment of priorities. It is the same distorted thinking that many female sports leaders fought so hard against in the decades before Title IX—the highly competitive model that they argued "damaged the few skilled female athletes while neglecting the many."[8] It is the same overemphasis on elite sports that draws fans to their television screens for hours on end, leads many athletes to make extraordinary sacrifices chasing unlikely dreams, and results in some communities investing in expensive stadiums that make little financial sense.

In his 2002 book *Sports: The All-American Addiction*, former college sports administrator and athlete John Gerdy argues that the elite sports model has a profoundly damaging impact on society.[9] Despite loving sports in general, Gerdy contends that modern spectator sports have become a costly, anti-intellectual industry that distracts people from much more valuable endeavors.[10] As he puts it:

> Sport in America has become more about money, winning, and ego than about education, sportsmanship, and ethics; more about commercialism, sneaker deals, and trash-talking than about personal development and educational opportunity; and more about being a passive spectator than an active participant.[11]

Gerdy's argument resonates with the views of many others whom we have encountered in this book. These thinkers include not only the female sports leaders already mentioned, but also the organizers of the 1936 Barcelona Olympics, the critics of the elite sports system in China, and the American scholars who suggest that the unrealistic sports dreams of underprivileged youth can hurt them greatly in the long run.

While reading this book, you may have found yourself siding with this view that elite sports have detrimental effects on athletes, spectators, and society at large. I believe there is much merit in this conclusion, which is a disheartening thought given that the elite sports model will not disappear anytime soon. However, I also believe that there are two reasons to be optimistic in this regard, and the first is quite simple: the lessons that you take away from this book can have a positive impact on your own life and the lives of the people you care about, even if broader social change is slow to come. If you simply make the decision to view your own relationship with sports more thoughtfully and encourage others to do the same, it may lead you and those around you to have much happier and more fulfilling experiences with sports.

The second reason for optimism is that the elite sports model's focus on winning might actually transform in a way that could make it have a much more positive impact on the world. To imagine how this might happen, we can look at the country that came in first place in the 2022 Beijing Winter Olympic medal count. It was not the United States, China, or Russia. Rather, it was Norway. This fact is striking given that Norway ranks 119th in the world in terms of total population with only about 5 million people. Its population is only about 1.6 percent of the U.S. population and 3.9 percent of Russia's. This was not Norway's first major sporting success either. It also ranked first in the total medal count at the 2018 PyeongChang Olympics. At the 2014 Sochi Olympics, Norway came in third place in terms of total number of medals, just behind Russia's state-sponsored doping operation and the U.S. team.

What exactly has Norway been doing that has proved so successful at winning medals? In Norway, sport is far less competitive than in most other countries. Norwegians often do not even keep score for young children, and as people grow older, the emphasis is on health and well-being rather than winning.[12] As the 2022 Norwegian gold medalist Vetle Sjaastad Christiansen explained, Norwegian sport is "a system for joy and happiness, to have joy with your sport and first of all be healthy. And maybe that's why we are so successful, because we really enjoy what we're doing and it's then easy to work hard—not every day but almost every day."[13]

Could Norway's less competitive, more health-focused approach to sports really account for its stunning performances? If so, it would suggest that the best strategy for success in elite sports might actually involve creating a health-focused participatory sports system that de-emphasizes the importance of winning. If this is true, we might see other countries adopt Norway's sports philosophy in the hopes of reaching similar levels of success. The lack of pressure that such a system puts on its top athletes could give them a major competitive advantage in international competition. It could help athletes avoid issues like anxiety, depression, and other mental health challenges that often occur when athletes take winning too seriously.

However, Norway is an unusual country in many other respects that might explain its success at the Winter Olympics. Besides being a wintery country with many mountains, it also stands out as an economic outlier in that it discovered very large oil reserves after having first developed a welfare state.[14] This meant that Norway could redistribute the benefits of its oil wealth to its citizens without facing the wealth distribution problems that often arise for economies heavily reliant on resource exports—a phenomenon that has come to be known as "the resource curse."[15] Clearly, having a relatively wealthy population in a country with plenty of snow, ice, and mountains could be the driving explanation for Norway's success.[16] We should therefore not rush to judgment about the Norway case, as its striking sports performances likely result from multiple factors. However, even if the hyper-competitive approach to sports remains widely pervasive well into the future, there are still ways that existing sporting events and institutions might be modified to accentuate their positive effects and minimize their downsides.

IMPROVING SPECTATOR SPORTS

Many people enjoy watching sports. No doubt, certain sports moments can prove inspirational. Yet improvements to the elite sports model could make sports even more inspiring. Imagine a world in which the Olympics included a longer swimming event between the best male and female distance swimmers in the world, and women competed against men in many other athletic competitions. Imagine a world in which major sporting events were as much about playing sports as watching them. Imagine a world in which you could fully enjoy the Olympics and World Cup and never worry that they were being exploited by dictators or harming local populations. Imagine a world in which sports spectators did not have a reputation for consuming large amounts of alcohol, getting overly invested in the results, and occasionally turning violent. Imagine a world in which fans were thoughtful about when and how they watched sports.

Jerry Seinfeld described spectator sports as rooting for laundry, since many fans support the players on their favorite teams primarily because of the jerseys they wear.[17] After all, when a team trades one of its players and acquires someone new, many fans simply root for the new player without putting much thought into it. Seinfeld's observation is clever and profound. It actually goes back to the Roman empire, the same civilization that gave us bread and circuses and the chariot race riots between supporters of the Reds, Whites, Blues, and Greens.

The Roman scholar Pliny the Younger mocked chariot-racing fans for cheering not the chariot racers but the clothes they wore. He even suggested that if the chariot racers traded clothes, the fans would immediately change their allegiances, because the cloth mattered more to them than the racers.[18] This observation, as true in Roman times as it is today, raises the question of whether deeply caring about a particular team makes sense. If it does not, then maybe sports spectators would be able to recognize their team fandom as somewhat superficial and might take the games they watch a little less seriously.

Beyond encouraging fans to adopt a more lighthearted approach to sports, several other potential policy recommendations are worth discussing. We can begin with the problem of dictators. An obvious improvement would be to stop allowing them to host major sporting events like the Olympics and World Cup. In Chapter 3, I went further by suggesting that it might be ethically indefensible to allow dictatorial regimes to even participate in international sports. However, banning non-democracies entirely would likely fragment the world of sports. Would it really be better to have one World Cup for democracies and another for non-democracies? It would certainly be different, and one could list the advantages and disadvantages of such a system. One drawback, for example, would be that this approach would make international sports a frequent reminder of how the world is split into friends and foes. On the other hand, an event that restricted the participants to democracies could greatly reduce concerns about state-sponsored doping and unethical authoritarian sports academy systems. At the very least, creating new institutions is a possibility that deserves careful consideration whenever sports officials prove to be uninterested in safeguarding the ethics and integrity of sports.

Another possibility would be to move toward a less nationalistic version of international sports. Many have suggested getting rid of the medal count at the Olympics. This may be a half-step in the right direction, but it could be very difficult to implement. Historically, the IOC has actually tried to discourage viewers from interpreting the medal count as a national ranking, but they could not stop the media from tracking it closely and framing it as a national competition. Since the media has the freedom in most countries to do this, it would be unlikely that the IOC would be able to prevent this practice. At best, the IOC could do more to try to de-emphasize the medal count, with some cooperating governments and media outlets potentially joining the effort.

A bolder move would be to restructure global sporting events so that they no longer feature competitions between nations. As we discussed in Chapter 1, having countries compete head-to-head can elevate nationalism to potentially dangerous levels, and it also creates other undesirable complications that sports might be better off without. Denationalizing global sporting events could keep sports organizations out of the sometimes-awkward position of having to decide which political communities qualify as nations. It could also avoid requiring athletes to compete for countries with which they strongly disagree on important human rights issues. Further, it could avoid the problem of having to decide whether countries that violate international law should be banned from international sports.

In short, the nation-based format causes many undesirable controversies. However, this is what happens when the founder of a major international sporting event is working with social science theory from the 1800s. Given that more than a hundred years later we can conclude with confidence that sporting competition between nations is not a reliable force for international peace, we should revisit the Olympic blueprint and consider alternative structures that would maintain fan interest, be fairer for athletes, and potentially allow events like the Olympics to have a more positive impact on the world.

One approach would simply be to have athletes compete as individuals rather than representatives of their countries. Competing as individuals would eliminate a major flaw in the Olympic rules. Currently, the world's third best athlete in certain events (like the women's 100-meter butterfly) might not even get to participate in the Olympics if she is from the same country as the world's top two athletes. In fact, there are many events at the Olympics in which no more than two athletes per country are allowed to compete. Meanwhile, in team sports, the world's best men's basketball player might miss the Olympics if he is from a country that lacks other great basketball players. Clearly, the current format of the Olympics can easily lead to people not being able to participate because of their nationalities.

Would it not make more sense to allow individuals to compete as individuals? In team sports, athletes could form their own teams without the current nationality constraints. This approach could lead to much more intense competition in sports that are currently dominated by specific countries, like the United States in basketball. For example, a group of NBA players who are friends could join together, even if they are not all from the same country. It might make the Olympics less interesting to fans who tune in mainly to see how well their country performs in the medal count—that is, fans who watch because of nationalism rather than simply wanting to see the best athletes in the world compete. However, it is the nationalistic impulse that has led to so many problems throughout Olympic history.

The Olympic movement certainly needs reform. The 2022 Beijing Olympics were marred with concerns over genocide, forced labor, doping, and athlete abuse. Even Thomas Bach, IOC president in 2022, expressed regret and disapproval for how the fifteen-year-old Russian figure skater Kamila Valieva, who tested positive for doping but was still allowed to compete, was treated by her coaches after finishing her routine. Bach said that he was "very disturbed" when he watched the competition.[19] He continued sorrowfully, "When afterwards I saw how she was received by her closest entourage, with what appeared to be a tremendous coldness, it was chilling to see this. Rather than giving her comfort, rather than trying to help her, you could feel this chilling atmosphere, this distance."[20]

Research on how international sports could have less damaging and more beneficial effects on the world should be a key focus moving forward. We will now turn our attention to briefly consider one way that the sports landscape has changed in recent years. This change involves the rise of competitive gaming, also known by the controversial term "esports."

THE RISE OF ESPORTS

As live streaming became more widespread on platforms like Twitch and YouTube in the early 2010s, esports grew to become a global phenomenon that now attracts hundreds of millions of spectators. In China and South Korea, esports have attained the same prominence as traditional sports.[21] In Europe, many of the major soccer clubs like Manchester City and Paris Saint-Germain now have esports teams, including in *Fortnight, League of Legends,* and *EA Sports FC* (the successor to the *FIFA* series). Esports have also been included at the 2022 Commonwealth Games and Asian Games. Meanwhile, many universities in the United States now recognize esports as a varsity sport and offer scholarships to promising gamers. Given the continued shift toward computers and online socialization, especially among the younger generations, it would not be surprising if esports eventually replaced traditional sports as the main cultural pastime of the modern world.

Before considering the implications of this new trend, a fundamental question confronts us: Do esports really qualify as sports? If you asked someone if they played any sports, and they responded, "Oh yes! I play video games," what would you think? In fact, scholars have long debated the definition of sports. I suggested in Chapter 4 that Eurovision, given its dancing component, might qualify as a sporting contest. What about other dancing competitions, like *Dancing with the Stars*? Do they really differ that much from Olympic figure skating or rhythmic gymnastics?[22] The IOC even included breakdancing at the 2024 Olympics. And what about other competitive contests of a physical nature—hot dog eating contests, art competitions, and student debate tournaments? These are all competitions with important physical elements, so might they count as sports?

In the 2019 book *Games, Sports, and Play: Philosophical Essays,* edited by

Thomas Hurka, scholars Mitchell Berman and David Papineau each put forward their own potential definitions of sports.[23] Berman proposes defining sports as activities that are performed for their own sake, that justify "warranted seriousness," and that include such elements as competitiveness, gameness, and physicality.[24] The "warranted seriousness" requirement rules out activities that people do not take seriously, such as pin the tail on the donkey and three-legged races.[25] It could also rule out activities that some people do take seriously but (arguably) without good reason (for example, hot dog eating contests).[26] Somewhat differently, Papineau defines sports as activities designed primarily to exercise physical skill.[27] This definition rules out activities like art competitions and bake-offs, because judges determine the winner based on the product itself rather than the process of making the product.[28] Note that neither of these definitions require sports to be games, so activities like recreational surfing and skiing can count as sports under both definitions.[29]

While the two scholars disagree to some extent on whether activities like chess and poker qualify as sports, they both view esports as sports.[30] After all, high-level esports competitions take place in arenas or stadiums in front of large audiences.[31] They require contestants to demonstrate key physical skills like hand-eye coordination and fast reaction times.[32] The top esports players train seriously and have coaches.[33] Moreover, the fact that many colleges and universities now offer scholarships for skilled esports players illustrates how seriously even academic institutions have come to regard competitive video games.

While I see much merit in Berman's and Papineau's thoughtful discussions on how best to define sports, I am somewhat skeptical of categorizing esports as sports. First, it seems somewhat awkward to think of video games as being primarily designed to exercise physical skill. Physical skill certainly factors in, but esports appear much more focused on dominance in the virtual realm. The real action takes place within the video game, and the physical movements of the players' hands are at most of secondary interest. Second, while many people take esports seriously, can we really view such seriousness as "warranted"? Certainly elite esports competitions showcase fast thinking, creativity, and teamwork. However, both training and competition can involve spending unhealthy amounts of time in front of a screen. In fact, I would go as far as to suggest that the efforts of some people in the gaming industry to link video games to sports constitute a new form of sportswashing. That is, such efforts try to improve the reputation of the gaming industry by tapping into many people's overly positive attitudes towards sports in general.

If esports do count as sports, I would classify them as one of the worst sports. As we have seen in this book, not all sports are created equal. In Chapter 4, we saw that sports that involve repetitive motions can lead to overuse injuries. Some sports can also cause respiratory problems, in particular cold-air sports and swimming (because of the chlorinated air). Many sports can also lead to eating disorders, such as when athletes want to look thin in revealing uniforms, believe that weighing less confers a competitive advantage, or simply want to make weight in sports like wrestling. Of course, sports that involve head trauma can lead to long-term brain damage.[34] Chapter 4 also discussed how certain types of sports can bring valuable benefits. In particular, sports that involve a ball typically require a wide variety of movements and cognitive tasks, which can benefit the body and mind.

Why would esports qualify as a bad sport? A major difference between esports and traditional sports is that video games can be highly addictive, and it might in fact require more self-discipline not to play than to play. When it comes to many traditional sports, most people do not find practice to be fun and addictive. It involves a lot of hard work, and the body also has limits in terms of how much time can be spent training before reaching the point of physical exhaustion. With esports, physical limits may exist, but not in the same way. In 2005, a twenty-eight-year-old Korean man died after playing esports almost non-stop for about fifty straight hours.[35] It is not uncommon for people training for esports competitions to play sixty hours or more per week.[36] Therefore, practicing esports is likely to take significantly more time than traditional sports, while also teaching players to give into their impulses rather than exercise impulse control. For these reasons, there seem to be some major differences between how traditional sports could impact individuals compared to esports.

Research on how video games influence personal health and well-being indicates that they can have a range of positive and negative effects. On the positive side, academic research has found that cooperative video games can increase various forms of prosocial behavior, such as the ability to build friendships.[37] On the negative side, playing video games for long periods may lead to anxiety, depression, and stress.[38] It can also cause some medical problems associated with sedentary lifestyles, excessive screen exposure, and repetitive hand movements.[39] In addition, violent video games have been linked to aggression.[40]

Despite the significant differences between esports and traditional sports, some esports competitions have started to resemble events like the Olympics and World Cup in their high levels of nationalism.[41] In particular, esports nationalism has played a prominent role in China, which having succeeded in the Olympics, has also sought to shine in the esports world as well.[42] In 2003, the Chinese state governing body for sports officially recognized esports as a formal sport.[43] Chinese companies have also recruited some of the best esports players in the world and acquired major gaming companies. As media and communication professor Haiqing Yu describes, "Live eSports competitions are presented as media spectacles that nurture the ideal patriotic citizen, just like any other major events—for instance, the Olympics or the national games; accordingly, eSports has become a platform to display carefully crafted nationalism and China's soft power."[44]

Another interesting feature of esports is that they might provide many more opportunities for women to compete with men. In theory, there is little reason to think that any sort of gender segregation makes sense in the esports realm, at least based on biological and cognitive differences between men and women.[45] Remarkably, however, women appear to be even more marginalized in esports than in traditional sports. According to a 2021 BBC report, there are no women in the top 300 highest-earning esports professionals.[46] The issue does not appear to be a lack of interest on the part of women—in general, they seem to play video games at similar rates as men.[47] Rather, the main obstacles appear to be widespread sexism and harassment in the gaming community, broader societal expectations that girls and women are less interested in video games, and the scarcity of women in positions of power in the esports industry.[48] The issue of notable gender imbalance at the top levels of esports also appears in professional chess, where the top-ranked players are almost exclusively men.[49]

As in the world of chess, some all-women's esports competitions have emerged to provide female gamers with more opportunity to compete. However, whether we should think positively about such efforts is debatable. Women should certainly have the same opportunities as men. Nonetheless, if playing video games excessively could have many long-term consequences, including poorer educational outcomes, then underrepresentation of women in esports could lead to greater female empowerment in other areas of life. From this perspective, the goal might be to get more men out of competitive gaming rather than to get more women into it.

Lastly, the incredible rise of esports suggests not only that they may become more popular than traditional sports, but also the more interesting possibility that esports and traditional sports could merge. In the movie *The Hunger Games: Catching Fire*, the protagonist Katniss Everdeen prepares for her looming gladiator battle by shooting arrows at hologram creatures that run at her in a mixed-reality simulation. As technology like this emerges in the coming years, it could create very popular games that can be enjoyed by casual participants while also serving as the basis for entertaining competitions between elite athletes. Focusing just on archery, current competitions involve participants aiming to hit stationary targets. If competitors instead shot at virtual reality monsters running towards them, archery might transform into one of the world's most popular sports. Therefore, the interesting question might not be whether traditional sports or esports will be more popular in the future, but how the two might combine to revolutionize the sports industry.

THE SHIFTING MOMENTUM

Whatever the future of sports looks like, there is little doubt that they will continue to serve as a cornerstone of modern civilization. Sports can help fulfill many fundamental human desires, in particular the desire to belong to a larger group, to play, and to be entertained.[50] We should not expect sports to decline in popularity anytime soon. Understanding how we can get the most out of them while also limiting their downsides remains a crucial task for academic researchers moving forward.

In his 1994 book *Soccer Against the Enemy*, Simon Kuper set out to understand how the world's most popular sport shapes society and politics.[51] For nine months, the young journalist traveled the world, sleeping in hostels to scrape by on his meager budget, and speaking with fans, managers, politicians, and many others involved in the game.[52] "I travelled for nine months, visiting 22 countries, from Ukraine to Cameroon to Argentina to Scotland," he recounts.[53] "But wherever I went I was told, 'Soccer and politics! You've come to the right place here.'"[54] Kuper likely would have received a similar answer had he studied hockey in Canada, baseball in Japan, cricket in India, or football in the United States.[55]

Yet there is one place that Kuper could have gone to learn about sports and politics in the 1990s and found surprisingly little interest in the topic: the field of political science. Fortunately, much has changed in the last three decades. The study of sports and politics has begun to consolidate as a major research focus within the field. Political scientists have joined sociologists, historians, economists, and many other scholars treating sports as a serious academic topic. This development was much needed.

I hope that this book will inspire further exploration of sports and politics, by both practitioners and academic researchers. Modern sports are far too important to treat with anything less than intellectual rigor, objective reflection, and deep curiosity. Such scholarly engagement can make sports better and the world better, deepening our understanding of how the world works and teaching us how we can shape it in more positive ways.

NOTES

Preface

1. For a rare exception, see Pollock, "Critical Moments."

2. Busby et al., "Political Relevance"; Potoski and Urbatsch, "Entertainment and Opportunity Cost"; Bertoli, "Nationalism and Conflict."

3. Gift and Miner, "'Dropping the Ball.'"

4. Alrababa'h et al., "Can Exposure"; Scharpf et al., "International Sports Events"; Kikuta and Uesugi, "Do Politically Irrelevant Events"; Gläßel et al., "Does Sportswashing Work?"; Rosenzweig and Zhou, "Team and Nation"; Busby and Druckman, "Football and Public Opinion"; Pinto, "Sports Nationalism and Xenophobia."

5. For example, see Elias, *Baseball and American Dream*; Mandelbaum, *Meaning of Sports*; Ring, *Stolen Bases*; Cha, *Beyond the Final Score*; Cha, "Theory of Sport and Politics": Elias, *The Empire Strikes Out*; Boykoff, *Celebration Capitalism*; Boykoff, *Activism and the Olympics*; Ring, *Game of Their Own*; Boykoff, *Power Games*. Also see Markovits and Rensmann, *Gaming the World*; Healy et al., "Irrelevant Events Affect Voters' Evaluations."

Introduction

1. Robert Summerscales, "FIFA World Cup Final Beat Super Bowl LVI by More Than One Billion Viewers in TV Ratings," *Sports Illustrated*, January 18, 2023, https://www.si.com/fannation/soccer/futbol/news/how-fifa-world-cup-final-beat-super-bowl-lvi-in-tv-ratings

2. Regarding audience size, see Julia Stoll, "Global TV Audience Olympic Summer Games 2008–2020," *Statista*, September 22, 2023, https://www.statista.com/statistics/280502/total-number-of-tv-viewers-of-olympic-summer-games-worldwide/

3. "Super Bowl LIX Makes TV History with over 127 Million Viewers," *Nielson*, Feb-

ruary 25, 2025, https://www.nielsen.com/news-center/2025/super-bowl-lix-makes-tv-history-with-over-127-million-viewers/

4. Chris Murphy, "Super Bowl LVIII Is the Modern Era's Most-Watched Telecast Ever," *Vanity Fair*, February 13, 2024, https://www.vanityfair.com/hollywood/super-bowl-lviii-is-the-modern-eras-most-watched-telecast-ever Also see Markovits and Albertson, *Sportista*, 1, 137–138; Paolantonio, *How Football Explains America*, 17.

5. For instance, see Guttmann, *The Olympics*, 2–3; Keys, *Globalizing Sport*, 7; Gift and Miner, "'Dropping the Ball,'" 129. In the context of the United States, see McDonagh and Pappano, *Playing with the Boys*, 2. Also see Foer, *How Soccer*, 4; Gerdy, *Sports*, xviii.

6. Markovits and Albertson, *Sportista*, 2; Hulteen et al., "Global Participation in Sport," 18–21; Feldman and Matjasko, "Role of School-Based," 163; Miller, *Greenwashing Sport*, 54.

7. Smith, *Race, Sport*, 74; Berglund, *Fastest Game*, 233–236.

8. On this point, see Zirin, *What's My Name*, 20–21; Gift and Miner, "'Dropping the Ball,'" 133–134; Goldblatt, *The Ball Is Round*, 905–906.

9. Aldrete, "'Bread and Circuses,'" 4.

10. Quoted in Aldrete, "'Bread and Circuses,'" 4.

11. Regarding the dearth of research in the fields of political science and international relations, see Gift and Miner, "'Dropping the Ball,'" 127–132; Bunting, *Democracy at the Ballpark*, 8. Regarding the academic field of history, which has taken sports more seriously than political science, see Keys, *Globalizing Sport*, 10. Also see Hunt, *Drug Games*, 1.

12. Cha, *Beyond the Final Score*, 2.

13. For more discussion of this widely held view, see Zirin, *What's My Name*, 20–35; Elias, *The Empire Strikes Out*, 1; Boykoff, *Power Games*, 5; Miller, *Greenwashing Sport*, 31–32; McDougall, "*Eulogy to Theft*," 125; Chappell, *Mexican American Fastpitch*, 10–11.

14. For example, see Bowman, "Futebol/Fútbol," 255.

15. Shaun Walker, "Successful World Cup Fails to Halt Slide in Vladimir Putin's Popularity," *Guardian*, July 6, 2018, https://www.theguardian.com/world/2018/jul/16/successful-world-cup-fails-to-halt-slide-in-vladimir-putins-popularity

16. Quoted in Elias, *The Empire Strikes Out*, 109. Also see Ruck, "Deflected Confrontations," 234.

17. Shaw, "Political Instrumentalization of Professional Football," 134, 172.

18. Shaw, "Political Instrumentalization of Professional Football," 134.

19. Huxley, *Brave New World*, 267–268; Aldrete, "'Bread and Circuses,'" 17–18.

20. Potoski and Urbatsch, "Entertainment and Opportunity Cost," 428–431.

21. Potoski and Urbatsch, "Entertainment and Opportunity Cost," 430–431.

22. Potoski and Urbatsch, "Entertainment and Opportunity Cost," 426.

23. Huxley, *Brave New World*, 267.

24. Zirin, *What's My Name*, 20–35; Elias, *The Empire Strikes Out*, 1–3; Boykoff, *Power Games*, 5; McDougall, "*Eulogy to Theft*," 125. Also see Kuper, *Soccer Against the Enemy*, 1–3; Bunting, *Democracy at the Ballpark*, 3, 7–8.

25. For instance, see Keys, "Introduction," 5–6; McDonagh and Pappano, *Playing with the Boys*, 39.

26. Tomlinson and Young, "Culture, Politics, and Spectacle," 5; Keys, "Introduction," 5–6; Guttmann, *The Olympics*, 1–3, 10–11.

27. Espy, *Politics of Olympic Games*, 3–8; Boykoff, *Activism and the Olympics*, 12–13; Zirin, *The Kaepernick Effect*, 4–7.

28. Putnam, *Bowling Alone*.

29. Putnam, *Bowling Alone*, 28.

30. Nicholson and Hoye, "Sport and Social Capital," 130.

31. For an earlier use of this term, see Korr, "Reviewed Work," 88. Also see Keys, "Introduction," 1.

32. On this topic, also see McDonagh and Pappano, *Playing with the Boys*, 1; Boykoff, *Activism and the Olympics*, 2; Keys, "Introduction," 1–7; Boykoff, *NOlympians*, 18; Hoberman, "Myth of Sport," 18; Berglund, *Fastest Game*, 20; Wenn and Barney, *Gold*, 8–9.

33. Quoted in Burke, "Peace," 85–88.

34. *Sport and the Sustainable Development Goals: An Overview Outlining the Contribution of Sport to the SDGs* (United Nations Office on Sport for Development and Peace (UNOSDP), 2014), 3–4, 7, 14–16, https://www.sport-for-development.com/imglib/downloads/unosdp2014-sport-and-the-sustainable-development-goals.pdf

35. "The Power of Sport: Scoring for People and the Planet," *United Nations*, April 5, 2023, https://www.un.org/en/information-centre-caribbean/power-sport-scoring-people-and-planet

36. For instance, see Coalter, "Sport-in-Development," 40–41, 47–48; Keys, "Introduction," 6–7; Mwaanga and Adeosun, "Reconceptualizing," 847.

37. On this point, see Keys, "Introduction," 1.

38. Suits, *The Grasshopper*, 1; Hurka, "Introduction," 4–9.

39. For instance, see Goldblatt, *The Games*, 25.

40. Bernstein, *Football*, 5; Goldblatt, *The Ball Is Round*, 17–18.

41. Zirin, *What's My Name*, 17.

42. Goldblatt, *The Ball Is Round*, 168–169.

43. Hokkanen, "'Christ and the Imperial Games Fields,'" 246, 253–256. Also see Bernstein, *Football*, 4; Gerdy, *Sports*, xiii.

44. Sansone, *Greek Athletics*, 130; Kyle, *Sport and Spectacle*, 176–179; Goldblatt, *The Games*, 2; Bunting, *Democracy at the Ballpark*, 9, 88–91; Gerdy, *Sports*, xix; Matthew Andrews, "Episode 1: The Religion of Sport," *The Untold History of Sports in America* (podcast), iHeartPodcasts, August 4, 2022, https://omny.fm/shows/the-untold-history-of-sports-in-america/the-untold-history-episode-1

45. Bunting, *Democracy at the Ballpark*, 9, 88–91.

46. Goldblatt, *The Ball Is Round*, 24–29; Guttmann, *The Olympics*, 8–9; Mandelbaum, *Meaning of Sports*, 13; Paolantonio, *How Football Explains America*, 19; Goldblatt, *The Games*, 31; Gerdy, *Sports*, xiii.

47. Markovits and Hellerman, *Offside*, 70.

48. On this point, also see Cha, *Beyond the Final Score*, 2.

49. Tunis, "The Dictators Discover Sport," 610.

50. Related to this distinction, also see Gerdy, *Sports*, xii.

51. Edelman and Young, "Introduction," 7–17; Shuman, "Learning from the Soviet Big Brother," 172–173.

52. Edelman and Young, "Introduction," 7–14; Dennis, "Sports, Politics, and 'Wild Doping,'" 129; Luther and Davidson, *Loving Sports*, 225.

53. Putnam, *Bowling Alone*, 109–113; Nicholson and Hoye, "Sport and Social Capital," 11.

54. For instance, see Dennis, "Sports, Politics, and 'Wild Doping,'" 126–129.

55. Hong et al., "Beijing Ambitions," 12–19. Also see Guttmann, *Sports*, 302–303.

56. Zirin, *What's My Name*, 222–227; Zirin, *Bad Sports*, 2–3, 10; Boykoff, *Activism and the Olympics*, 11; Crepeau, *NFL Football*, ix; Berglund, *Fastest Game*, 216; Luther and Davidson, *Loving Sports*, 209–226; Guridy, *The Stadium*, 2; Dinces, *Bull Markets*, 2.

57. I use "tribalism" here in the sense that it is commonly used in everyday language, and in particular in how it emphasizes the negative feelings toward perceived outsiders that arise from passionate in-group loyalty. By "tribalism," I do not simply mean the human tendency for group identification.

58. Festle, *Playing Nice*, 84; Wagg and Andrews, "Introduction," 2–4; Boykoff, *Power Games*, 81–82; Prozumenshikov, "Action in the Era of Stagnation," 74.

59. Nye, *Soft Power*, 40, 74–76, 88; Cha, *Beyond the Final Score*, 47–50; Edelman and Young, "Introduction," 1–3; Dennis, "Sports, Politics, and 'Wild Doping,'" 129; Morris, "'Communist Bandits,'" 188.

60. Nye, *Soft Power*, x.

61. Related to this point, see Cha, *Beyond the Final Score*, 40.

62. Huizinga, *Homo Ludens*, 50, 63, 196–198.

63. Huizinga, *Homo Ludens*, 46–76; Kyle, *Sport and Spectacle*, 3, 55.

64. On this point, also see Ross and Szymanski, *Fans*, 10; deMause and Cagan, *Field of Schemes*, xi–xvi; Boykoff, *Celebration Capitalism*, 11–17; Miller, *Greenwashing Sport*, 29; Luther and Davidson, *Loving Sports*, 223–226; Boykoff, *NOlympians*, 15–18. Also see Zirin, *Brazil's Dance*, 29, 39.

65. Zirin, *What's My Name*, 293.

66. Ross and Szymanski, *Fans*, 2, 11–13; deMause and Cagan, *Field of Schemes*, 38; Boykoff, *Celebration Capitalism*, 11–17, 116; Zirin, *Brazil's Dance*, 30; Luther and Davidson, *Loving Sports*, 209–210.

67. On this topic, see Miller, *Greenwashing Sport*, 31; Boykoff, *NOlympians*, 15–16; Guridy, *The Sports Revolution*, 5; Guridy, *The Stadium*, 239–242.

68. Markovits and Albertson, *Sportista*, 80–81.

69. Luther and Davidson, *Loving Sports*, 1. Also see Elias and Dreier, *Major League Rebels*, x.

Chapter 1

This chapter was adapted from Andrew D. Bertoli, "Nationalism and Conflict: Lessons from International Sports," *International Studies Quarterly* 61, no. 4 (2017): 835–849, https://doi.org/10.1093/isq/sqx029. I thank Oxford University Press for facilitating the reuse of this material.

1. For instance, see Foo, "Interview with Benedict Anderson," 21. Also see "Ahead of Sochi Olympic Games, Ban Praises Power of Sport to Unite All People," *UN News*, February 6, 2014, https://news.un.org/en/story/2014/02/461342; Creak, "Friendship and Mutual Understanding," 21.

2. George Orwell, "The Sporting Spirit," *London Tribune*, December 4, 1945, https://www.orwellfoundation.com/the-orwell-foundation/orwell/essays-and-other-works/the-sporting-spirit/; Christopher Hitchens, "Why the Olympics and Other Sports Cause Conflict," *Newsweek*, February 4, 2010, https://www.newsweek.com/why-olympics-and-other-sports-cause-conflict-75043

3. Burke, "Peace," 86; Zimbalist, *Circus Maximus*, 10.

4. Guttmann, *The Olympics*, 1–3, 10–11, 16; Goldblatt, *The Games*, 5, 35–36, 38–39.

5. Guttmann, *The Olympics*, 7–10.

6. Guttmann, *The Olympics*, 10–11; MacAloon, *The Great Symbol*, 187, 300; Boykoff, *Power Games*, 15; Creak, "Friendship and Mutual Understanding," 21.

7. Hoberman, "Myth of Sport," 18–19.

8. Bushman et al., "Catharsis," 367–368; Sipes, "War, Sports and Aggression," 64.

9. Bushman et al., "Catharsis," 368.

10. Bushman et al., "Catharsis," 368, 373–375.

11. "Ahead of Sochi Olympic Games"; Janice Turner, "Thwack! Kerpoww! I'm Purging My Anger," *The Times*, February 3, 2007, https://www.thetimes.com/article/thwack-kerpoww-im-purging-my-anger-cs8jh3nx3c6; Foo, "Interview with Benedict Anderson," 21. Also see Hoberman, "Myth of Sport," 19–20.

12. Quoted in Foo, "Interview with Benedict Anderson," 21.

13. Tomlinson and Young, "Culture, Politics, and Spectacle," 5.

14. Philip Barker, "The Olympic Rings and the Oval Office: From Teddy to Donald," *Inside the Games*, January 15, 2017, https://www.insidethegames.biz/articles/1045832/the-olympic-rings-and-the-oval-office-from-teddy-to-donald; James Gerstenzang, "'You Represent Peace,' Bush Tells Olympic Team," *Los Angeles Times*, February 9, 2002, https://www.latimes.com/archives/la-xpm-2002-feb-09-mn-27179-story.html; "Full Text of Obama Olympics Speech," *NBC* (Chicago), September 16, 2009, https://www.nbcchicago.com/news/politics/full-text-of-obama-olympics-speech/1861625/

15. Mark Oliver, "Blair Going 'All-Out' for London," *Guardian*, July 4, 2005, https://www.theguardian.com/uk/2005/jul/04/olympics2012.olympics2012; Keys, "Introduction," 1; Pope John Paul II, "Homily," 21–22.

16. Haas, "International Integration," 366–374, 377–378.

17. Torres, "Morally Incompatible?," 8–9.

18. Morgan, "Sports as Moral Discourse," 65, 72.

19. Espy, *Politics of Olympic Games*, 28–31, 163–164.

20. For example, see Boykoff, *The 1936 Berlin Olympics*, 90.

21. Cha, *Beyond the Final Score*, 9–11.

22. Espy, *Politics of Olympic Games*, 29; Keys, *Globalizing Sport*, 7–8; Cha, *Beyond the Final Score*, 11; Goldblatt, *The Games*, 213–14, 292.

23. Cha, *Beyond the Final Score*, 11.

24. Boykoff, *Power Games*, 92–95; Morris, "'Communist Bandits,'" 175–176.

25. Morris, "'Communist Bandits,'" 175.

26. For instance, see Archetti, "Argentina 1978," 137; Boykoff, *Power Games*, 2; Boykoff, *The 1936 Berlin Olympics*, 96.

27. For instance, see Elsey, "Ambivalent Solidarities," 240; Creak, "New Regional Order," 194.

28. For example, see Espy, *Olympic Games*, 3; Hong and Sun, "Butterfly Effect,'" 429; Murray and Pigman, "Mapping International Sport and Diplomacy," 1101.

29. Jonathan Kay, "War in Lycra," *National Post*, August 12, 2008; Chris Howells, "Dynamo Moscow's 1945 Tour of Britain: Was It Really 'War Minus the Shooting?,'" *BBC Sport*, November 13, 2020, https://www.bbc.com/sport/football/54839305

30. Orwell, "The Sporting Spirit"; Kay, "War in Lycra."

31. Sherif et al., *Intergroup Conflict and Cooperation*, 96–149.

32. Garland and Rowe, "War Minus the Shooting?," 81; Vincent et al., "England Expects," 209–218. On this topic, also see Keys, "Introduction," 7.

33. For instance, see Gruffydd-Jones, "Dangerous Days," 698. Also see Mansfield and Snyder, "Democratization," 6–7, 19–20.

34. For instance, see Cha, *Beyond the Final Score*, 8–9; Goldblatt, *The Ball Is Round*, 533–534; Hitchens, "Why Sports Cause Conflict."

35. Espy, *Olympic Games*, 3. Also see Cha, *Beyond the Final Score*, 8–9.

36. Kapuscinski, *The Soccer War*, 157–161; Hitchens, "Why Sports Cause Conflict."

37. Kapuscinski, *The Soccer War*, 158.

38. For this paragraph and the following one, see Goldblatt, *The Ball Is Round*, 533–534.

39. Elias, *The Empire Strikes Out*, 109.

40. James Montague, "Egypt Versus Algeria: Inside the Storm," *CNN*, November 27, 2009, https://edition.cnn.com/2009/SPORT/football/11/20/egypt.algeria.inside.story/

41. Ursula Lindsey, "The Soccer Wars," *Foreign Policy*, December 3, 2009, https://foreignpolicy.com/2009/12/03/the-soccer-wars/; Jack Shenker, "More to Egypt Riots Than Football," *Guardian*, November 25, 2009, https://www.theguardian.com/commentisfree/2009/nov/25/egypt-riots-football-world-cup

42. Montague, "Egypt Versus Algeria."

43. Hitchens, "Why Sports Cause Conflict."

44. Bertoli, "Nationalism and Conflict," 838.

45. Dan Bilesfky, "Albanian Premier Postpones Serbia Trip After Episode at Soccer Match," *New York Times*, October 20, 2014, https://www.nytimes.com/2014/10/21/world/europe/albania-edi-rama-belgrade-trip-soccer-match-drone.html; Guy de Launey, "Serbia-Albania: Football and Politics Prove Toxic Mix," *BBC News*, November 14, 2014, https://www.bbc.com/news/world-europe-30046273

46. Quoted in Melodie Bouchaud, "Video Shows Fans Brawling on Field with Albanian and Serbian Soccer Teams," *Vice News*, October 15, 2014, https://www.vice.com/en/article/video-shows-fans-brawling-on-field-with-albanian-and-serbian-soccer--teams/

47. Bilesfky, "Albanian Premier Postpones."

48. Bilesfky, "Albanian Premier Postpones"; de Launey, "Serbia-Albania."

49. de Launey, "Serbia-Albania."

50. David Willetts, "Putin Sends Attack Submarine into English Channel Just Days Before England's Russia Clash at Euro 2016," *The Sun*, June 7, 2016, https://www.thesun .co.uk/news/uknews/1246785/putin-sends-attack-submarine-into-english-channel -just-days-before-englands-russia-clash-at-euro-2016/

51. Quoted in Jack de Menezes, "Euro 2016: Russian Official Tells Hooligans 'Well Done Lads, Keep It Up' After Marseilles Violence," *The Independent*, June 13, 2016, https://www.independent.co.uk/sport/football/international/russia-fan-violence-rus sian-official-tells-hooligans-well-done-lads-keep-it-up-after-condoning-euro-2016-vio lence-a7079861.html

52. Daniel Boffey, "Whitehall Fears Russian Football Hooligans Had Kremlin Links," *Guardian*, June 18, 2016, https://www.theguardian.com/football/2016/jun/18/whitehall -suspects-kremlin-links-to-russian-euro-2016-hooligans-vladimir-putin

53. Quoted in Fionn Hargreaves, "Putin Makes Sick Jibe About 200 Russian Hooli- gans Beating Up 'Thousands' of England Football Fans," *The Sun*, June 17, 2016, https:// www.thesun.co.uk/news/1299849/euro-2016putin-makes-sick-jibe-about-200-russian -hooligans-beating-up-thousands-of-england-football-fans/

54. Frith, *Bodyline Autopsy*, 7–9, 378–390; Swan, "Bodyline's Final Legacy May Be an Australian Republic," *Sydney Morning Herald*, January 25, 2014, https://www.smh.com .au/politics/federal/bodylines-final-legacy-may-be-an-australian-republic-20130124-- 2d9nr.html

55. On this topic, also see Goldblatt, *The Ball Is Round*, 253–259.

56. Cha, "Theory of Sport and Politics," 12. In particular, see Boykoff, *The 1936 Berlin Olympics*, 100–101.

57. Ian Willoughby, " 'Things Really Went Wild': The 1969 Czechoslovak Ice Hockey Riots," *Radio Prague International*, March 27, 2024, https://english.radio.cz/things -really-went-wild-1969-czechoslovak-ice-hockey-riots-8812513; Berglund, *Fastest Game*, 140–143. Also see Hardy and Holman, *Hockey*, 336–337.

58. For the full article, see Bertoli, "Nationalism and Conflict."

59. Also see Oyer, *Economist Goes*, 9.

60. For this paragraph, see Thistlethwaite and Campbell, "Regression-Discontinuity Analysis," 309–315.

61. Oyer, *Economist Goes*, 9.

62. Note that many experts prefer not to call regression discontinuities "natural experiments." The main reason is that units just above and just below the cut point may differ in small but systematic ways. For example, students who scored 50 might be, on average, a little smarter than students who scored 49. One way to mitigate this concern is to look at the change in the outcome variable (when doing so is possible), since this approach should clean up small baseline differences between the two groups. I take this approach in the empirical analysis in this chapter. For further reading, see Sekhon and Titiunik, "Regression Discontinuity," 175–180.

63. Ghosn et al., "The MID3 Data Set," 133.

64. Regarding the common use of militarized interstate disputes, see Dafoe et al., "The Democratic Peace," 203–205, 211–212.

65. Quoted in Ralph, "'Crimes of History,'" 201.

66. Bertoli, "Nationalism and Conflict," 844–846.

67. Bertoli, "Nationalism and Conflict," 846.

68. Bell, "Roman Chariot Racing," 493. Also see Kyle, *Sport and Spectacle*, 248–249, 292–297.

69. Bell, "Roman Chariot Racing," 500.

70. Bell, "Roman Chariot Racing," 500.

71. Markovits and Hellerman, *Offside*, 70–74; Bernstein, *Football*, 9–12.

72. Bernstein, *Football*, x–xi.

73. Bernstein, *Football*, x–xi.

74. Mandelbaum, *Meaning of Sports*, 156.

75. Mandelbaum, *Meaning of Sports*, 156.

76. Sherif et al., *Intergroup Conflict and Cooperation*, 34–35.

77. For the details of the study included in this paragraph, see Sherif et al., *Intergroup Conflict and Cooperation*, 34–62, 120–198.

78. Powers, *Nationalisms in International Politics*, 1–7.

79. Hoberman, "Myth of Sport," 17–27.

80. Orwell, "The Sporting Spirit."

81. Keys, "Introduction," 7.

82. Markovits and Rensmann, *Gaming the World*, 29–30.

83. Note that such programs have been criticized for ignoring the difficult challenges that fuel complex political conflicts, instead assuming that peace can prevail if people simply get to know one another. Related to this point, also see Keys, "Introduction," 1–7.

Chapter 2

1. For a discussion of this topic, see Jaksa, "Sports and Collective Identity," 41; Olivier Guiberteau, "Didier Drogba: How Ivory Coast Striker Helped to Halt Civil War in His Home Nation," *BBC Sport*, March 31, 2020, https://www.bbc.com/sport/football/52072592

2. For example, see Markovits and Rensmann, *Gaming the World*, 72–73; Zirin, *Brazil's Dance*, 107–108.

3. On this point, see Luther and Davidson, *Loving Sports*, 226.

4. Zirin, *Brazil's Dance*, 115–116; Kuper and Szymanski, *Soccernomics*, 237.

5. Markovits and Albertson, *Sportista*, 2–3. Also see Luther and Davidson, *Loving Sports*, 173–174.

6. Markovits and Albertson, *Sportista*, 10, 136–147.

7. Markovits and Albertson, *Sportista*, 92.

8. Markovits and Albertson, *Sportista*, 93. Also see Hobsbawm, *Nations and Nationalism*, 143.

9. Kuper and Szymanski, *Soccernomics*, 229.

10. Kuper and Szymanski, *Soccernomics*, 227–228.

11. Kuper and Szymanski, *Soccernomics*, 236.

12. Kuper and Szymanski, *Soccernomics*, 233–236.

13. Kuper and Szymanski, *Soccernomics*, 238.

14. Kuper and Szymanski, *Soccernomics*, 237.

15. On this point, see Kuper and Szymanksi, *Soccernomics*, 239. On the close links between sports and alcohol, see Collins and Vamplew, *Mud, Sweat and Beers*, 1–2.

16. Vamplew, *Games People Played*, 25, 431–434.

17. Vamplew, *Games People Played*, 25, 431–434.

18. Vamplew, *Games People Played*, 24.

19. For instance, see Glassman et al., "Extreme Alcohol Consumption," 413; Glassman et al., "Blood (Breath) Alcohol," 55; Erickson et al., "Can We Assess Blood Alcohol Levels," 689.

20. Zerhouni et al., "How Alcohol Advertising," 395–396.

21. See Collins and Vamplew, *Mud, Sweat and Beers*, 1.

22. Deakin et al., "Effects of International Football," 405–406; Quigg et al., "Effects of the 2010 World Cup," 383–384; Bellis et al., "Nighttime Assaults," 1, 4.

23. Deakin et al., "Effects of International Football," 406; Rees and Schnepel, "College Football," 68, 73–76. Also see Bellis et al., "Nighttime Assaults," 4.

24. Block, "Professional Sports and Crime," 2069, 2076–2079.

25. Pyun, "Exploring Major League Baseball and Crime," 365, 376.

26. Rees and Schnepel, "College Football," 68, 73–76.

27. For instance, see Deakin et al., "Effects of International Football," 405; Quigg et al., "Effects of the 2010 World Cup," 384.

28. On emotional stress, see Quigg et al., "Effects of the 2010 World Cup," 384. Also see Van der Meij et al., "Testosterone and Cortisol Release," 1, 4–6.

29. Kirby et al., "Can FIFA World Cup Football," 269–270; Brimicombe and Cafe, "Beware, Win or Lose," 35; Kirby and Birdsall, "Kicking Off," 378, 383–385; Card and Dahl, "Family Violence and Football," 121, 129; Trendl et al., "Role of Alcohol," 1. Also see Ivandić et al., "Football," 2, 13.

30. Card and Dahl, "Family Violence and Football," 103, 129; Kirby et al., "Can FIFA World Cup Football," 269–270; Brimicombe and Cafe, "Beware, Win or Lose," 35; Kirby and Birdsall, "Kicking Off," 378, 383–385.

31. Healy et al., "Irrelevant Events Affect Voters' Evaluations," 12804; Busby et al., "Political Relevance," 347.

32. Healy et al., "Irrelevant Events Affect Voters' Evaluations."

33. Healy et al., "Irrelevant Events Affect Voters' Evaluations," 12804.

34. Healy et al., "Irrelevant Events Affect Voters' Evaluations," 12805–12806.

35. Healy et al., "Irrelevant Events Affect Voters' Evaluations," 12805–12806.

36. Healy et al., "Irrelevant Events Affect Voters' Evaluations," 12806.

37. Healy et al., "Irrelevant Events Affect Voters' Evaluations," 12806.

38. Busby et al., "Political Relevance."

39. Busby et al., "Political Relevance," 347.

40. Kikuta and Uesugi, "Do Politically Irrelevant Events," 201–210.

41. Goldblatt, *The Age of Football*, 34–37.

42. Kikuta and Uesugi, "Do Politically Irrelevant Events," 179, 188.

43. Kikuta and Uesugi, "Do Politically Irrelevant Events," 192–197, 201–210.

44. Kikuta and Uesugi, "Do Politically Irrelevant Events," 192, 201.

45. Kikuta and Uesugi, "Do Politically Irrelevant Events," 194, 202.

46. Note that I exclude 1992 in this analysis because Toronto won the World Series that year.

47. Berrett, *Pigskin Nation*, 2.

48. Depetris-Chauvin et al., "Building Nations," 1579, 1592.

49. Depetris-Chauvin et al., "Building Nations," 1589, online appendix, table A.13.

50. For this analysis, my measure of incidents of civil unrest comes from the Historical Phoenix Event dataset that was constructed using content from the *New York Times*. See Althaus et al., *Historical Phoenix Event Data*.

51. Depetris-Chauvin et al., "Building Nations," 1576–1577, 1589.

52. Depetris-Chauvin et al., "Building Nations," 1579, 1596.

53. Rosenzweig and Zhou, "Team and Nation," 2137–2139.

54. Rosenzweig and Zhou, "Team and Nation," 2139–2143.

55. Depetris-Chauvin et al., "Building Nations," 1579, 1596.

56. Steenveld and Strelitz, "1995 Rugby World Cup," 609–611.

57. Grundlingh, "From Redemption to Recidivism?," 71–72.

58. Grundlingh, "From Redemption to Recidivism?," 75–76.

59. Grundlingh, "From Redemption to Recidivism?," 75–76.

60. Grundlingh, "From Redemption to Recidivism?," 76.

61. Quoted in Grundlingh, "From Redemption to Recidivism?," 76.

62. Steenveld and Strelitz, "1995 Rugby World Cup," 625.

63. Christopher Hitchens, "Why the Olympics and Other Sports Cause Conflict," *Newsweek*, February 4, 2010, https://www.newsweek.com/why-olympics-and-other -sports-cause-conflict-75043

64. Jaksa, "Sports and Collective Identity," 41.

65. Cha, *Beyond the Final Score*, 41–42.

66. Cha, *Beyond the Final Score*, 41–42.

67. Andrew Bertoli, "Here's How the Euro Soccer Tournament Will Affect the Brexit Vote," *Washington Post*, June 22, 2016, https://www.washingtonpost.com/news/monkey -cage/wp/2016/06/22/why-is-the-brexit-vote-happening-smack-in-the-middle-of-a-eu ropean-soccer-championship-good-question/

68. Quoted in Keys, "Introduction," 1.

69. Quoted in Keys, "Introduction," 1.

Chapter 3

1. Sagan, *Contact*, 85–88.

2. On the speed of the transmission, see Sagan, *Contact*, 85.

3. Boykoff, *The 1936 Berlin Olympics*, 1–3.

4. Related to this point, see Johnson and Ali, "Tale of Two Seasons," 986–987; Dawn Brancati and William C. Wohlforth, "Why Authoritarians Love the Olympics: A Boycott of Beijing 2022 Will Do Little to Deter China," *Foreign Affairs*, March 25, 2021, https://www.foreignaffairs.com/articles/china/2021-03-25/why-authoritarians-love-olympics

5. Regarding the success of single-party and communist systems at the Olympics, see Johnson and Ali, "Tale of Two Seasons," 986–987. Related to the other points, see Zirin, *Brazil's Dance*, 163–165; Jaksa, "Sports and Collective Identity," 41; Brancati and Wohlforth, "Authoritarians." In addition, see Bason et al., "Fifa," 425.

6. Tunis, "The Dictators Discover Sport," 608.

7. Prozumenshikov, "Action in the Era of Stagnation," 74.

8. Vamplew, *Games People Played*, 40–41; Fisher, *Lacrosse*, 13–14.

9. Quoted in Mandelbaum, *Meaning of Sports*, 13. Also see Gerdy, *Sports*, xiii.

10. Elias, *The Empire Strikes Out*, 34–35; Paolantonio, *How Football Explains America*, 56–60; Matthew Andrews, "College Football and the Strenuous Life," *The Untold History of Sports in America* (podcast), August 18, 2022, https://omny.fm/shows/the-untold-history-of-sports-in-america/college-football-and-the-strenuous-life; Matthew Andrews, "Babe Ruth and the American Dream," *The Untold History of Sports in America* (podcast), iHeartPodcasts, September 8, 2022, https://omny.fm/shows/the-untold-history-of-sports-in-america/babe-ruth-and-the-american-dream. Also see Mandelbaum, *Meaning of Sports*, 128–143; McDonagh and Pappano, *Playing with the Boys*, 203–204; Gerdy, *Sports*, xiv.

11. Rowley, "Sport," 1324.

12. See Tunis, "The Dictators Discover Sport," 610–611.

13. See Tunis, "The Dictators Discover Sport," 610.

14. Tunis, "The Dictators Discover Sport," 609.

15. Rowley, "Sport," 1314, 1319–1332.

16. Goldblatt, *The Games*, 211–212.

17. Parks, "Verbal Gymnastics," 31–32, 36–37, 39.

18. Belloni, "Birth of the Sport Nation," 54.

19. Perales, "Politics and Play," 247; Elias, *The Empire Strikes Out*, 27–28, 31–33.

20. Belloni, "Birth of the Sport Nation," 54.

21. Tunis, "The Dictators Discover Sport," 610–611; Belloni, "Birth of the Sport Nation," 54; Erminio Fonzo, "Italian Fascism and the Olympic Games," paper presented at the Second Annual Conference of the Center for Sociocultural Sport and Olympic Research, 15–16, Fullerton, CA, March 2019, 1–2, 4, https://www.researchgate.net/publication/332015183_Italian_Fascism_and_Olympic_Games

22. Pujadas, "Sport Under Authoritarian Regimes," 10.

23. Tunis, "The Dictators Discover Sport," 612; Goldblatt, *The Ball Is Round*, 215; Belloni, "Birth of the Sport Nation," 56.

24. Goldblatt, *The Ball Is Round*, 215–216; Belloni, "Birth of the Sport Nation," 57; Foot, *Calcio*, 389–390.

25. Goldblatt, *The Ball Is Round*, 216; Foot, *Calcio*, 427.

26. Quoted in Fonzo, "Italian Fascism," 3.

27. Tunis, "The Dictators Discover Sport," 613–614.

28. Goldblatt, *The Ball Is Round*, 254.

29. Goldblatt, *The Ball Is Round*, 254.

30. Fonzo, "Italian Fascism," 2.

31. Fonzo, "Italian Fascism," 2–3.

32. Goldblatt, *The Ball Is Round*, 255.

33. Goldblatt, *The Ball Is Round*, 254.

34. Martin, *Football and Fascism*, 189.

35. Belloni, "Birth of the Sport Nation," 59.

36. Quoted in Goldblatt, *The Ball Is Round*, 260.

37. Belloni, "Birth of the Sport Nation," 58–59.

38. William Tuohy, "50th Anniversary of Berlin Olympics: Hitler Is Recalled, but So Too Is Owens," *Los Angeles Times*, August 1, 1986, https://www.latimes.com/archives/la-xpm-1986-08-01-sp-18870-story.html

39. Guttmann, *The Olympics*, 3–4, 12.

40. Tunis, "The Dictators Discover Sport," 615–617.

41. Boykoff, *Power Games*, 69.

42. Guttmann, *The Olympics*, 51.

43. Guttmann, *The Olympics*, 55.

44. Boykoff, *Power Games*, 69.

45. Boykoff, *The 1936 Berlin Olympics*, 11, 70, 100.

46. Boykoff, *The 1936 Berlin Olympics*, 41–47.

47. Boykoff, *The 1936 Berlin Olympics*, 43; Goldblatt, *The Games,* 176–177.

48. Boykoff, *Power Games*, 70.

49. Goldblatt, *The Games*, 178–179.

50. Boykoff, *Power Games*, 63.

51. Also see Zirin, *Brazil's Dance*, 157; Boykoff, *The 1936 Berlin Olympics*, 6, 8, 79.

52. Quoted in "The Nazi Games: Berlin 1936," *PBS America*, YouTube, posted November 12, 2022, https://www.youtube.com/watch?v=nCA0s3sMc6Q; this video is not currently available in the United States.

53. Guttmann, *Women's Sports*, 107–108.

54. Goldblatt, *The Games,* 174.

55. Boykoff, *The 1936 Berlin Olympics*, 3, 77–78; Zirin, *Brazil's Dance*, 156.

56. Boykoff, *The 1936 Berlin Olympics*, 3, 77–79; Zirin, *Brazil's Dance,* 156.

57. Zirin, *Brazil's Dance,* 154–157; Goldblatt, *The Games,* 154; Boykoff, *Power Games*, 72.

58. Boykoff, *Power Games*, 72.

59. Quoted in "The Nazi Games."

60. Quoted in "The Nazi Games."

61. Quoted in "The Nazi Games."

62. Regarding Germany, see Goldblatt, *The Games,* 191; Boykoff, *The 1936 Berlin Olympics*, 10.

63. Boykoff, *The 1936 Berlin Olympics*, 51.

64. For instance, see Boykoff, *Power Games*, 97–102, 112–113.

65. Espy, *Olympic Games*, 4; Wagg and Andrews, "Introduction," 2–4; Boykoff, *Power Games*, 81–82; Prozumenshikov, "Action in the Era of Stagnation," 74; Festle, *Playing Nice*, 84; Matthew Andrews, "Cold War Olympics," *The Untold History of Sports in America* (podcast), iHeartPodcasts, September 22, 2022, https://omny.fm/shows/the-untold -history-of-sports-in-america/cold-war-olympics

66. Prozumenshikov, "Action in the Era of Stagnation," 74.

67. Related to this point, see Guttmann, *Women's Sports*, 175.

68. Also see Rider, *Cold War Games*, 2.

69. Regarding Soviet specialized sports schools, see Guttmann, *Women's Sports*, 175.

70. Llewellyn and Gleaves, *Rise and Fall of Olympic Amateurism*, 113. Also see Guttmann, *Women's Sports*, 174.

71. Beamish and Ritchie, "Totalitarian Regimes," 14, 16–17, 19. Also see Hunt, *Drug Games*, 7–9.

72. Parks, "Verbal Gymnastics," 31–32, 36–37, 39.

73. Parks, "Verbal Gymnastics," 36–37, 39.

74. Parks, "Verbal Gymnastics," 39–40.

75. Guttmann, *Women's Sports*, 256.

76. Goldblatt, *The Games*, 294–295.

77. Guttmann, "Cold War," 554, 565–566; Guttmann, *Women's Sports*, 245; Guttmann, *Sports*, 267; Cottrell and Nelson, "Not Just the Games?," 738; Andrews, "Cold War Olympics."

78. Espy, *Olympic Games*, 81.

79. Kobierecki, "Sport as Tool," 106.

80. Boykoff, *Power Games*, 95.

81. Quoted in Boykoff, *Power Games*, 95.

82. Goldblatt, *The Games*, 239.

83. Russell Field, "A Third World Olympics: Sport, Politics, and the Developing World in the 1963 Games of the New Emerging Forces (GANEFO)," *Verso* (blog), August 9, 2016, https://www.versobooks.com/blogs/news/2799-a-third-world-olympics-sport -politics-and-the-developing-world-in-the-1963-games-of-the-new-emerging-forces -ganefo; Pauker, "Ganefo I," 171–172.

84. Kobierecki, "Sport as Tool," 114.

85. Boykoff, *Power Games*, 96.

86. Espy, *Olympic Games*, 82.

87. Pauker, "Ganefo I," 180.

88. Kobierecki, "Sport as Tool," 113.

89. Kobierecki, "Sport as Tool," 115–117, 119.

90. Boykoff, *Power Games*, 97; Kobierecki, "Sport as Tool," 119.

91. Kobierecki, "Sport as Tool," 118–119.

92. Quoted in Scharpf et al., "International Sports Events," 914.

93. Paula Canelo, "The EAM and the 'Magnificent Party,'" *Papelitos*, 2018, https:// papelitos.com.ar/nota/la-interna-de-la-dictadura-frente-al-mundial-78

94. Quoted in Canelo, "The EAM."

95. Tim Pears, "Salvation Army: Part Two," *Guardian*, June 4, 2006, https://www.theguardian.com/sport/2006/jun/04/worldcup2006.football4

96. Pears, "Salvation Army."

97. For the details of my discussion of this article, see Scharpf et al., "International Sports Events," 913–922.

98. Quoted in Scharpf et al., "International Sports Events," 920.

99. Aaron O'Neill, "Population in the Former Territories of the Federal Republic of Germany and the German Democratic Republic from 1950 to 2016," *Statista*, August 9, 2024, https://www.statista.com/statistics/1054199/population-of-east-and-west-germany/; Anderson and Silver, "Growth and Diversity," 158.

100. Singer et al., "Capability Distribution."

101. Sleifer, *Planning Ahead*, 13.

102. Edelman and Young, "Introduction," 11; Dennis, "Sports, Politics, and 'Wild Doping,'" 126.

103. Hunt, *Drug Games*, 51.

104. Dennis, "Sports, Politics, and 'Wild Doping,'" 129.

105. Dennis, "Sports, Politics, and 'Wild Doping,'" 135–136; Marc Fisher, "E. German Sports: Ruled by Steroids," *Washington Post*, September 7, 1991, https://www.washingtonpost.com/archive/politics/1991/09/07/e-german-sports-ruled-by-steroids/22edb482-664a-4513-8672-c87581b166d7/; Lucas Aykroyd, "Fall of Berlin Wall Brought Curtain Down on GDR's Doping Program," *Global Sport Matters*, November 6, 2019, https://globalsportmatters.com/culture/2019/11/06/fall-of-berlin-wall-brought-curtain-down-on-gdrs-doping-program/

106. Aykroyd, "Fall of Berlin."

107. Fisher, "E. German Sports."

108. Aykroyd, "Fall of Berlin."

109. Fisher, "E. German Sports."

110. Fisher, "E. German Sports."

111. Aykroyd, "Fall of Berlin."

112. Dennis, "Sports, Politics, and 'Wild Doping,'" 142.

113. Fisher, "E. German Sports."

114. Reuters Staff, "Factbox-Timeline of the Russia Doping Case," *Reuters*, December 17, 2020, https://www.reuters.com/article/sports/factbox-timeline-of-the-russia-doping-case-idUSKBN28R2HR/

115. Julia Ioffe, "How the Kremlin Tried to Rig the Olympics, and Failed," *Atlantic*, December 6, 2017, https://www.theatlantic.com/international/archive/2017/12/kremlin-doping-scandal-sochi-winter-olympics/547616/

116. Kalyeena Makortoff, "What You Need to Know About Russia's Doping Scandal," *CNBC*, November 12, 2015, https://www.cnbc.com/2015/11/12/what-you-need-to-know-about-russias-doping-scandal.html

117. Luther and Davidson, *Loving Sports*, 33.

118. Christian Lowe and Aleksandar Vasovic, "Exclusive: Scrutiny on Global Sport

Bodies as They Decide Russians' Olympic Fates," *Reuters*, July 26, 2016, https://www.reuters.com/article/sports/olympics/exclusive-scrutiny-on-global-sport-bodies-as-they-decide-russians-olympic-fate-idUSKCN1062ER/

119. Steven Taranto, "2020 Tokyo Olympics: Ryan Murphy Becomes Latest Olympian to Question Integrity of ROC's Athletes," *CBS Sports*, July 30, 2021, https://www.cbssports.com/olympics/news/2020-tokyo-olympics-ryan-murphy-becomes-latest-olympian-to-question-integrity-of-rocs-athletes/

120. Adam Taylor, "We Treat Him Like He's Mad, but Vladimir Putin's Popularity Has Just Hit a 3-Year High," *Washington Post*, March 13, 2014, https://www.washingtonpost.com/news/worldviews/wp/2014/03/13/we-treat-him-like-hes-mad-but-vladimir-putins-popularity-has-just-hit-a-3-year-high/

121. Alec Luhn, "Ukraine Crisis and Olympics Boost Vladimir Putin's Popularity in Russia," *Guardian*, March 6, 2014, https://www.theguardian.com/world/2014/mar/06/ukraine-olympics-vladimir-putin-russia-crimea

122. Shaun Walker, "Successful World Cup Fails to Halt Slide in Vladimir Putin's Popularity," *Guardian*, July 6, 2018, https://www.theguardian.com/world/2018/jul/16/successful-world-cup-fails-to-halt-slide-in-vladimir-putins-popularity

123. On this point, also see Berglund, *Fastest Game*, 222–224.

124. Alissa de Carbonnel, "Billions Stolen in Sochi Olympics Preparations—Russian Opposition," *Reuters*, May 30, 2013, https://www.reuters.com/article/sports/billions-stolen-in-sochi-olympics-preparations-russian-opposition-idUSBRE94T0RU/; Zirin, *Brazil's Dance*, 186–187; Barney Ronay, "UEFA and FIFA Are Too Late: Russia's Sportswashing Has Served Its Purpose," *Guardian*, February 25, 2022, https://www.theguardian.com/football/2022/feb/25/uefa-and-fifa-are-too-late-russias-sportswashing-has-served-its-purpose

125. Müller, "After Sochi 2014," 641–642. Also see Mark Ellwood, "Why Oligarch Cash Is Vanishing from This Billionaire Resort in the French Alps," *New York Post*, March 30, 2022, https://nypost.com/2022/03/30/oligarch-billions-are-vanishing-from-french-alps-resort/

126. Ronay, "UEFA and FIFA."

127. Steve Rosenberg, "Is Russia the Real Winner of World Cup 2018?," *BBC News*, July 14, 2018, https://www.bbc.com/news/world-europe-44812175

128. Quoted in Rosenberg, "Is Russia."

129. Shuman, "Learning from the Soviet Big Brother," 164, 172–174.

130. Boykoff, *Power Games*, 92–95; Morris, "'Communist Bandits,'" 175–176.

131. Morris, "'Communist Bandits,'" 175–176.

132. Hong et al., "Beijing Ambitions," 11–19.

133. Hong et al., "Beijing Ambitions," 17.

134. On China's sports academies for children, see Hong et al., "Beijing Ambitions," 12–17.

135. Hong et al., "Beijing Ambitions," 17, 20–21.

136. Hong et al., "Beijing Ambitions," 12–13, 19.

137. Hong et al., "Beijing Ambitions," 19.

138. Hong et al., "Beijing Ambitions," 13, 20–21.

139. Xu, "Modernizing China," 90–91.

140. On this topic, see Chen et al., "2008 Beijing Olympics," 188.

141. Preuss and Alfs, "Signaling," 55.

142. Brady, "The Beijing Olympics," 1, 5–6.

143. Victor D. Cha, "The Biden Boycott of the 2022 Beijing Winter Olympics," *Center for Strategic and International Studies*, January 18, 2022, https://www.csis.org/analysis/ biden-boycott-2022-beijing-winter-olympics; Associated Press, "World Leaders: Who's Coming, Who Isn't to Beijing Olympics," *AP News*, February 3, 2022, https://apnews .com/article/winter-olympics-dignitaries-attending-beijing-2022-7b8a52f7bab22720de 2b90895e008ea1

144. "The Hermit Kingdom," *Vice News*, YouTube, posted February 23, 2014, https:// www.youtube.com/watch?v=IrCQh1usdzE

145. Kim Tong-Hyung, "Highlights of Dennis Rodman's Past Visits to North Korea," *AP News*, June 13, 2017, https://apnews.com/article/9ba134a5e9c046f78712da589fa12921

146. Daniel Etchells, "Bach Claims Pyeongchang 2018 'Opened the Door' as Agreement to End Korean War Announced," *Inside the Games*, April 27, 2018, https://www.in sidethegames.biz/articles/1064433/bach-claims-pyeongchang-2018-opened-the-door -as-agreement-to-end-korean-war-announced; Michael Pavitt, "Bach Welcomes 'Historic Initiative' of Joint Korean Bid for 2032 Olympic Games as Unified Teams at Tokyo 2020 Discussed," *Inside the Games*, February 15, 2019, https://www.insidethegames.biz/ articles/1075569/bach-welcomes-historic-initiative-of-joint-korean-bid-for-2032 -olympic-games-as-unified-teams-at-tokyo-2020-discussed

147. Jaime Tarabay, "North Korea Is Winning the Olympics—and It's Not Because of Sports," *CNN*, February 11, 2018, https://edition.cnn.com/2018/02/09/asia/south -korea-north-korea-spotlight-fight-intl/index.html

148. Berglund, *Fastest Game*, 7–10.

149. Timothy W. Martin, "Kim Yo Jong: What We Know About Kim Jong Un's Sister and Her Role in North Korea," *Wall Street Journal*, December 21, 2023, https://www.wsj .com/world/asia/kim-jong-un-sister-kim-yo-jong-11607524273

150. Motoko Rich and Choe Sang-Hun, "Kim Jong-un's Sister Turns on the Charm, Taking Pence's Spotlight," *New York Times*, February 18, 2018, https://www.nytimes. com/2018/02/11/world/asia/kim-yo-jong-mike-pence-olympics.html

151. Morgan Winsor, "North Korea's 200-Plus Cheerleaders Command Spotlight at 2018 Winter Olympics with Synchronized Chants," *ABC News*, February 10, 2018, https:// abcnews.go.com/International/north-koreas-cheerleaders-steal-spotlight-2018-winter -olympics/story?id=52983432

152. "North Korea Judged Winner of Diplomatic Gold at Olympics," *Reuters*, February 11, 2018, https://www.reuters.com/article/sports/olympics/north-korea-judged-win ner-of-diplomatic-gold-at-olympics-idUSL4N1Q1oDI/

153. Paul Chiasson, "North Korean Sport Diplomacy: The Olympic Event Where Everyone Loses," *The Conversation*, February 18, 2018, https://theconversation.com/ north-korean-sport-diplomacy-the-olympic-event-where-everyone-loses-91894; Tim-

othy Bynion, "Glamorizing Dictators," *Towson University Journal of International Affairs*, February 21, 2018, https://wp.towson.edu/iajournal/2018/02/21/glamorizing-dicta tors/

154. Quoted in Aamer Madhani, "Pence Arrives for Winter Olympics, Sounds Alarm About North Korea's Record on Human Rights," *USA Today*, February 8, 2018, https://eu.usatoday.com/story/sports/winter-olympics-2018/2018/02/08/mike-pence-north -korea-south-korea-cooperation-human-rights/318614002/

155. Quoted in Madhani, "Pence Arrives."

156. Martin Pengelly, "Mike Pence to Stop North Korea 'Hijacking' Winter Olympics, Aide Says," *Guardian*, February 4, 2018, https://www.theguardian.com/world/2018/feb/04/mike-pence-north-korea-winter-olympics

157. Bynion, "Glamorizing Dictators."

158. Karim Zidan, "Saudi Arabia Has Bought into Soccer and Golf. Will the NBA and NFL Be Next?," *Guardian*, June 9, 2023, https://www.theguardian.com/sport/2023/jun/09/saudi-arabia-soccer-golf-nba-nfl-sportswashing

159. R. García, "Newcastle Spend 46m Euros on Gordon . . . Taking Their Expenditure to 283m Under Saudi Arabian Owners," *Marca*, January 29, 2023, https://www.marca.com/en/football/newcastle-united/2023/01/29/63d6be87e2704ec6408b45a3.html

160. For the financial figures, see Sean L. Yom, "The Long Game: Saudi Arabia and Professional Golf," *Foreign Policy Research Institute*, June 21, 2023, https://www.fpri.org/article/2023/06/the-long-game-saudi-arabia-and-professional-golf/

161. Quoted in Noah Berman, "Saudi Arabia's Investments Raise Questions of 'Sportswashing,'" *Council on Foreign Relations*, July 13, 2023, https://www.cfr.org/in -brief/saudi-arabias-investments-raise-questions-sportswashing

162. Yom, "The Long Game."

163. Berman, "Saudi Arabia's Investments."

164. Zidan, "Saudi Arabia Has Bought into Soccer and Golf."

165. On this topic, see Guttmann, *Women's Sports*, 255–258. Also see Luther and Davidson, *Loving Sports*, 34.

166. Also see Luther and Davidson, *Loving Sports*, 34, 43.

167. Keys, "Introduction," 1–6.

168. On this point, also see Hoberman, "Myth of Sport," 21–23.

169. This quote comes from Boykoff, *NOlympians*, 4. Also see Zirin, *Brazil's Dance*, 4; Boykoff, *The 1936 Berlin Olympics*, 12.

Chapter 4

1. McDonagh and Pappano, *Playing with the Boys*, 30–31; Ware, *Game, Set, Match*, 1. Also see Guttmann, *Women's Sports*, 210–211; Schultz, *Qualifying Times*, 130.

2. Ware, *Game, Set, Match*, 4.

3. Chatziefstathiou, "Reading Coubertin," 98–105.

4. Chatziefstathiou, "Reading Coubertin," 100, 102–103; Schultz, *Women's Sports*, 17–19.

5. Chatziefstathiou, "Reading Coubertin," 99–101.

6. Quoted in Chatziefstathiou, "Reading Coubertin," 101–102. Also see Boykoff, *What Are the Olympics For?*, 13.

7. Boykoff, *Power Games*, 17.

8. Kyle, *Sport and Spectacle*, 214–215. Note that there may have been some exceptions where specific women were allowed to watch the ancient Olympics, such as priestesses.

9. Folk football was a chaotic game dating back to the Middle Ages in which two villages competed to move a ball into the portal of the other side's parish church. See Guttmann, *Sports,* 64–65; see also Guttmann, *Women's Sports,* 1–2, 7–8, 47–48, 61–63, 71–79.

10. Guttmann, *Women's Sports*, 20–21, 27; Kyle, "Ancient Greek and Roman Sport," 87.

11. Guttmann, *Women's Sports*, 25.

12. Guttmann, *Women's Sports*, 33–84.

13. McDonagh and Pappano, *Playing with the Boys*, 200.

14. For a more ambivalent view, see Guttmann, *Women's Sports*, 210.

15. Quoted in Ware, *Game, Set, Match*, 2.

16. McDonagh and Pappano, *Playing with the Boys*, 31.

17. McDonagh and Pappano, *Playing with the Boys*, 31.

18. Aaron O'Neill, "Distribution of Male and Female Athletes Participating at the Summer Olympics from 1896 to 2024," *Statista*, July 4, 2024, https://www.statista.com/statistics/1090616/olympics-share-athletes-by-gender-since-1896/; Statista Research Department, "Olympic Winter Games Number of Participating Athletes from 1924 to 2022, by Gender," *Statista*, February 19, 2024, https://www.statista.com/statistics/266368/number-of-winter-olympic-games-participants-since-1924-by-gender/

19. Hargreaves, "Olympic Women," 3.

20. Guttmann, *Women's Sports*, 85–105.

21. Schultz, *Women's Sports*, 5; Luther and Davidson, *Loving Sports*, 27.

22. Park, "Sport, Gender, and Society," 59, 61, 69–76.

23. On this topic, see Dunning, "Sport as a Male Preserve;" Guttmann, *Women's Sports*, 251–254.

24. McDonagh and Pappano, *Playing with the Boys*, 17–18, 63, 73–74, 197–200; Schultz, *Women's Sports*, 67–68.

25. Schultz, *Women's Sports*, 6.

26. Markovits and Albertson, *Sportista*, 48.

27. Also see McDonagh and Pappano, *Playing with the Boys*, 236; Ring, *Stolen Bases*, 8.

28. "What Impact Did WW1 Have on Women's Football?," *BBC*, November 2018, https://www.bbc.co.uk/bitesize/articles/zjxywty

29. "What Impact."

30. "What Impact."

31. Lauren Zumbach, "How Women's Track and Field Fought Their Way into the Olympics—by Staging Their Own," *Women's Running*, July 29, 2021, https://www.womensrunning.com/events/olympics/womens-track-and-field-olympics-history/

32. Guttmann, *Women's Sports*, 165–168.

33. Guttmann, *Women's Sports*, 168–169; Hargreaves, "Olympic Women," 8.

34. Schultz, *Women's Sports*, 94–95; Hargreaves, "Olympic Women," 11; Ware, *Game, Set, Match*, 121.

35. Guttmann, *Women's Sports*, 142–146.

36. O'Reilly and Cahn, "Timeline," xxv.

37. Markovits and Albertson, *Sportista*, 76–78; Dreier and Elias, *Baseball Rebels*, 164–165.

38. Guttmann, *Women's Sports*, 135–142.

39. Festle, *Playing Nice*, 79–80; Hargreaves, "Olympic Women," 9–11.

40. Festle, *Playing Nice*, 79–80; Guttmann, *Women's Sports*, 136–142.

41. Guttmann, *Women's Sports*, 136–142; Festle, *Playing Nice*, 79–80; Suggs, *Place*, 7, 20–27.

42. O'Reilly and Cahn, "Introduction," xi.

43. For instance, see Festle, *Playing Nice*, 12, 16–18; Hargreaves, "Olympic Women," 9–11; Ware, *Game, Set, Match*, 121–122.

44. Festle, *Playing Nice*, 79–84.

45. Festle, *Playing Nice*, 12.

46. Festle, *Playing Nice*, 12, 16.

47. Markovits and Albertson, *Sportista*, 74–75, 78.

48. Guttmann, *Women's Sports*, 136–137.

49. Markovits and Albertson, *Sportista*, 81; Ware, *Game, Set, Match*, 8.

50. For instance, see Guttmann, *Women's Sports*, 140; Suggs, *Place*, 48, 59; Festle, *Playing Nice*, 20, 80–83.

51. Festle, *Playing Nice*, 80–83.

52. Related to this point, see Festle, *Playing Nice*, 81.

53. Druckman and Sharrow, *Equality Unfulfilled*, 5–6; Guttmann, *Women's Sports*, 220–223.

54. Druckman and Sharrow, *Equality Unfulfilled*, 15–16.

55. For more discussion on this topic, see Suggs, *Place*, 105–124; McDonagh and Pappano, *Playing with the Boys*, 28–29, 108–111, 180–81; Druckman and Sharrow, *Equality Unfulfilled*, 5–23; Guttmann, *Women's Sports*, 220–221.

56. Ware, *Game, Set, Match*, 11.

57. Festle, *Playing Nice*, 222, 286–287.

58. Festle, *Playing Nice*, 286–287; Will, "Train Wreck," 346–348; Markovits and Albertson, *Sportista*, 81.

59. For instance, see Ware, *Game, Set, Match*, 13, 141; Guttmann, *Women's Sports*, 222–223; Druckman and Sharrow, *Equality Unfulfilled*, 17.

60. Suggs, *Place*, 59–62.

61. Druckman and Sharrow, *Equality Unfulfilled*, 15.

62. For instance, see Theberge and Birrell, "Structural Constraints," 170–171; Druckman and Sharrow, *Equality Unfulfilled*, 13–14; Suggs, *Place*, 59.

63. Part of this trend might also be explained by male administrators preferring to hire male coaches instead of female ones. See Festle, *Playing Nice*, 224; Zirin, *What's My*

Name, 189; Markovits and Smith, *Sports Culture Among Undergraduates;* Cooky and Messner, "Introduction," 2; Druckman and Sharrow, *Equality Unfulfilled,* 15.

64. Ware, *Game, Set, Match,* 163.

65. For more discussion of this topic, see McDonagh and Pappano, *Playing with the Boys,* 105, 211–214, 216.

66. Also see Druckman and Sharrow, *Equality Unfulfilled,* 13.

67. On this topic, see McDonagh and Pappano, *Playing with the Boys,* 214–215.

68. Druckman and Sharrow, *Equality Unfulfilled,* 14; Suggs, *Place,* 5.

69. Bialystok and Kingwell, "Fragility of Fairness," 155; Schultz, *Women's Sports,* 84; Luther and Davidson, *Loving Sports,* 92–97.

70. Zirin, *Game Over,* 139; Schultz, *Qualifying Times,* 103, 111–112; McDonagh and Pappano, *Playing with the Boys,* 42–44.

71. Schultz, *Women's Sports,* 78–79.

72. Schultz, *Women's Sports,* 80.

73. Schultz, *Qualifying Times,* 103, 108–118; Schultz, *Women's Sports,* 80; McDonagh and Pappano, *Playing with the Boys,* 43–44.

74. Schultz, *Women's Sports,* 80.

75. Luther and Davidson, *Loving Sports,* 40–43.

76. Schultz, *Women's Sports,* 83.

77. Zirin, *Game Over,* 138–144; Luther and Davidson, *Loving Sports,* 40–43.

78. McDonagh and Pappano, *Playing with the Boys,* 7–8.

79. McDonagh and Pappano, *Playing with the Boys,* 195–200, 213–214, 216–218.

80. For this paragraph, see McDonagh and Pappano, *Playing with the Boys,* 12–14, 17, 22, 59–60, 73–74, 132–134, 195–200. Also see Druckman and Sharrow, *Equality Unfulfilled,* 9.

81. For instance, see Markovits and Albertson, *Sportista,* 242; Luther and Davidson, *Loving Sports,* 97. For this paragraph, also see Schultz, *Women's Sports,* 68.

82. McDonagh and Pappano, *Playing with the Boys,* 59–60.

83. For instance, see Festle, *Playing Nice,* 46–47, 91–94, 255–258; Zirin, *What's My Name,* 188–191.

84. Zirin, *Game Over,* 135–138.

85. Hargreaves, *Sporting Females,* 158–167; Zirin, *Game Over,* 136–137.

86. Festle, *Playing Nice,* 255–262.

87. Festle, *Playing Nice,* 49–50. Regarding revealing uniforms, see Festle, *Playing Nice,* 256–257; Krane et al., "Living the Paradox," 87–89.

88. Guttmann, *Women's Sports,* 258–265; Markovits and Albertson, *Sportista,* 97–104; Timm, "'Beautiful Face,'" 156–58. Also see the statement by Mary Jo Kane in Zirin, *Game Over,* 138.

89. Guttmann, *Women's Sports,* 260.

90. Related to this point, see Festle, *Playing Nice,* 257; Luther and Davidson, *Loving Sports,* 72–73.

91. See Elias, *The Empire Strikes Out,* 270, 272. Also see Markovits and Rensmann, *Gaming the World,* 91.

92. Zirin, *Game Over*, 137. Also see Kane et al., "Exploring Sport Media Images," 282–284.

93. Goldblatt, *The Age of Football*, 306–308.

94. Goldblatt, *The Age of Football*, 306–308.

95. *From Moment to Mainstream: What Consumers in 7 Countries Really Think About Women's Sports* (Parity and SurveyMonkey, 2024), https://paritynow.co/report-2024-parity-surveymonkey

96. For example, see Guttmann, *Women's Sports*, 224–230; Goldblatt, *The Age of Football*, 306–308; *From Moment to Mainstream*.

97. Goldblatt, *The Age of Football*, 307.

98. Goldblatt, *The Age of Football*, 307.

99. Goldblatt, *The Age of Football*, 145.

100. Goldblatt, *The Age of Football*, 145.

101. Regarding the cases of Chile and Argentina, see Goldblatt, *The Age of Football*, 145.

102. Goldblatt, *The Age of Football*, 146.

103. Regarding China, see the previous chapter and Hong et al., "Beijing Ambitions," 12–17, 20–21.

104. See Rosato, "Flawed Logic," 585.

105. Schultz, *Women's Sports*, 3–4.

106. Schultz, *Women's Sports*, 2; Luther and Davidson, *Loving Sports*, 238.

107. Schultz, *Women's Sports*, 3.

108. For instance, see the *New York Times* quote in Ware, *Game, Set, Match*, 2.

109. Luther and Davidson, *Loving Sports*, 118; Cooky et al., "One and Done," 347–348, 351–356; Elsey and Nadel, *Futbolera*, 5.

110. Schultz, *Women's Sports*, 109. Regarding "symbolic annihilation," Schultz cites Tuchman, "Symbolic Annihilation."

111. Schultz, *Women's Sports*, 109.

112. Billings et al., "'Man, That Was a Pretty Shot,'" 308–309; Luther and Davidson, *Loving Sports*, 118–119.

113. Jones and Greer, "You Don't Look Like an Athlete," 360–362.

114. Jones and Greer, "You Don't Look Like an Athlete," 361; Schultz, *Women's Sports*, 110; Cooky et al., "'It's Dude Time!,'" 274–276; Cooky et al., "One and Done," 367.

115. Schultz, *Women's Sports*, 112–113.

116. Schultz, *Women's Sports*, 112, 115.

117. Schultz, *Women's Sports*, 116.

118. Schultz, *Women's Sports*, 118.

119. Cooky et al., "One and Done."

120. Cooky et al., "One and Done," 352.

121. Cooky et al., "One and Done," 352.

122. Cooky et al., "One and Done," 348.

123. Cooky et al., "One and Done," 350, 353.

124. Cooky et al., "One and Done," 367.

125. Cooky et al., "One and Done," 368.

126. Suggs, *Place*, 1–2.

127. Bob Cook, "If Sports Teaches Kids Life Lessons, Often They're the Wrong Ones," *Forbes*, September 29, 2018, https://www.forbes.com/sites/bobcook/2018/09/29/if-sports-teaches-kids-life-lessons-often-theyre-the-wrong-ones/

128. On this topic, also see Suggs, *Place*, 10; Ring, *Stolen Bases*, 10.

129. For this paragraph and the following one, see Feldman and Matjasko, "Role of School-Based," 161–193; Farb and Matjasko, "Recent Advances," 4–43.

130. Also see Oyer, *Economist Goes*, 9–10.

131. Also see Oyer, *Economist Goes*, 8.

132. Nagle and Brooks, "Systematic Review," 235–236, 239, 242; Tenforde et al., "Participation in Ball Sports," 222; Vlachopoulos et al., "Effect of Program of Short Bouts," 2.

133. Tenforde and Fredericson, "Influence of Sports Participation," 861–862; Nagle and Brooks, "Systematic Review," 235, 239; Tenforde et al., "Participation in Ball Sports," 222–223; Andreoli et al., "Effects of Different Sports," 507.

134. Tomporowski and Pesce, "Exercise, Sports, and Performance Arts," 94; Madinabeitia-Cabrera et al., "Cognitive Benefits," 1, 6–9. Also see Zhang et al., "Ping Pong," 1104, 1110–1112.

135. For instance, see Lavie et al., "Exercise and the Heart," 104–105, 107–109; Möhlenkamp et al., "Running," 1800.

136. Aicale et al., "Overuse Injuries in Sport," 6–7.

137. An important reason is that playing several different sports can reduce the chances of overuse injuries. Related to this topic, see Rugg et al., "Effects of Playing Multiple High School Sports," 402.

138. Sue-Chu, "Winter Sports Athletes," 397–400; Bougault et al., "Asthma and Cold-Air Athletes," 740; Kennedy and Faulhaber, "Respiratory Function," 43–44, 48–50.

139. For example, see Maron et al., "Cardiovascular Preparticipation Screening."

140. See Feldman and Matjasko, "Role," 180–181; Farb and Matjasko, "Recent Advances," 2, 29–30, 33, 38, 41–43.

141. Festle, *Playing Nice*, 270–272; O'Reilly and Cahn, "Introduction," xviii–xix; Suggs, *Place*, 3.

142. Schultz, *Women's Sports*, 152–153.

143. Schultz, *Women's Sports*, 152.

144. Schultz, *Women's Sports*, 155–159.

145. Farmer, "Student-Athlete," 121, 133.

146. For the estimates reported in this paragraph, see "The Odds of Success—Betting on Fame and Fortune," *Online Casino*, accessed April 6, 2025, https://www.onlinecasino.ca/odds-of-success/

147. For example, see Elsey and Nadel, *Futbolera*, 1.

148. Sarah Pruitt, "How Title IX Transformed Women's Sports," *History*, June 23, 2022, https://www.history.com/news/title-nine-womens-sports

149. Troy Brock, "College Athletes' Average NIL Earnings Shockingly Low Despite Headline Deals," *Sports Illustrated*, December 30, 2024, https://www.si.com/fannation/name-image-likeness/nil-news/college-athlete-average-nil-earnings-shockingly-low-despite-headline-deals

150. Oyer, *Economist Goes*, 12; Robert Farrington, "Athletic Scholarships Aren't Enough to Pay for College," *Forbes*, May 22, 2023, https://www.forbes.com/sites/robert farrington/2023/05/22/athletic-scholarships-arent-enough-to-pay-for-college/

151. Farrington, "Athletic Scholarships."

152. Also see Carlos, *The John Carlos Story*, 75; Luther and Davidson, *Loving Sports*, 206.

153. Kevin B. Blackistone, "Naomi Osaka, Simone Biles and the Enduring Sports Message of 2021," *Washington Post*, December 28, 2021, https://www.washingtonpost.com/sports/2021/12/26/simone-biles-naomi-osaka-mental-health/; Boykoff, *What Are the Olympics For?*, 12.

154. Matt Lavietes, "Soccer Star Megan Rapinoe Receives Presidential Medal of Freedom," *NBC Sports*, July 7, 2022, https://www.nbcnews.com/nbc-out/nbc-out-proud/soccer-star-megan-rapinoe-receives-presidential-medal-freedom-rcna37141

155. For instance, see Smith, "Stand Up, Show Respect," 2378–2379, 2384–2390; Sanderson et al., "When Athlete Activism," 303–306, 309–317.

156. Cooky and Antunovic, "'This Isn't Just About Us,'" 702–707.

157. Cooky and Antunovic, "'This Isn't Just About Us,'" 702–707.

158. McClearen and Fischer, "Maya Moore," 64–66.

159. Festle, *Playing Nice*, xxiv; Cooky and Antunovic, "'This Isn't Just About Us,'" 692, 695, 701–702. On this point, also see Luther and Davidson, *Loving Sports*, 255.

160. "World Fame 100," *ESPN*, accessed April 6, 2025, https://www.espn.com/espn/feature/story/_/id/26113613/espn-world-fame-100-2019

161. Cooky et al., "One and Done," 360.

162. Cooky and Antunovic, "'This Isn't Just About Us,'" 695.

163. Festle, *Playing Nice*, 231–233.

164. Sean Gregory, "Chloe Kim Is Ready to Win Olympic Gold Again—On Her Own Terms," *Time*, January 19, 2022, https://time.com/6140099/chloe-kim-2022-olympics-snowboarder/

165. David Axelrod, "Ep. 228—Michael Phelps," *The Axe Files with David Axelrod* (podcast), CNN Audio, March 26, 2018, https://edition.cnn.com/audio/podcasts/axe-files/episodes/c3dca1fd-298f-458c-9f94-ab850114e7bd

166. Jarrett Bell, "Tom Brady Voices Support for Naomi Osaka, Simone Biles on Mental Health Issues," *USA Today*, September 7, 2021, https://eu.usatoday.com/story/sports/nfl/buccaneers/2021/09/07/tom-brady-naomi-osaka-simone-biles-mental-health/5747577001/

167. Axelrod, "Ep. 228—Michael Phelps."

168. Axelrod, "Ep. 228—Michael Phelps."

169. Sheldon and Lyubomirsky, "Is It Possible," 134.

170. Sheldon and Lyubomirsky, "Is It Possible," 134–135.

171. Sheldon and Lyubomirsky, "Is It Possible," 138; Bao and Lyubomirsky, "Making Happiness Last," 371.

172. Sheldon and Lyubomirsky, "Is It Possible," 120.

173. See Sheldon and Lyubomirsky, "Is It Possible," 140.

174. See Sheldon and Lyubomirsky, "Is It Possible," 139, 141.

175. Jong Hee Park and Andrew D. Martin, "Did the 'Red Devils' Help Diversify the Korean Legal Profession?," unpublished manuscript, 2012, 4. The study is discussed in this book with permission from the study's lead author.

176. Park and Martin, "'Red Devils,'" 4.

177. Park and Martin, "'Red Devils,'" 8.

Chapter 5

1. For instance, see Gorn, "'No Quarrel,'" 42; Dreier and Elias, *Baseball Rebels*, 15; Matthew Andrews, "The Sweet Science," *The Untold History of Sports in America* (podcast), iHeartPodcasts, August 16, 2022, https://omny.fm/shows/the-untold-history-of -sports-in-america/the-sweet-science; Matthew Andrews, "The Return of the Great White Hope," *The Untold History of Sports in America* (podcast), iHeartPodcasts, October 25, 2022, https://omny.fm/shows/the-untold-history-of-sports-in-america/the-re turn-of-the-great-white-hope; also see Elias, *The Empire Strikes Out*, 275.

2. On this point, see Kuper, *Soccer Against the Enemy*, 4–18, 248–266.

3. Wiggins and Miller, *The Unlevel Playing Field*, 67; Zirin, *What's My Name,* 54; Matthew Andrews, "Jim Crow's Impact on Sports," *The Untold History of Sports in America* (podcast), iHeartPodcasts, August 23, 2022, https://omny.fm/shows/the-untold-history -of-sports-in-america/jim-crows-impact-on-sports

4. See Matthew Andrews, "Jack Johnson vs. The Great White Hopes," *The Untold History of Sports in America* (podcast), iHeartPodcasts, August 25, 2022, https://omny .fm/shows/the-untold-history-of-sports-in-america/jack-johnson-vs-the-great-white -hopes; also see Zirin, *What's My Name,* 55.

5. Zirin, *What's My Name,* 55.

6. For instance, see Widener, "Race and Sport," 466–467.

7. For instance, see Harris, *Red Card to Racism*, 132–156, 363–364.

8. Luther and Davidson, *Loving Sports*, 3.

9. Edwards, *Revolt,* 77–78; Prozumenshikov, "Action in the Era of Stagnation," 86–87.

10. Edwards, *Revolt,* 86.

11. Edwards, *Revolt,* 89.

12. Nicholson and Hoye, "Sport and Social Capital," 7.

13. On this topic, see Nicholson and Hoye, "Sport and Social Capital," 12.

14. On this point, see Luther and Davidson, *Loving Sports*, 1. Also see Chappell, *Mexican American Fastpitch*, 4–8.

15. In particular, see Ring, *Stolen Bases*, 1–14.

16. Nicholson and Hoye, "Sport and Social Capital," 12.

17. Crabbe, "Avoiding the Numbers Game," 25.

18. Mousa, "Building Social Cohesion."

19. Mousa, "Building Social Cohesion," 866–868.

20. Mousa, "Building Social Cohesion," 867–868.

21. Mousa, "Building Social Cohesion," 867.

22. For a related study involving men from different castes in India, see Lowe, "Types of Contact."

23. Markovits and Albertson, *Sportista*, 142–147.

24. Regarding sports talk, see Markovits and Albertson, *Sportista*, 142–47.

25. Related to this point, see Dreier and Elias, *Baseball Rebels*, 12–13; Zirin, *Jim Brown*, 132–137.

26. Related to this point, also see Dreier, "Jackie Robinson's Legacy," 47–48.

27. Alrababa'h et al., "Can Exposure," 1111.

28. See Moore, *We Will Win the Day*, 1–11.

29. Quoted in Mike Bertha, "Martin Luther King Jr. and Jackie Robinson: Friends and Civil Rights Icons," *Cut4*, January 18, 2016, https://www.mlb.com/cut4/mlk-jr-and -jackie-robinson-were-good-friends-c162102154

30. For further discussion of this topic, see Matthew Andrews, "Air Jordan," *The Untold History of Sports in America* (podcast), iHeartPodcasts, October 27, 2022, https:// omny.fm/shows/the-untold-history-of-sports-in-america/air-jordan

31. "TV Executive 1st Black Member at Augusta," *Los Angeles Times*, September 12, 1990, https://www.latimes.com/archives/la-xpm-1990-09-12-sp-242-story.html

32. For further discussion of this topic, see Matthew Andrews, "Cheating and Sports," *The Untold History of Sports in America* (podcast), iHeartPodcasts, November 3, 2022, https://omny.fm/shows/the-untold-history-of-sports-in-america/cheating-and-sports

33. Obama also associated himself with many prominent Black athletes. See Zirin, *Jim Brown*, 5.

34. Alrababa'h et al., "Can Exposure."

35. Alrababa'h et al., "Can Exposure," 1116.

36. Alrababa'h et al., "Can Exposure," 1119.

37. Widener, "Race and Sport," 466.

38. Zirin, *What's My Name*, 33–34.

39. Festle, *Playing Nice*, 60–61.

40. On this topic, see Rider, "In the 'Twilight Warzone,'" 33.

41. Maraniss, *Rome 1960*, xii–xiii; Edelman and Young, "Introduction," 24; Luther and Davidson, *Loving Sports*, 250; Matthew Andrews, "The Greatest: Muhammad Ali," *The Untold History of Sports in America* (podcast), iHeartPodcasts, September 27, 2022, https:// omny.fm/shows/the-untold-history-of-sports-in-america/the-greatest-muhammad-ali

42. For example, see Harris, *Red Card to Racism*, 281–283.

43. Ben Morse, "Racist Abuse Directed at England Players After Euro 2020 Final Defeat Is Described as 'Unforgivable' by Manager Gareth Southgate," *CNN*, July 12, 2021, https://edition.cnn.com/2021/07/12/football/england-racist-abuse-bukayo-saka-jadon -sancho-marcus-rashford-euro-2020-final-spt-intl/index.html

44. "Marcus Rashford Mural Defaced After England Euro 2020 Defeat," *BBC*, July 12, 2021, https://www.bbc.com/news/uk-england-manchester-57803161

45. Mandelbaum, *Meaning of Sports*, 94; Harris, *Red Card to Racism*, 248–249; Dreier and Elias, *Baseball Rebels*, 19.

46. Harris, *Red Card to Racism*, 325, 338, 354, 357.

47. Related to this topic, see Smith, *Sport*, xxvi–xxvii; Harrison and Valdez, "Uneven View of African American Ballers," 186. Also see Dexter Blackman's comments in "The Story Behind This Iconic Olympics Protest," *Vox*, YouTube, posted July 9, 2020, https://www.youtube.com/watch?v=1ACXn-BD0g8

48. Hoberman, *Darwin's Athletes*, xxiii–xxx, xxxiii–xxxv; Brooks and Blackman, "Introduction"; Harris, *Red Card to Racism*, 247.

49. "Celtics/Lakers: Best of Enemies (Part 1)," *ESPN Films*, June 13, 2017, https://www.espn.com/espnplus/collections/44816b37-411a-11ee-9ec0-02571ed8de13/celtics-lakers-best-of-enemies

50. "Celtics/Lakers."

51. Bob Cook, "If Sports Teaches Kids Life Lessons, Often They're the Wrong Ones," *Forbes*, September 29, 2018, https://www.forbes.com/sites/bobcook/2018/09/29/if-sports-teaches-kids-life-lessons-often-theyre-the-wrong-ones/; Luther and Davidson, *Loving Sports*, 84.

52. See the discussion about the personal development of athletes in Chapter 4 and Feldman and Matjasko, "Role of School-Based," 163–193; Farb and Matjasko, "Recent Advances," 4–43.

53. Edwards, "Decline," 440; Brooks and Blackman, "Introduction," 443.

54. Oyer, *Economist Goes*, 20–21. Also see Ring, *Stolen Bases*, 5; Ring, *A Game of Their Own*, ix.

55. "40% of Americans Think They're Fit Enough to Be an Olympian," *Yahoo News*, August 5, 2021, https://uk.news.yahoo.com/40-americans-think-theyre-fit-180400774.html

56. "A Fifth of Men Think They Could Have Become a Pro Athlete," *SWNS Digital*, May 12, 2016, https://swnsdigital.com/uk/2016/05/a-fifth-of-men-think-they-could-have-been-a-pro-athlete/

57. Jake New, "A Long Shot," *Inside Higher Ed*, January 26, 2015, https://www.insidehighered.com/news/2015/01/27/college-athletes-greatly-overestimate-their-chances-playing-professionally; Luther and Davidson, *Loving Sports*, 207.

58. New, "A Long Shot."

59. Luther and Davidson, *Loving Sports*, 207.

60. Zang, "Interview," 367–369.

61. Brooks and Blackman, "Introduction," 441, 444; also see Harris, *Red Card to Racism*, 247.

62. Hoberman, *Darwin's Athletes*, xxxiv.

63. Smith, *Sport*, 86.

64. Carlson et al., "Bankruptcy Rates," 381, 384. Also see McGraw et al., "NFL," 461–465.

65. Carlson et al., "Bankruptcy Rates," 381.

66. Dreier and Elias, *Baseball Rebels*, 2; Elias, *The Empire Strikes Out*, 180–182. On more recent cases, see Zirin, *The Kaepernick Effect*, 1–8.

67. Crepeau, *NFL Football*, 24–25.

68. Crepeau, *NFL Football*, 25.

69. Elias, *The Empire Strikes Out*, 180–182.

70. Quoted in Elias, *The Empire Strikes Out*, 180.

71. Elias, *The Empire Strikes Out*, 180–181.

72. Elias, *The Empire Strikes Out*, 181–182.

73. Quoted in Dave Zirin, "Don't Remember Muhammad Ali as a Sanctified Sports Hero. He Was a Powerful, Dangerous Political Force," *Los Angeles Times*, June 4, 2016, https://www.latimes.com/opinion/op-ed/la-oe-zirin-muhammad-ali-legacy-20160603-snap-story.html

74. Quoted in Krishnadev Calamur, "Muhammad Ali and Vietnam," *Atlantic*, June 4, 2016, https://www.theatlantic.com/news/archive/2016/06/muhammad-ali-vietnam/485717/

75. Hartmann, *Race, Culture, and the Revolt*, 5–6.

76. Quoted in Martin Rodgers, "American Simone Manuel Speaks Out on Police Brutality, Race After Earning Olympic Gold," *USA Today*, August 12, 2016, https://eu.usatoday.com/story/sports/olympics/rio-2016/2016/08/12/simone-manuel-gold-medalist-police-brutality-african-american-swimmer/88603406/

77. Alrababa'h et al., "Can Exposure," 1124–1125.

78. Smith, "Stand Up, Show Respect," 2376–2377; Sanderson et al., "When Athlete Activism," 309–315; Luther and Davidson, *Loving Sports*, 246–247, 252; Harris, *Red Card to Racism*, 294–299.

79. Sanderson et al., "When Athlete Activism," 309–315; Hartmann, *Race, Culture, and the Revolt*, 233.

80. Emily Sullivan, "Laura Ingraham Told LeBron James to Shut Up and Dribble; He Went to the Hoop," *NPR*, February 19, 2018, https://www.npr.org/sections/thetwo-way/2018/02/19/587097707/laura-ingraham-told-lebron-james-to-shutup-and-dribble-he-went-to-the-hoop

81. Quoted in Sullivan, "Shut Up and Dribble."

82. Zirin, *What's My Name*, 61–71, 73–78; Carlos, *The John Carlos Story*, 1, 122–137; Zirin, *Jim Brown*, 146, 154–155.

83. For instance, see Carlos, *The John Carlos Story*, 132–133.

84. Sullivan, "Shut Up and Dribble."

85. For instance, see the discussion of Naomi Osaka and Simone Biles in Chapter 4.

86. Kate Nalepinski and Dan Gooding, "What Is Tiger Woods' Political Affiliation? What We Know," *Newsweek*, February 21, 2025, https://www.newsweek.com/tiger-woods-donald-trump-relationship-political-liv-golf-2034134

87. Zirin, *What's My Name*, 64–69.

88. Carlos, *The John Carlos Story*, 122–137.

89. For more discussion of barriers to athlete activism, see Sanderson et al., "When Athlete Activism," 303–304.

90. Quoted in Tim Bontemps, "Michael Jordan Stands Firm on 'Republicans Buy Sneakers, Too' Quote, Says It Was Made in Jest," *ABC News*, May 4, 2020, https://

abcnews.go.com/Sports/michael-jordan-stands-firm-republicans-buy-sneakers-quote/story?id=70483289

91. On Gu's economic interests in China, see John Branch, "Eileen Gu Is Trying to Soar over the Geopolitical Divide," *New York Times*, February 3, 2022, https://www.nytimes.com/2022/02/03/sports/olympics/eileen-gu-china-freeski.html

92. For more discussion of the controversy surrounding Eileen Gu's decision to compete for China, see Lincoln Mitchell, "Controversy over Gold Medalist Eileen Gu Skiing for China Misses the Point," *CNN*, February 10, 2022, https://edition.cnn.com/2022/02/08/opinions/eileen-gu-gold-medal-for-china-mitchell/index.html

93. For instance, see Zirin, *What's My Name,* 214–217; Zirin, *Jim Brown,* 7; Burns, *Maradona,* 6; Boykoff, *The 1936 Berlin Olympics,* 90, 104.

94. Gorn, "'No Quarrel,'" 48–52; Andrews, "The Greatest."

95. "The Hermit Kingdom," *Vice News,* YouTube, posted February 23, 2014, https://www.youtube.com/watch?v=IrCQh1usdzE

96. "The Hermit Kingdom."

97. "Rodman: For Better or Worse," *ESPN Films,* September 10, 2019, https://www.espn.com/espnplus/player/_/id/adfd4fa7-1b51-485d-a65c-99768821ca49

98. Quoted in Associated Press, "Dennis Rodman: Kim's Great Leaders," *ESPN*, March 1, 2013, https://www.espn.com/nba/story/_/id/9002026/dennis-rodman-calls-north-korea-kim-jong-un-awesome-guy

99. Quoted in Boykoff, *The 1936 Berlin Olympics,* 90, 104.

100. Zirin, *Jim Brown,* 1–2, 7, 119–120, 79–80, 137–138.

101. Zirin, *What's My Name,* 215–217.

102. For instance, see Zirin, *Jim Brown,* 132–136; Zirin, *What's My Name,* 214.

103. Jai Lennard, "Harry Edwards Is Not Who You Think He Is," *Victory Journal 13,* accessed June 9, 2025, https://victoryjournal.com/stories/harry-edwards/

104. Edwards, *Revolt,* 46–47, 53; Moore, *We Will Win the Day,* 161; Boykoff, *Power Games,* 104.

105. Related to this point, also see Alrababa'h et al., "Can Exposure," 1124.

106. Goldblatt, *The Ball Is Round,* 91, 487–488.

107. Perales, *Politics and Play,* 247–248; Elias, *The Empire Strikes Out,* 27–28, 31–33.

108. Goldblatt, *The Ball Is Round,* 487–488.

109. For instance, see Goldblatt, *The Ball Is Round,* 91; Elias, *The Empire Strikes Out,* 29; Ruck, "Deflected Confrontations," 233.

110. On this topic, see Elias, *The Empire Strikes Out,* 28–29.

111. Goldblatt, *The Ball Is Round,* 91; Perales, *Politics and Play,* 252–255.

112. Goldblatt, *The Ball Is Round,* 487; Elias, *The Empire Strikes Out,* 32.

113. James, *Beyond a Boundary,* 72.

114. For example, see Goldblatt, *The Ball Is Round,* 487.

115. Goldblatt, *The Ball Is Round,* 91.

116. Elias, *The Empire Strikes Out,* 29, 61–65, 67, 216–217; also see Perales, *Politics and Play,* 241–255.

117. Quoted in Elias, *The Empire Strikes Out,* 193.

118. Related to this point, see Perales, *Politics and Play*, 249. Also see Hobsbawm, *Nations and Nationalism*, 143.

119. Also see Elias, *The Empire Strikes Out*, 61–68, 230–231; Morris, "'Communist Bandits,'" 176; Ruck, "Deflected Confrontations," 232.

120. Foer, *How Soccer*, 2; Goldblatt, *The Age of Football*, 34–40.

121. Goldblatt, *The Age of Football*, 34–37.

122. Goldblatt, *The Age of Football*, 39.

123. Goldblatt, *The Age of Football*, 31, 46, 49.

124. Goldblatt, *The Age of Football*, 44–45.

125. Goldblatt, *The Age of Football*, 31.

126. Goldblatt, *The Age of Football*, 138–139.

127. Goldblatt, *The Age of Football*, 138.

128. Goldblatt, *The Age of Football*, 315–316.

129. Goldblatt, *The Age of Football*, 314, 322–325, 330.

130. On baseball, see Elias, *The Empire Strikes Out*, 270–271.

131. For example, see Forsyth et al., "Ways of Knowing," 9.

Chapter 6

1. For instance, see Thomas Bach's comments in Boykoff, *NOlympians*, 1–2.

2. For example, see Zirin, *Brazil's Dance*, 3–4, 167–190; Boykoff, *NOlympians*, 1–7; Zimbalist, *Circus Maximus*, xiii–xv.

3. Zirin, *Brazil's Dance*, 45–54, 167–190; Boykoff, *NOlympians*, 18–25, 142.

4. Related to this point, see Zirin, *Bad Sports*, 10. Also see McGillivray et al., "Mega Sport Events and Spatial Management," 280.

5. In particular, see Zirin, *Brazil's Dance*, 3; Müller, "The Mega-Event Syndrome," 9.

6. Zirin, *Brazil's Dance*, 19–54.

7. For instance, see Flyvbjerg et al., "Oxford Olympics Study 2016," 2, 5, 16; Baade and Matheson, "Going for the Gold," 202; Mitchell and Stewart, "What Should You Pay to Host a Party," 1550–1556; Miller, *Greenwashing Sport*, 44; Boykoff, *NOlympians*, 5; Zimbalist, *Circus Maximus*, xiii–xv; Oyer, *Economist Goes*, 138–157; Luther and Davidson, *Loving Sports*, 227–243. Also see Ross and Szymanski, *Fans*, 12–13; deMause and Cagan, *Field of Schemes*, xi–xvi; Zirin, *Bad Sports*, 9; Dinces, *Bull Markets*, 2–3.

8. Flyvbjerg et al., "Oxford Olympics Study 2016," 2, 5, 16; Baade and Matheson, "Going for the Gold," 202; Mitchell and Stewart, "What Should You Pay to Host a Party," 1550–1556.

9. Mitchell and Stewart, "What Should You Pay to Host a Party," 1550–1556; Müller, "The Mega-Event Syndrome," 7.

10. Storm et al., "Impact of Formula One," 827.

11. Matheson and Baade, "Economic Slam Dunk."

12. Zirin, *Bad Sports*, 9; Baade et al., "Selling the Game," 794.

13. Storm and Jakobsen, "National Pride," 163.

14. Baade and Matheson, "Going for the Gold," 202.

15. Quoted in Zimbalist, *Circus Maximus*, 18.

16. Müller, "How Mega-Events Capture," 1114–1115.

17. For instance, see Mark Koba, "World Cup by the Numbers: Most Expensive Ever!," *CNBC*, June 12, 2014, https://www.cnbc.com/2014/06/11/conomics-by-the-numbers. html; Flyvbjerg et al., "Oxford Olympics Study 2016," 11; Leila Ugincius, "What We Learned About Sports and Athletes—and Ourselves—at the Tokyo Summer Olympics," *VCU News*, August 6, 2021, https://www.news.vcu.edu/article/2021/08/what-we-learned -about-sports-and-athletes--and-ourselves--at-the-tokyo-summer-olympics; Associated Press, "Russia's 2018 World Cup Costs Grow by $600 Million," *ESPN*, October 24, 2022, https://www.espn.co.uk/football/story/_/id/37536816/russia-says-2018-world-cup -costs-grown-600-million

18. Flyvbjerg et al., "Oxford Olympics Study 2016," 9; Zimbalist, *Circus Maximus*, 49.

19. Zimbalist, *Circus Maximus*, 49.

20. Zimbalist, *Circus Maximus*, 49; Lee and Taylor, "Critical Reflections," 595.

21. Zimbalist, *Circus Maximus*, 63–69.

22. Zimbalist, *Circus Maximus*, 30, 40; also see Luther and Davidson, *Loving Sports*, 220–221.

23. Flyvbjerg et al., "Oxford Olympics Study 2016."

24. Flyvbjerg et al., "Oxford Olympics Study 2016," 2, 13. Also see Müller, "The Mega-Event Syndrome," 7, 14–15; Zirin, *Brazil's Dance*, 169, 173; Müller, "How Mega-Events Capture," 1115–1116; Müller and Gaffney, "Comparing Urban Impacts," 247, 251–252.

25. Flyvbjerg et al., "Oxford Olympics Study 2016," 2.

26. Müller, "The Mega-Event Syndrome," 6–7.

27. Müller, "The Mega-Event Syndrome," 7, 14–15; Zirin, *Brazil's Dance*, 169, 173; Müller, "How Mega-Events Capture," 1115–1116; Müller and Gaffney, "Comparing Urban Impacts," 247, 251–252.

28. Müller, "The Mega-Event Syndrome," 9–10; Müller and Gaffney, "Comparing Urban Impacts," 255.

29. Müller, "The Mega-Event Syndrome," 9.

30. For instance, see Zirin, *What's My Name*, 220–221; Zirin, *Brazil's Dance*, 22–26, 168, 188–189. Also see Luther and Davidson, *Loving Sports*, 237.

31. Müller, "The Mega-Event Syndrome," 9–10.

32. Müller, "The Mega-Event Syndrome," 9.

33. Flyvbjerg et al., "Oxford Olympics Study 2016," 13.

34. Zimbalist, "Economic Legacy," 209.

35. Müller and Gaffney, "Urban Impacts," 255.

36. Müller, "The Mega-Event Syndrome," 9.

37. Müller, "The Mega-Event Syndrome," 8–9; Müller, "How Mega-Events Capture," 1114.

38. For example, see Zirin, *Brazil's Dance*, 47; Müller and Gaffney, "Urban Impacts," 252, 260–261.

39. Johnson, "The World Cup"; Boykoff, *NOlympians*, 20.

40. Zimbalist, *Circus Maximus*, 73–78.

41. For this paragraph, see Müller, "The Mega-Event Syndrome," 10–11; Müller, "How Mega-Events Capture," 1113–1114, 1116.

42. Müller, "The Mega-Event Syndrome," 10; Müller, "How Mega-Events Capture," 1116; Müller and Gaffney, "Urban Impacts," 259–260.

43. Müller, "Mega-Events Capture," 1115–1116.

44. Müller and Gaffney, "Urban Impacts," 259.

45. Müller and Gaffney, "Urban Impacts," 259–260; Müller, "How Mega-Events Capture," 1121–1123.

46. For this paragraph, see Müller, "How Mega-Events Capture," 1115, 1118, 1127–1128; Orttung and Zhemukhov, "2014 Sochi Olympic Mega-Project," 175–176.

47. Müller and Gaffney, "Urban Impacts," 262.

48. Goldblatt, The Games, 311; Boykoff, Power Games, 67, 132.

49. Goldblatt, The Games, 149, 311–313; Zimbalist, Circus Maximus, 1–2, 20.

50. Oyer, Economist Goes, 142–143.

51. For example, see Jennifer Cole, "For Moral and Practical Reasons, the Olympics Need a Permanent Home," Toronto Star, January 3, 2022, https://www.thestar.com/opinion/contributors/for-moral-and-practical-reasons-the-olympics-need-a-permanent-home/article_e97d83e3-6b95-58fd-a538-bf522cb06f1a.html; Luther and Davidson, Loving Sports, 243.

52. Boykoff, What Are the Olympics For?, 103–104; Boykoff, NOlympians, 2–4; Zimbalist, Circus Maximus, 166; Duignan et al., "'Summer of Discontent,'" 355; Luther and Davidson, Loving Sports, 227–228.

53. Müller and Gaffney, "Urban Impacts," 247, 262–263.

54. For this paragraph, see Matheson and Baade, "Mega-Sporting Events," 1091–1095; Dowse and Fletcher, "Sport Mega-Events"; Müller and Gaffney, "Urban Impacts," 247, 262–263. Also see Zirin, Brazil's Dance, 23, 27; Luther and Davidson, Loving Sports, 230–131.

55. Zimbalist, Circus Maximus, 80–86.

56. Grix, "Image Leveraging," 306–307; Oshimi and Harada, "Effects of City Image," 90–91; Liu and Gratton, "Impact of Mega Sporting Events," 629, 632–633; Kassens-Noor et al., "Good Games, Bad Host?," 229.

57. Grix, "Image Leveraging," 306–307.

58. Kassens-Noor et al., "Good Games, Bad Host?," 229, 233–334.

59. Liu and Gratton, "Impact of Mega Sporting Events," 636–644.

60. Kenyon and Bodet, "Exploring Mega-Events and Destination Image," 232, 239, 244–247.

61. Kenyon and Bodet, "Exploring Mega-Events and Destination Image," 245.

62. Kang and Perdue, "Long-Term Impact," 205.

63. See Zimbalist, Circus Maximus, 64.

64. Scharpf et al., "Repression in Autocracies," 911–912.

65. "Beijing Winter Olympics Boycott: Why Are the Games So Controversial?," BBC, February 4, 2022, https://www.bbc.com/news/explainers-59644043

66. Adam Kilgore, "At Beijing's Big Air Venue, the Setting Is Post-Apocalyptic and the Jump Is 'Perfect,'" *Washington Post*, February 13, 2022, https://www.washingtonpost.com/sports/olympics/2022/02/13/beijing-nuclear-power-plant-olympics/

67. Mason Bissada, "'Not Getting Food': China Under Fire for Treatment of Olympic Athletes," *Forbes*, February 7, 2022, https://www.forbes.com/sites/masonbissada/2022/02/06/not-getting-food-china-under-fire-for-treatment-of-olympic-athletes/

68. Conn, *Fall of House of FIFA*, 18, 73; Geoffrey Skelley, "How Americans Feel About Qatar Hosting the World Cup," *FiveThirtyEight*, December 2, 2022, https://fivethirtyeight.com/features/how-americans-feel-about-qatar-hosting-the-world-cup

69. Also see Tom McTague, "The Qatar World Cup Exposes Soccer's Shame," *Atlantic*, November 19, 2022, https://www.theatlantic.com/international/archive/2022/11/qatar-hosting-fifa-world-cup-soccer/672171/

70. "Qatar: Male Guardianship Severely Curtails Women's Rights," *Human Rights Watch*, March 29, 2021, https://www.hrw.org/news/2021/03/29/qatar-male-guardianship-severely-curtails-womens-rights

71. "Qatar."

72. Gläßel et al., "Does Sportswashing Work?"

73. Matt Craig, "The Money Behind the Most Expensive World Cup in History: Qatar 2022 by the Numbers," *Forbes*, November 19, 2022, https://www.forbes.com/sites/mattcraig/2022/11/19/the-money-behind-the-most-expensive-world-cup-in-history-qatar-2022-by-the-numbers/; Pete Pattisson et al., "Revealed: 6,500 Migrant Workers Have Died in Qatar Since World Cup Awarded," *Guardian*, February 23, 2021, https://www.theguardian.com/global-development/2021/feb/23/revealed-migrant-worker-deaths-qatar-fifa-world-cup-2022

74. Pattisson et al., "Revealed."

75. Wesley Stephenson, "Have 1,200 World Cup Workers Really Died in Qatar?," *BBC News*, June 6, 2015, https://www.bbc.com/news/magazine-33019838; Zirin, *Brazil's Dance*, 188–189; Pattisson et al., "Revealed."

76. Stephenson, "Have 1,200 Workers."

77. Pattisson et al., "Revealed."

78. Baxter, Kevin, "The World Will Be Watching as Qatar Hosts the 2022 World Cup . . . for Better or Worse," *Los Angeles Times*, August 11, 2022, https://www.latimes.com/sports/soccer/story/2022-08-11/controversial-world-cup-sparked-positive-change-qatar-2022-fifa

79. Peter Raven, "Britons' Views of Qatar Remain Very Negative Following 2022 World Cup," *YouGov*, January 16, 2023, https://yougov.co.uk/sport/articles/44942-britons-views-qatar-remain-very-negative-following

80. Matthew Smith, "Europeans and Americans on Hosting the World Cup in Qatar," *YouGov*, November 11, 2022, https://yougov.co.uk/sport/articles/44382-europeans-and-americans-hosting-world-cup-qatar

81. Skelley, "How Americans Feel About Qatar Hosting."

82. Simon Burnton, "Why Not Everyone Remembers the 1966 World Cup as Fondly

as England," *Guardian*, July 24, 2016, https://www.theguardian.com/football/blog/2016/jul/24/1966-world-cup-final-conspiracy-refereeing-50-years

83. Quoted in Burnton, "Why Not Everyone Remembers."

84. Quoted in Burnton, "Why Not Everyone Remembers."

85. Quoted in Burnton, "Why Not Everyone Remembers."

86. Quoted in Burnton, "Why Not Everyone Remembers."

87. Hiller and Wanner, "Public Opinion," 891–895; Mitchell and Stewart, "What Should You Pay to Host a Party," 1556, 1559; Pfitzner and Koenigstorfer, "Quality of Life," 1, 4–7; Schlegel et al., "Impact of Atmosphere," 605; Dolan et al., "Quantifying the Intangible Impact," 3, 6–10; Luther and Davidson, *Loving Sports*, 226; Oyer, *Economist Goes*, 149–150.

88. Related to this point, see Mitchell and Stewart, "What Should You Pay to Host a Party," 1559.

89. Mitchell and Stewart, "What Should You Pay to Host a Party," 1560. Also see Oyer, *Economist Goes*, 150.

90. Zirin, *Brazil's Dance*, 30; Oyer, *Economist Goes*, 151–154; Mitchell and Stewart, "What Should You Pay to Host a Party," 1559.

91. Orttung and Zhemukhov, "2014 Sochi Olympic Mega-Project," 175–176; Zirin, *Brazil's Dance*, 186–187.

92. Mitchell and Stewart, "What Should You Pay to Host a Party," 1559.

93. Zirin, *Brazil's Dance*, 30–33; Keys, "Introduction," 13; Boykoff, *NOlympians*, 21–22; Luther and Davidson, *Loving Sports*, 229, 234–235. Regarding the displacement of local businesses, see Duignan, "London's Local Olympic Legacy," 142, 150–156.

94. Zirin, *Brazil's Dance*, 42, 47, 170, 176–177, 188, 191–224; Boykoff, *NOlympians*, 21–22; Müller and Gaffney, "Urban Impacts," 252, 256–257.

95. Boykoff, *NOlympians*, 21–22; Müller and Gaffney, "Urban Impacts," 256–257.

96. Müller and Gaffney, "Urban Impacts," 256.

97. For instance, see Mundim and Silva, "The World Cup and Presidential Popularity," 1.

98. Chris Arsenault, "Victory for Olympic Displaced Despite Rio's 'Biggest Eviction Cycle,'" *Reuters*, August 4, 2016, https://www.reuters.com/article/world/victory-for-olympic-displaced-despite-rio-s-biggest-eviction-cycle-idUSKCN10E1QV/

99. "Brazilian Discontent Ahead of World Cup," *Pew Research Center*, June 3, 2014, https://www.pewresearch.org/global/2014/06/03/brazilian-discontent-ahead-of-world-cup/

100. Reuters Staff, "Most Brazilians Expect Rio Olympics to Hurt Brazil: Poll," *Reuters*, July 27, 2016, https://www.reuters.com/article/olympics-rio-pessimism/most-brazilians-expect-rio-olympics-to-hurt-brazil-poll-idINKCN1071IO/

101. Statista Research Department, "Approval Rates of Brazilian Presidents 2002–2023," *Statista*, December 4, 2024, https://www.statista.com/statistics/781916/presidents-approval-rate-brazil/

102. Mundim and Silva, "The World Cup and Presidential Popularity," 1.

103 For instance, see Müller, "The Mega-Event Syndrome," 11; Zirin, *Brazil's Dance*, 184, 226.

104. Cha, *Beyond the Final Score*, 12–14.

105. Cha, *Beyond the Final Score*, 13; Espy, *Olympic Games*, 141; Boykoff, *Power Games*, 111–113; Goldblatt, *The Games*, 285–286.

106. Cha, *Beyond the Final Score*, 13.

107. Cha, *Beyond the Final Score*, 13.

108. Cha, *Beyond the Final Score*, 13.

109. Boykoff, *NOlympians*, 22–23; Luther and Davidson, *Loving Sports*, 234.

110. Zirin, *Brazil's Dance*, 150–152, 183–185; Boykoff, *NOlympians*, 22–23; Luther and Davidson, *Loving Sports*, 229.

111. Zirin, *Brazil's Dance*, 48–53; Boykoff, *NOlympians*, 22–23.

112. Zimbalist, *Circus Maximus*, 16–17; Goldblatt, *The Games*, 267; Zirin, *Brazil's Dance*, 158, 232.

113. Goldblatt, *The Games*, 265–267; Boykoff, *Power Games*, 103.

114. In particular, see Goldblatt, *The Games*, 266–267.

115. Goldblatt, *The Games*, 267.

116. See Zirin, *Brazil's Dance*, 177. Countries also sometimes deviate from their own laws before or during major sporting events, viewing these events as "states of exception." For instance, see Zirin, *What's My Name*, 221; Zirin, *Brazil's Dance*, 31–32, 54, 192–193. Also see Miller, *Greenwashing Sport*, 44.

117. "Beer 'Must be Sold' at Brazil World Cup, Says FIFA," *BBC News*, January 19, 2012, https://www.bbc.com/news/world-latin-america-16624823

118. "Mass Brawls, Attacks as Football Violence Spreads in Latin America," *France 24*, March 15, 2022, https://www.france24.com/en/live-news/20220315-mass-brawls-attacks -as-football-violence-spreads-in-latin-america

119. "Beer 'Must be Sold.'"

120. Ben Church, "Soaking Up the Atmosphere at Qatar 2022: What It's Like at a 'Dry' World Cup," *CNN*, November 30, 2022, https://edition.cnn.com/2022/11/30/foot ball/alcohol-world-cup-fans-qatar-2022-spt-intl/index.html

121. Related to this topic, see Geeraert and Gauthier, "Out-of-Control Olympics," 16.

122. Miller, *Greenwashing Sport*, 2.

123. Karamichas, "Olympics," 381–393.

124. Zirin, *Brazil's Dance*, 45.

125. On this case, see Boykoff, *NOlympians*, 142.

126. Boykoff, *NOlympians*, 142.

127. Goldblatt, *The Games*, 442; Mitchell and Stewart, "What Should You Pay to Host a Party," 1551; Grix et al., "State Strategies." Note that Goldblatt discusses how aspirations to reach the highest levels of sports motivate some young athletes, particularly in poorer communities.

128. For instance, see Goldblatt, *The Games*, 313.

Conclusion

1. Alan Abrahamson, "AI Comes to the IOC and Says It and Olympic Movement Need, Uh-Oh, Radical Overhaul," *Wire Sports*, October 15, 2023, https://www.3wiresports .com/articles/2023/10/15/d8a8nfygl94wroqo3zcqoq3wz40sk7

2. Quoted in Abrahamson, "AI Comes."

3. Quoted in Abrahamson, "AI Comes."

4. Quoted in Abrahamson, "AI Comes." Note that Alan Abrahamson used Professor Scott Galloway's AI chatbot ProfG.ai.

5. Quoted in Abrahamson, "AI Comes."

6. Boykoff, *What Are the Olympics For?*, 103.

7. Christopher Hitchens, "Why the Olympics and Other Sports Cause Conflict," *Newsweek*, February 4, 2010, https://www.newsweek.com/why-olympics-and-other -sports-cause-conflict-75043

8. O'Reilly and Cahn, "Introduction," xi.

9. Gerdy, *Sports*, xvii, xix–xxii.

10. Gerdy, *Sports*, xi, xvii, xix–xxii.

11. Gerdy, *Sports*, 235.

12. Chuck Culpepper, "How Does Norway Dominate the Winter Olympics? By Not Worrying About Success," *Washington Post*, February 16, 2022, https://www.washington post.com/sports/olympics/2022/02/15/norway-biathlon-medals-lead/

13. Quoted in Culpepper, "How Does Norway Dominate."

14. On this topic, see Kumah-Abiwu et al., "Oil Wealth," 63, 67.

15. Ross, "Political Economy of Resource Curse," 297–298.

16. Oyer, *Economist Goes*, 25–30.

17. See Markovits and Albertson, *Sportista*, 92–93.

18. Kyle, *Sport and Spectacle*, 296.

19. Quoted in Sean Ingle, "'Tremendous Coldness': IOC President Condemns Kamila Valieva's Entourage," *Guardian*, February 18, 2022, https://www.theguardian.com/ sport/2022/feb/18/tremendous-coldness-ioc-president-slams-kamila-valievas-entour age-over-skaters-treatment

20. Quoted in Ingle, "'Tremendous Coldness.'"

21. Regarding South Korea, see Taylor, *Raising the Stakes*, 211.

22. On this topic, see Papineau, "Nature and Value," 131.

23. Hurka, *Games, Sports, and Play*, 99–134.

24. Berman, "Sport as a Thick Cluster Concept," 109–116.

25. Berman, "Sport as a Thick Cluster Concept," 110–111.

26. Berman, "Sport as a Thick Cluster Concept," 111–112.

27. Papineau, "Nature and Value," 126.

28. Papineau, "Nature and Value," 131–132.

29. Berman, "Sport as a Thick Cluster Concept," 115; Papineau, "Nature and Value," 125, 128.

30. Berman, "Sport as a Thick Cluster Concept," 108–109, 111, 115; Papineau, "Nature and Value," 130–131.

31. Papineau, "Nature and Value," 130–131.

32. Berman, "Sport as a Thick Cluster Concept," 111; Papineau, "Nature and Value," 130–131.

33. Papineau, "Nature and Value," 130–131.

34. For instance, see Luther and Davidson, *Loving Sports*, 9–24.

35. Philippe Naughton, "Korean Drops Dead After 50 Hour Gaming Marathon," *The Times Online*, August 10, 2005, https://www.thetimes.com/article/korean-drops-dead-after-50-hour-gaming-marathon-skd6cow7hbm

36. Naughton, "Korean Drops Dead."

37. Halbrook et al., "When and How Video Games," 1096–1098.

38. See Halbrook et al., "When and How Video Games," 1098.

39. Kohorst et al., "Obesity," 1, 3; Emara et al., "Gamer's Health Guide," 537–539.

40. Bushman and Gibson, "Violent Video Games," 30–31.

41. Kim and Kim, "Show Must Go On," 6.

42. Kim and Kim, "Show Must Go On," 6.

43. Yu, "Game On," 93.

44. Yu, "Game On," 93.

45. Jay Castello, "Why Do Female Pro Gamers Earn Millions Less than Men?," *Guardian*, December 2, 2021, https://www.theguardian.com/games/2021/dec/02/why-do-female-pro-gamers-earn-less-than-men-esports

46. "Esports: Why Are There So Few Professional Women Gamers?," *BBC News*, September 7, 2021, https://www.bbc.com/news/av/technology-58466374

47. Mary Brune, "Zooming in on Female Gamers with Consumer Insights Data," *Newzoo*, March 8, 2022, https://newzoo.com/resources/blog/zooming-in-on-female-gamers-with-consumer-insights-data

48. Castello, "Why Do Female"; "Women in the Gaming Industry: Nine Questions for Scientist and Gamer Natalie Denk," *owayo*, accessed June 17, 2025, https://www.owayo.com/magazine/esports-women-us.htm

49. For more on gender disparities in elite chess, see Markovits and Albertson, *Sportista*, 51–61.

50. On the topic of group identification, see Markovits and Rensmann, *Gaming the World*, 14, 49–50; Dietz-Uhler and Lanter, "Consequences of Fan Identification," 103–104; Mumford, *Philosopher*, 71. On the topic of play, see Goldblatt, *The Ball Is Round*, 908–911.

51. Kuper, *Soccer Against the Enemy*, 1–3.

52. Kuper, *Soccer Against the Enemy*, 2–3.

53. Kuper, *Soccer Against the Enemy*, 2.

54. Kuper, *Soccer Against the Enemy*, 3.

55. Regarding hockey, see Berglund, *Fastest Game*, 10–11; Hardy and Holman, *Hockey*, 7, 401–402. For baseball, see Kelly, *Sportsworld of Hanshin Tigers*, 2. On cricket (specifically in the West Indies), see James, *Beyond a Boundary*, 71–72. Respecting football, see Berrett, *Pigskin Nation*, 3–8.

REFERENCES

Aicale, Rocco, Domiziano Tarantino, and Nicola Maffulli. "Overuse Injuries in Sport: A Comprehensive Overview." *Journal of Orthopaedic Surgery and Research* 13, no. 1 (2018): 1–11. https://doi.org/10.1186/s13018-018-1017-5

Aldrete, Gregory S. "'Bread and Circuses': Ancient Rome, Modern Science Fiction, and the Art of Political Distraction." *Film & History: An Interdisciplinary Journal* 51, no. 2 (2021): 4–20. https://muse.jhu.edu/article/842291

Alrababa'h, Ala', William Marble, Salma Mousa, and Alexandra A. Siegel. "Can Exposure to Celebrities Reduce Prejudice? The Effect of Mohamed Salah on Islamophobic Behaviors and Attitudes." *American Political Science Review* 115, no. 4 (2021): 1111–1128. https://doi.org/10.1017/S0003055421000423

Althaus, Scott, Joseph Bajjalieh, John F. Carter, Buddy Peyton, and Dan A. Shalmon. *Cline Center Historical Phoenix Event Data*. Version 1.3.0. Cline Center for Advanced Social Research. University of Illinois Urbana-Champaign. May 4, 2020. https://doi.org/10.13012/B2IDB-0647142_V3

Anderson, Barbara A., and Brian D. Silver. "Growth and Diversity of the Population of the Soviet Union." *Annals of the American Academy of Political and Social Science* 510, no. 1 (1990): 155–177. https://doi.org/10.1177/0002716290510001

Andreoli, Angella, Maurizio Monteleone, Marta Van Loan, Luigi Promenzio, Umberto Tarantino, and Antonio de Lorenzo. "Effects of Different Sports on Bone Density and Muscle Mass in Highly Trained Athletes." *Medicine and Science in Sports and Exercise* 33, no. 4 (2001): 507–511. https://doi.org/10.1097/00005768-200104000-00001

Archetti, Eduardo P. "Argentina 1978: Military Nationalism, Football Essentialism, and Moral Ambivalence." In *National Identity and Global Sports Events: Culture, Politics, and Spectacle in the Olympics and Football World Cup*, edited by Alan Tomlinson and Christopher Young. State University of New York Press, 2006.

Baade, Robert A., Robert Baumann, and Victor A. Matheson. "Selling the Game: Estimating the Economic Impact of Professional Sports Through Taxable Sales." *Southern Economic Journal* 74, no. 3 (2008): 794–810. https://doi.org/10.1002/j.2325-8012.2008.tb00864.x

Baade, Robert A., and Victor A. Matheson. "Going for the Gold: The Economics of the Olympics." *Journal of Economic Perspectives* 30, no. 2 (2016): 201–218. https://doi.org/10.1257/jep.30.2.201

Bao, Katherine Jacobs, and Sonja Lyubomirsky. "Making Happiness Last: Using the Hedonic Adaptation Prevention Model to Extend the Success of Positive Interventions." In *The Wiley Blackwell Handbook of Positive Psychological Interventions*, edited by Acacia C. Parks and Stephen M. Schueller. John Wiley & Sons, 2014. https://doi.org/10.1002/9781118315927.ch21

Bason, Tom, Paul Salisbury, and Simon Gerard. "Fifa." In *Routledge Handbook of Football Business and Management*, edited by Simon Chadwick, Daniel Parnell, Paul Widdop, and Christos Anagnostopoulos. Routledge, 2018.

Beamish, Rob, and Ian Ritchie. "Totalitarian Regimes and Cold War Sport: Steroid 'Übermenschen' and 'Ball-Bearing Females.'" In *East Plays West: Sport and the Cold War*, edited by Stephen Wagg and David L. Andrews. Routledge, 2007.

Bell, Sinclair. "Roman Chariot Racing: Charioteers, Factions, Spectators." In *A Companion to Sport and Spectacle in Greek and Roman Antiquity*, edited by Paul Christesen and Donald G. Kyle. John Wiley & Sons, 2014.

Bellis, Mark A., Nicola Leckenby, Karen Hughes, Chris Luke, Sacha Wyke, and Zara Quigg. "Nighttime Assaults: Using a National Emergency Department Monitoring System to Predict Occurrence, Target Prevention and Plan Services." *BMC Public Health* 12, no. 1 (2012): 1–13. https://doi.org/10.1186/1471-2458-12-746

Belloni, Eleonora. "The Birth of the Sport Nation: Sports and Mass Media in Fascist Italy." *Revista de Psicologia, Ciències de l'Educació i de l'Esport* 32, no. 2 (2014): 53–61. https://www.revistaaloma.blanquerna.edu/index.php/aloma/article/view/228

Berglund, Bruce. *The Fastest Game in the World: Hockey and the Globalization of Sports.* University of California Press, 2021.

Berman, Mitchell. "Sport as a Thick Cluster Concept." In *Games, Sports, and Play: Philosophical Essays*, edited by Thomas Hurka. Oxford University Press, 2019.

Bernstein, Mark F. *Football: The Ivy League Origins of an American Obsession.* University of Pennsylvania Press, 2001.

Berrett, Jesse. *Pigskin Nation: How the NFL Remade American Politics.* University of Illinois Press, 2018.

Bertoli, Andrew D. "Nationalism and Conflict: Lessons from International Sports." *International Studies Quarterly* 61, no. 4 (2017): 835–849. https://doi.org/10.1093/isq/sqx029

Bialystok, Lauren, and Mark Kingwell. "The Fragility of Fairness: Rethinking the Ethics of Women's Categories in Sports." In *Games, Sports, and Play: Philosophical Essays*, edited by Thomas Hurka. Oxford University Press, 2019.

Billings, Andrew C., Kelby K. Halone, and Bryan E. Denham. "'Man, That Was a Pretty

Shot': An Analysis of Gendered Broadcast Commentary Surrounding the 2000 Men's and Women's NCAA Final Four Basketball Championships." *Mass Communication & Society* 5, no. 3 (2002): 295–315. https://doi.org/10.1207/S15327825MCS0503_4

Block, Kristina. "Professional Sports and Crime: Do Professional Hockey Games Increase City-Level Crime Rates?" *Crime & Delinquency* 67, no. 12 (2021): 2069–2087. https://doi.org/10.1177/00111287211010491

Bougault, Valérie, Julie Turmel, Julie St-Laurent, Mylene Bertrand, and Louis-Philippe Boulet. 2009. "Asthma, Airway Inflammation and Epithelial Damage in Swimmers and Cold-Air Athletes." *European Respiratory Journal* 33, no. 4 (2009): 740–746. https://doi.org/10.1183/09031936.00117708

Bowman, Kirk. "Futebol/Fútbol, Identity, and Politics in Latin America." *Latin American Research Review* 50, no. 3 (2015): 254–264. https://doi.org/10.1353/lar.2015.0037

Boykoff, Jules. *Activism and the Olympics: Dissent at the Games in Vancouver and London.* Rutgers University Press, 2014.

———. *Celebration Capitalism and the Olympic Games.* Routledge, 2013.

———. *The 1936 Berlin Olympics: Race, Power, and Sportswashing.* Common Ground Research Networks, 2023.

———. *NOlympians: Inside the Fight Against Capitalist Mega-Sports Events in Los Angeles, Tokyo, and Beyond.* Fernwood Publishing, 2020.

———. *Power Games: A Political History of the Olympics.* Verso, 2016.

———. *What Are the Olympics For?* Bristol University Press, 2024.

Brady, Anne-Marie. "The Beijing Olympics as a Campaign of Mass Distraction." *China Quarterly* 197 (2009): 1–24. https://doi.org/10.1017/S0305741009000058

Brimicombe, Allan, and Rebecca Cafe. "Beware, Win or Lose: Domestic Violence and the World Cup." *Significance* 9, no. 5 (2012): 32–35. https://doi.org/10.1111/j.1740-9713.2012.00606.x

Brooks, Scott N., and Dexter Blackman. "Introduction: African Americans and the History of Sport—New Perspectives." *Journal of African American History* 96, no. 4 (2011): 441–447. https://doi.org/10.5323/jafriamerhist.96.4.0441

Bunting, Thomas David. *Democracy at the Ballpark: Sport, Spectatorship, and Politics.* State University of New York Press, 2021.

Burke, Roland. "Peace: The United Nations, the International Olympic Committee, and the Renovation of the Olympic Truce." In *The Ideals of Modern Sport: From Peace to Human Rights*, edited by Barbara Keys. University of Pennsylvania Press, 2019.

Burns, Jimmy. *Maradona: The Hand of God.* Bloomsbury Publishing, 2021.

Busby, Ethan C., and James N. Druckman. "Football and Public Opinion: A Partial Replication and Extension." *Journal of Experimental Political Science* 5, no. 1 (2018): 4–10. https://doi.org/10.1017/XPS.2017.22

Busby, Ethan C., James N. Druckman, and Alexandria Fredendall. "The Political Relevance of Irrelevant Events." *Journal of Politics* 79, no. 1 (2017): 346–350. https://doi.org/10.1086/688585

Bushman, Brad J., Roy F. Baumeister, and Angela D. Stack. "Catharsis, Aggression, and Persuasive Influence: Self-Fulfilling or Self-Defeating Prophecies?" *Journal of*

Personality and Social Psychology 76, no. 3 (1999): 367–376. https://doi.org/10.1037/0022-3514.76.3.367

Bushman, Brad J., and Bryan Gibson. "Violent Video Games Cause an Increase in Aggression Long After the Game Has Been Turned Off." *Social Psychological and Personality Science* 2, no. 1 (2011): 29–32. https://doi.org/10.1177/1948550610379506

Card, David, and Gordon B. Dahl. "Family Violence and Football: The Effect of Unexpected Emotional Cues on Violent Behavior." *Quarterly Journal of Economics* 126, no. 1 (2011): 103–143. https://doi.org/10.1093/qje/qjr001

Carlos, John. *The John Carlos Story: The Sports Moment That Changed the World.* With Dave Zirin. Haymarket Books, 2013.

Carlson, Kyle, Joshua Kim, Annamaria Lusardi, and Colin F. Camerer. "Bankruptcy Rates Among NFL Players with Short-Lived Income Spikes." *American Economic Review* 105, no. 5 (2015): 381–84. https://doi.org/10.1257/aer.p20151038

Cha, Victor D. *Beyond the Final Score: The Politics of Sport in Asia.* Columbia University Press, 2009.

———. "A Theory of Sport and Politics." *International Journal of the History of Sport* 26, no. 11 (2009): 1581–1610. https://doi.org/10.1080/09523360903132972

Chappell, Ben. *Mexican American Fastpitch: Identity at Play in Vernacular Sport.* Stanford University Press, 2021.

Chatziefstathiou, Dikaia. "Reading Baron Pierre de Coubertin: Issues of Gender and Race." *Aethlon: The Journal of Sport Literature* 25, no. 2 (2008): 95–116.

Chen, Chwen Chwen, Cinzia Colapinto, and Qing Luo. "The 2008 Beijing Olympics Opening Ceremony: Visual Insights into China's Soft Power." *Visual Studies* 27, no. 2 (2012): 188–195. https://doi.org/10.1080/1472586X.2012.677252

Coalter, Fred. "Sport-in-Development: Development for and Through Sport?" In *Sport and Social Capital,* edited by Matthew Nicholson and Russell Hoye. Routledge, 2008.

Collins, Tony, and Wray Vamplew. *Mud, Sweat and Beers: A Cultural History of Sport and Alcohol.* Berg, 2002.

Conn, David. *The Fall of the House of FIFA.* Yellow Jersey Press, 2017.

Cooky, Cheryl, and Dunja Antunovic. "'This Isn't Just About Us': Articulations of Feminism in Media Narratives of Athlete Activism." *Communication and Sport* 8, no. 4–5 (2020): 692–711. https://doi.org/10.1177/2167479519896360

Cooky, Cheryl, LaToya D. Council, Maria A. Mears, and Michael A. Messner. "One and Done: The Long Eclipse of Women's Televised Sports, 1989–2019." *Communication & Sport* 9, no. 3 (2021): 347–371. https://doi.org/10.1177/21674795211003524

Cooky, Cheryl, and Michael A. Messner. "Introduction." In *No Slam Dunk: Gender, Sport, and the Unevenness of Social Change,* edited by Cheryl Cooky and Michael A. Messner. Rutgers University Press, 2018.

Cooky, Cheryl, Michael A. Messner, and Michela Musto. 2015. "'It's Dude Time!': A Quarter Century of Excluding Women's Sports in Televised News and Highlight Shows." *Communication & Sport* 3, no. 3 (2015): 261–287. https://doi.org/10.1177/2167479515588761

Cottrell, M. Patrick, and Travis Nelson. "Not Just the Games? Power, Protest and Politics at the Olympics." *European Journal of International Relations* 17, no. 4 (2011): 729–753. https://doi.org/10.1177/1354066110380965

Crabbe, Tim. "Avoiding the Numbers Game: Social Theory, Policy, and Sport's Role in the Art of Relationship Building." In *Sport and Social Capital*, edited by Matthew Nicholson and Russell Hoye. Routledge, 2008.

Creak, Simon. "Friendship and Mutual Understanding: Sport and Regional Relations in Southeast Asia." In *The Ideals of Modern Sport: From Peace to Human Rights*, edited by Barbara Keys. University of Pennsylvania Press, 2019.

———. "New Regional Order: Sport, Cold War Culture, and the Making of Southeast Asia." In *The Whole World Was Watching: Sport in the Cold War*, edited by Robert Edelman and Christopher Young. Stanford University Press, 2019.

Crepeau, Richard C. *NFL Football: A History of America's New National Pastime.* University of Illinois Press, 2020.

Dafoe, Allan, John R. Oneal, and Bruce Russett. "The Democratic Peace: Weighing the Evidence and Cautious Inference." *International Studies Quarterly* 57, no. 1 (2013): 201–214. https://doi.org/10.1111/isqu.12055

Deakin, Charles D., Fizz Thompson, Caroline Gibson, and Mark Green. "Effects of International Football Matches on Ambulance Call Profiles and Volumes During the 2006 World Cup." *Emergency Medicine Journal* 24, no. 6 (2007): 405–407. https://doi.org/10.1136/emj.2007.046920

deMause, Neil, and Joanna Cagan. *Field of Schemes: How the Great Stadium Swindle Turns Public Money into Private Profits*, rev. ed. University of Nebraska Press, 2008.

Dennis, Mike. "Sports, Politics, and 'Wild Doping' in the East Germany Sporting 'Miracle.'" In *The Whole World Was Watching: Sport in the Cold War*, edited by Robert Edelman and Christopher Young. Stanford University Press, 2019.

Depetris-Chauvin, Emilio, Ruben Durante, and Filipe Campante. "Building Nations Through Shared Experiences: Evidence from African Football." *American Economic Review* 110, no. 5 (2020): 1572–1602. https://doi.org/10.1257/aer.20180805

Dietz-Uhler, Beth, and Jason R. Lanter. "The Consequences of Sports Fan Identification." In *Sports Mania: Essays on Fandom and the Media in the 21st Century*, edited by Lawrence W. Hugenberg, Paul M. Haridakis, and Adam C. Earnheardt. McFarland & Company, 2008.

Dinces, Sean. *Bull Markets: Chicago's Basketball Business and the New Inequality.* University of Chicago Press, 2018.

Dolan, Paul, Georgios Kavetsos, Christian Krekel, et al. "Quantifying the Intangible Impact of the Olympics Using Subjective Well-Being Data." *Journal of Public Economics* 177 (2019): 104043. https://doi.org/10.1016/j.jpubeco.2019.07.002

Dowse, Suzanne, and Thomas Fletcher. "Sport Mega-Events, the Non-West and the Ethics of Event Hosting." *Sport in Society* 21, no. 5 (2018): 745–761. https://doi.org/10.1080/17430437.2018.1401359

Dreier, Peter. "Jackie Robinson's Legacy: Baseball, Race, and Politics." In *Baseball and the American Dream*, edited by Robert Elias. M. E. Sharpe, 2001.

Dreier, Peter, and Robert Elias. *Baseball Rebels: The Players, People, and Social Move-*

ments That Shook Up the Game and Changed America. University of Nebraska Press, 2022.

Druckman, James N., and Elizabeth A. Sharrow. *Equality Unfulfilled: How Title IX's Policy Design Undermines Change in College Sports.* Cambridge University Press, 2023.

Duignan, Michael B. "London's Local Olympic Legacy: Small Business Displacement, 'Clone Town' Effect and the Production of 'Urban Blandscapes.'" *Journal of Place Management and Development* 12, no. 2 (2019): 142–163. https://dx.doi.org/10.1108/JPMD -05-2018-0033

Duignan, Michael B., Ilaria Pappalepore, and Sally Everett. "The 'Summer of Discontent': Exclusion and Communal Resistance at the London 2012 Olympics." *Tourism Management* 70 (2019): 355–367. https://doi.org/10.1016/j.tourman.2018.08.029

Dunning, Eric. "Sport as a Male Preserve: Notes on the Social Sources of Masculine Identity and Its Transformations." *Theory, Culture & Society* 3, no. 1 (1986): 79–90. https://doi.org/10.1177/0263276486003001007

Edelman, Robert, and Christopher Young. "Introduction: Explaining Cold War Sport." In *The Whole World Was Watching: Sport in the Cold War*, edited by Robert Edelman and Christopher Young. Stanford University Press, 2019.

Edwards, Harry. "The Decline of the Black Athlete." In *The Unlevel Playing Field: A Documentary History of the African American Experience in Sport*, edited by David K. Wiggins and Patrick B. Miller. University of Illinois Press, 2005.

———. *The Revolt of the Black Athlete.* 50th anniversary ed. University of Illinois Press, 2018.

Elias, Robert, ed. *Baseball and the American Dream.* M. E. Sharpe, 2001.

———. *The Empire Strikes Out: How Baseball Sold US Foreign Policy and Promoted the American Way Abroad.* New Press, 2010.

Elias, Robert, and Peter Dreier. *Major League Rebels: Baseball Battles over Workers' Rights and American Empire.* Rowman & Littlefield, 2022.

Elsey, Brenda. "Ambivalent Solidarities: Cultural Diplomacy, Women, and South-South Cooperation at the 1950s Pan American Games." In *The Whole World Was Watching: Sport in the Cold War*, edited by Robert Edelman and Christopher Young. Stanford University Press, 2019.

Elsey, Brenda, and Joshua Nadel. *Futbolera: A History of Women and Sports in Latin America.* University of Texas Press, 2019.

Emara, Ahmed K., Mitchell K. Ng, Jason A. Cruickshank, et al. "Gamer's Health Guide: Optimizing Performance, Recognizing Hazards, and Promoting Wellness in Esports." *Current Sports Medicine Reports* 19, no. 12 (2020): 537–545. https://doi.org/10 .1249/JSR.0000000000000787

Erickson, Darin J., Traci L. Toomey, Kathleen M. Lenk, Gunna R. Kilian, and Lindsey E. A. Fabian. "Can We Assess Blood Alcohol Levels of Attendees Leaving Professional Sporting Events?" *Alcoholism: Clinical and Experimental Research* 35, no. 4 (2011): 689–694. https://doi.org/10.1111/j.1530-0277.2010.01386.x

Espy, Richard. *The Politics of the Olympic Games.* University of California Press, 1979.

Farb, Amy Feldman, and Jennifer L. Matjasko. "Recent Advances in Research on

School-Based Extracurricular Activities and Adolescent Development." *Developmental Review* 32, no. 1 (2012): 1–48. https://doi.org/10.1016/j.dr.2011.10.001

Farmer, Angela S. "Student-Athlete to Professional Athlete: Confronting the Brutal Facts." *Athens Journal of Sports* 6, no. 3 (2019): 121–138. https://doi.org/10.30958/ajspo.6-3-1

Feldman, Amy F., and Jennifer L. Matjasko. "The Role of School-Based Extracurricular Activities in Adolescent Development: A Comprehensive Review and Future Directions." *Review of Educational Research* 75, no. 2 (2005): 159–210. https://doi.org/10.3102/00346543075002159

Festle, Mary Jo. *Playing Nice: Politics and Apologies in Women's Sports.* Columbia University Press, 1996.

Fisher, Donald M. *Lacrosse: A History of the Game.* Johns Hopkins University Press, 2002.

Flyvbjerg, Bent, Allison Stewart, and Alexander Budzier. "The Oxford Olympics Study 2016: Cost and Cost Overrun at the Games." Said Business School, University of Oxford, July 14, 2016. https://arxiv.org/pdf/1607.04484

Foer, Franklin. *How Soccer Explains the World: An Unlikely Theory of Globalization.* Harper Perennial, 2006.

Foo, Cynthia. "Interview with Benedict Anderson." *Invisible Culture: An Electronic Journal for Visual Culture* 13 (2009): 4–21. https://www.rochester.edu/in_visible_culture/Issue_13_/foo/index.html

Foot, John. *Calcio: A History of Italian Football.* Fully updated ed. Harper Perennial, 2007.

Forsyth, Janice, Christine O'Bonsawin, Russell Field, and Murray G. Phillips. "Ways of Knowing: Sport, Colonialism, and Decolonization." In *Decolonizing Sport*, edited by Janice Forsyth, Christine O'Bonsawin, Russell Field, and Murray G. Phillips. Fernwood Publishing, 2023.

Frith, David. *Bodyline Autopsy: The Full Story of the Most Sensational Test Cricket Series: Australia v England 1932–33.* Aurum Press Limited, 2013.

Garland, Jon, and Mike Rowe. "War Minus the Shooting? Jingoism, the English Press, and Euro 96." *Journal of Sport and Social Issues* 23, no. 1 (1999): 80–95. https://doi.org/10.1177/0193723599231006

Geeraert, Arnout, and Ryan Gauthier. "Out-of-Control Olympics: Why the IOC Is Unable to Ensure an Environmentally Sustainable Olympic Games." *Journal of Environmental Policy & Planning* 20, no. 1 (2018): 16–30. https://doi.org/10.1080/1523908X.2017.1302322

Gerdy, John R. *Sports: The All-American Addiction.* University Press of Mississippi, 2010.

Ghosn, Faten, Glenn Palmer, and Stuart Bremer. "The MID3 Data Set, 1993–2001: Procedures, Coding Rules, and Description." *Conflict Management and Peace Science* 21, no. 2 (2004): 133–154. https://doi.org/10.1080/07388940490463861

Gift, Thomas, and Andrew Miner. "'Dropping the Ball': The Understudied Nexus of Sports and Politics." *World Affairs* 180, no. 1 (2017): 127–161. https://doi.org/10.1177/0043820017715569

Gläßel, Christian, Adam Scharpf, and Pearce Edwards. "Does Sportswashing Work? First Insights from the 2022 World Cup in Qatar." *Journal of Politics* 87, no. 1 (2025): 388–392. https://doi.org/10.1086/730728

Glassman, Tavis, Robert Braun, Diana M. Reindl, and Aubrey Whewell. "Blood (Breath) Alcohol Concentration Rates of College Football Fans on Game Day." *Journal of Alcohol and Drug Education* 55, no. 2 (2011): 55–73. https://www.jstor.org/stable/45128447

Glassman, Tavis J., Virginia J. Dodd, Jiunn-Jye Sheu, Barbara A. Rienzo, and Alex C. Wagenaar. "Extreme Ritualistic Alcohol Consumption Among College Students on Game Day." *Journal of American College Health* 58, no. 5 (2010): 413–423. https://doi.org/10.1080/07448480903540473

Goldblatt, David. *The Age of Football: The Global Game in the Twenty-First Century.* Pan Macmillan, 2019.

———. *The Ball Is Round: A Global History of Soccer.* Penguin, 2007.

———. *The Games: A Global History of the Olympics.* Pan Macmillan, 2016.

Gorn, Elliot J. " 'No Quarrel with Them Vietcong': Muhammad Ali's Cold War." In *The Whole World Was Watching: Sport in the Cold War,* edited by Robert Edelman and Christopher Young. Stanford University Press, 2019.

Grix, Jonathan. "Image Leveraging and Sports Mega-Events: Germany and the 2006 FIFA World Cup." *Journal of Sport & Tourism* 17, no. 4 (2012): 289–312. https://doi.org/10.1080/14775085.2012.760934

Grix, Jonathan, Paul Michael Brannagan, Hannah Wood, and Ceri Wynne. "State Strategies for Leveraging Sports Mega-Events: Unpacking the Concept of 'Legacy.' " *International Journal of Sport Policy and Politics* 9, no. 2 (2017): 203–218. https://doi.org/10.1080/19406940.2017.1316761

Gruffydd-Jones, Jamie. "Dangerous Days: The Impact of Nationalism on Interstate Conflict." *Security Studies* 26, no. 4 (2017): 698–728. https://doi.org/10.1080/09636412.2017.1336393

Grundlingh, Albert. "From Redemption to Recidivism? Rugby and Change in South Africa During the 1995 Rugby World Cup and Its Aftermath." *Sporting Traditions* 14, no. 2 (1998): 67–86.

Guridy, Frank A. *The Sports Revolution: How Texas Changed the Culture of American Athletics.* University of Texas Press, 2021.

———. *The Stadium: An American History of Politics, Protest, and Play.* Basic Books, 2024.

Guttmann, Allen. "The Cold War and the Olympics." *International Journal* 43, no. 4 (1988): 554–568. https://doi.org/10.1177/002070208804300402

———. *The Olympics: A History of the Modern Games,* 2nd ed. University of Illinois Press, 2002.

———. *Sports: The First Five Millennia.* University of Massachusetts Press, 2004.

———. *Women's Sports: A History.* Columbia University Press, 1991.

Haas, Ernst B. "International Integration: The European and the Universal Process." *International Organization* 15, no. 3 (1961): 366–392. https://doi.org/10.1017/S0020818300002198

Halbrook, Yemaya J., Aisling T. O'Donnell, Rachel M. Msetfi. "When and How Video Games Can Be Good: A Review of the Positive Effects of Video Games on Well-Being." *Perspectives on Psychological Science* 14, no. 6 (2019): 13031–13038. https://doi.org/10 .1177/1745691619863807

Hardy, Stephan, and Andrew C. Holman. *Hockey: A Global History.* University of Illinois Press, 2018.

Hargreaves, Jennifer. "Olympic Women: A Struggle for Recognition." In *Women and Sports in the United States: A Documentary Reader,* edited by Jean O'Reilly and Susan K. Cahn. Northeastern University Press, 2007.

———. *Sporting Females: Critical Issues in the History and Sociology of Women's Sports.* Routledge, 1994.

Harris, Harry. *Red Card to Racism: The Fight for Equality in Football.* Ad Lib Publishers, 2021.

Harrison, C. Keith, and Alicia Valdez. "The Uneven View of African American Ballers." In *Race and Sport: The Struggle for Equality On and Off the Field,* edited by Charles K. Ross. University Press of Mississippi, 2004.

Hartmann, Douglas. *Race, Culture, and the Revolt of the Black Athlete: The 1968 Olympic Protests and Their Aftermath.* University of Chicago Press, 2003.

Healy, Andrew J., Neil Malhotra, and Cecilia Hyunjung Mo. "Irrelevant Events Affect Voters' Evaluations of Government Performance." *Proceedings of the National Academy of Sciences* 107, no. 29 (2010): 12804–12809. https://doi.org/10.1073/pnas.100742 0107

Hiller, Harry H., and Richard A. Wanner. "Public Opinion in Host Olympic Cities: The Case of the 2010 Vancouver Winter Games." *Sociology* 45, no. 5 (2011): 883–899. https:// doi.org/10.1177/0038038511413414

Hoberman, John. *Darwin's Athletes: How Sport Has Damaged Black America and Preserved the Myth of Race.* Mariner Books, 1997.

———. "The Myth of Sport as a Peace-Promoting Political Force." *SAIS Review of International Affairs* 31, no. 1 (2011): 17–29. https://doi.org/10.1353/sais.2011.0001

Hobsbawm, Eric J. *Nations and Nationalism Since 1780: Programme, Myth, Reality.* Cambridge University Press, 1992.

Hokkanen, Markku. 2007. "'Christ and the Imperial Games Fields' in South-Central Africa—Sport and the Scottish Missionaries in Malawi, 1880–1914." In *Modern Sport: The Global Obsession,* edited by Boria Majumdar and Fan Hong. Routledge, 2007.

Hong, Fan, Ping Wu, and Huan Xiong. 2007. "Beijing Ambitions: An Analysis of the Chinese Elite Sports System and Its Olympic Strategy for the 2008 Olympic Games." In *Modern Sport: The Global Obsession,* edited by Boria Majumdar and Fan Hong. Routledge, 2007.

Hong, Zhaohui, and Yi Sun. "The Butterfly Effect and the Making of 'Ping-Pong Diplomacy.'" *Journal of Contemporary China* 9, no. 25 (2000): 429–448. https://doi.org/10 .1080/713675951

Huizinga, Johan. *Homo Ludens: A Study of the Play Element in Culture.* Angelico Press, 2016.

Hulteen, Ryan M., Jordan J. Smith, Philip J. Morgan, et al. "Global Participation in Sport and Leisure-Time Physical Activities: A Systematic Review and Meta-Analysis." *Preventive Medicine* 95 (2017): 14–25. https://doi.org/10.1016/j.ypmed.2016 .11.027

Hunt, Thomas M. *Drug Games: The International Olympic Committee and the Politics of Doping, 1960–2008.* University of Texas Press, 2011.

Hurka, Thomas, ed. *Games, Sports, and Play: Philosophical Essays.* Oxford University Press, 2019.

———. "Introduction." In *Games, Sports, and Play: Philosophical Essays*, edited by Thomas Hurka. Oxford University Press, 2019.

Huxley, Aldous. *Brave New World and Brave New World Revisited.* Harper Perennial Modern Classics, 2004.

Ivandić, Ria, Tom Kirchmaier, Yasaman Saeidi, and Neus Torres Blas. "Football, Alcohol, and Domestic Abuse." *Journal of Public Economics* 230 (2024): 105031. https:// doi.org/10.1016/j.jpubeco.2023.105031

Jaksa, Kari L. "Sports and Collective Identity: The Effects of Athletics on National Unity." *SAIS Review of International Affairs* 31, no. 1 (2011): 39–41. https://dx.doi.org/ 10.1353/sais.2011.0007

James, C. L. R. *Beyond a Boundary.* Stanley Paul, 1986.

Johnson, Daniel K. N., and Ayfer Ali. 2002. "A Tale of Two Seasons: Participation and Medal Counts at the Summer and Winter Olympic Games." *Social Science Quarterly* 85, no. 4 (2004): 974–993. https://doi.org/10.1111/j.0038-4941.2004.00254.x

Johnson, R. W. "The World Cup." *London Review of Books* 31, no. 4 (2009). https://www .lrb.co.uk/the-paper/v31/n24/r.w.-johnson/diary

Jones, Amy, and Jennifer Greer. "You Don't Look Like an Athlete: The Effects of Feminine Appearance on Audience Perceptions of Female Athletes and Women's Sports." *Journal of Sport Behavior* 34, no. 4 (2011): 358–377.

Kane, Mary Jo, Nicole M. LaVoi, and Janet S. Fink. "Exploring Elite Female Athletes' Interpretations of Sport Media Images: A Window into the Construction of Social Identity and 'Selling Sex' in Women's Sports." *Communication & Sport* 1, no. 3 (2013): 269–298. https://doi.org/10.1177/2167479512473585

Kang, Yong-Soon, and Richard Perdue. "Long-Term Impact of a Mega-Event on International Tourism to the Host Country: A Conceptual Model and the Case of the 1988 Seoul Olympics." *Journal of International Consumer Marketing* 6, no. 3–4 (1994): 205–225. https://doi.org/10.1300/J046v06n03_11

Kapuscinski, Ryszard. *The Soccer War.* Granta Books, 2007.

Karamichas, John. "The Olympics and the Environment." In *The Palgrave Handbook of Olympic Studies*, edited by Helen Jefferson Lenskyj and Stephen Wagg. Palgrave Macmillan, 2012.

Kassens-Noor, Eva, Joshua Vertalka, and Mark Wilson. "Good Games, Bad Host? Using Big Data to Measure Public Attention and Imagery of the Olympic Games." *Cities* 90 (2019): 229–236. https://doi.org/10.1016/j.cities.2019.02.009

Kelly, William W. *The Sportsworld of the Hanshin Tigers: Professional Baseball in Modern Japan*. University of California Press, 2019.

Kennedy, Michael D., and Martin Faulhaber. "Respiratory Function and Symptoms Post Cold Air Exercise in Female High and Low Ventilation Sport Athletes." *Allergy, Asthma & Immunology Research* 10, no. 1 (2018): 43–51. https://doi.org/10.4168/aair .2018.10.1.43

Kenyon, James Andrew, and Guillaume Bodet. "Exploring the Domestic Relationship Between Mega-Events and Destination Image: The Image Impact of Hosting the 2012 Olympic Games for the City of London." *Sport Management Review* 21, no. 3 (2018): 232–249. https://doi.org/10.1016/j.smr.2017.07.001

Keys, Barbara. *Globalizing Sport: National Rivalry and International Community in the 1930s*. Harvard University Press, 2006.

———. "Introduction: The Ideals of International Sport." In *The Ideals of Modern Sport: From Peace to Human Rights*, edited by Barbara Keys. University of Pennsylvania Press, 2019.

Kikuta, Kyosuke, and Mamoru Uesugi. "Do Politically Irrelevant Events Cause Conflict? The Cross-Continental Effects of European Professional Football on Protests in Africa." *International Organization* 77, no. 1 (2023): 179–216. https://doi.org/10 .1017/S0020818322000261

Kim, Hyung-Min, and Seongcheol Kim. "The Show Must Go On: Why Korea Lost Its First-Mover Advantage in Esports and How It Can Become a Major Player Again." *Technological Forecasting and Social Change* 179 (2022): 121649. https://doi.org/10 .1016/j.techfore.2022.121649

Kirby, Stuart, and Nathan Birdsall. "Kicking Off: Is the Association Between the FIFA World Cup and Domestic Abuse an International Phenomenon?" *Police Journal: Theory, Practice and Principles* 95, no. 2 (2021): 378–390. https://doi.org/10.1177/00 32258X211007182

Kirby, Stuart, Brian Francis, and Rosalie O'Flaherty. "Can the FIFA World Cup Football (Soccer) Tournament Be Associated with an Increase in Domestic Abuse?" *Journal of Research in Crime and Delinquency* 51, no. 3 (2014): 259–276. https://doi .org/10.1177/0022427813494843

Kobierecki, Michał Marcin. "Sport as a Tool of Building Political Alliances: The Case of the Games of New Emerging Forces (GANEFO)." *Polish Quarterly of International Affairs* 25, no. 4 (2016): 105–121. https://www.ceeol.com/search/article-detail?id= 526790

Kohorst, Mira A., Deepti M. Warad, Amulya A. Nageswara Rao, and Vilmarie Rodriguez. "Obesity, Sedentary Lifestyle, and Video Games: The New Thrombophilia Cocktail in Adolescents." *Pediatric Blood & Cancer* 65, no. 7 (2018): 1–4. https://doi .org/10.1002/pbc.27041

Korr, Charles P. "Reviewed Work: *Barbarians, Gentlemen and Players: A Sociological Study of Rugby Football* by Eric Dunning, Kenneth Sheard." *Journal of Social History* 14, no. 2 (1980): 87–90. https://www.jstor.org/stable/43609049

Krane, Vikki, Y. L. Choi, Shannon M. Baird, Christine M. Aimar, and Kerrie J. Kauer. "Living the Paradox: Female Athletes Negotiate Femininity and Muscularity." In *Women and Sports in the United States: A Documentary Reader,* edited by Jean O'Reilly and Susan K. Cahn. Northeastern University Press, 2007.

Kumah-Abiwu, Felix, Edward Brenya, and James Agbodzakey. "Oil Wealth, Resource Curse and Development: Any Lessons for Ghana?" *Journal of Economics and Sustainable Development* 6, no. 1 (2015): 62–73. https://thekeep.eiu.edu/afriamer_fac/5/

Kuper, Simon. *Soccer Against the Enemy.* Bold Type Books, 2010.

Kuper, Simon, and Stefan Szymanski. *Soccernomics: Why European Men and American Women Win and Billionaire Owners Are Destined to Lose.* 2022 World Cup ed. Bold Type Books, 2022.

Kyle, Donald G. "Ancient Greek and Roman Sport." In *The Oxford Handbook of Sports History,* edited by Robert Edelman and Wayne Wilson. Oxford University Press, 2017.

———. *Sport and Spectacle in the Ancient World,* 2nd ed. Wiley Blackwell, 2015.

Lavie, Carl J., James H. O'Keefe, and Robert E. Sallis. "Exercise and the Heart—The Harm of Too Little and Too Much." *Current Sports Medicine Reports* 14, no. 2 (2015): 104–109. https://doi.org/10.1249/JSR.0000000000000134

Lee, Choong-Ki, and Tracy Taylor. "Critical Reflections on the Economic Impact Assessment of a Mega-Event: The Case of 2002 FIFA World Cup." *Tourism Management* 26, no. 4 (2005): 595–603. https://doi.org/10.1016/j.tourman.2004.03.002

Liu, Dongfeng, and Chris Gratton. "The Impact of Mega Sporting Events on Live Spectators' Images of a Host City: A Case Study of the Shanghai F1 Grand Prix." *Tourism Economics* 16, no. 3 (2010): 629–645. https://doi.org/10.5367/000000010792278347

Llewellyn, Matthew P., and John Gleaves. *The Rise and Fall of Olympic Amateurism.* University of Illinois Press, 2016.

Lowe, Matt. "Types of Contact: A Field Experiment on Collaborative and Adversarial Caste Integration." *American Economic Review* 111, no. 6 (2021): 1807–1844. https://doi.org/10.1257/aer.20191780

Luther, Jessica, and Kavitha A. Davidson. *Loving Sports When They Don't Love You Back: Dilemmas of the Modern Fan.* University of Texas Press, 2020.

MacAloon, John J. *The Great Symbol: Pierre de Coubertin and the Origins of the Modern Olympics.* Routledge, 2008.

Madinabeitia-Cabrera, Iker, Francisco Alarcón-López, Luis J. Chirosa-Ríos, Ignacio Pelayo-Tejo, and David Cárdenas-Vélez. "The Cognitive Benefits of Basketball Training Compared to a Combined Endurance and Resistance Training Regimen: A Four-Month Intervention Study." *Nature Scientific Reports* 13, no. 1 (2023): 11132. https://doi.org/10.1038/s41598-023-32470-2

Mandelbaum, Michael. *The Meaning of Sports: Why Americans Watch Baseball, Football, and Basketball and What They See When They Do.* PublicAffairs, 2004.

Mansfield, Edward, and Jack Snyder. "Democratization and the Danger of War." *International Security* 20, no. 1 (1995): 5–38. https://doi.org/10.2307/2539213

Maraniss, David. *Rome 1960: The Olympics That Changed the World.* Simon & Schuster, 2008.

Markovits, Andrei S., and Emily Albertson. *Sportista: Female Fandom in the United States.* Temple University Press, 2012.

Markovits, Andrei S., and Steven L. Hellerman. *Offside: Soccer and American Exceptionalism.* Princeton University Press, 2001.

Markovits, Andrei S., and Lars Rensmann. *Gaming the World: How Sports Are Reshaping Global Politics and Culture.* Princeton University Press, 2010.

Markovits, Andrei S., and David T. Smith. *Sports Culture Among Undergraduates: A Study of Student Athletes and Students at the University of Michigan.* Scholarly Publishing Office, University of Michigan University Library, 2007. https://dx.doi.org/10.3998/spobooks.5099288.0001.001

Maron, Barry J., Paul D. Thompson, James C. Puffer, et al. "Cardiovascular Preparticipation Screening of Competitive Athletes: A Statement for Health Professionals from the Sudden Death Committee (Clinical Cardiology) and Congenital Cardiac Defects Committee (Cardiovascular Disease in the Young), American Heart Association." *Circulation* 94, no. 4 (1996): 850–856. https://doi.org/10.1161/01.CIR.94.4.850

Martin, Simon. *Football and Fascism: The National Game Under Mussolini.* Berg, 2004.

Matheson, Victor A., and Robert A. Baade. "An Economic Slam Dunk or March Madness? Assessing the Economic Impact of the NCAA Basketball Tournament." In *The Economics of College Sports,* edited by John Fizel and Rodney Fort. Praeger Publishers, 2004.

———. "Mega-Sporting Events in Developing Nations: Playing the Way to Prosperity?" *South African Journal of Economics* 72, no. 5 (2004): 1085–1096. https://doi.org/10.1111/j.1813-6982.2004.tb00147.x

McClearen, Jennifer, and Mia Fischer. "Maya Moore, Black Lives Matter, and the Visibility of Athlete Activism." *The Velvet Light Trap* 87, no. 1 (2021): 64–68. https://muse.jhu.edu/article/786162

McDonagh, Eileen, and Laura Pappano. *Playing with the Boys: Why Separate Is Not Equal in Sports.* Oxford University Press, 2007.

McDougall, Alan. "*Eulogy to Theft*: Berliner FC Dynamo, East German Football, and the End of Communism." In *The Whole World Was Watching: Sport in the Cold War,* edited by Robert Edelman and Christopher Young. Stanford University Press, 2019.

McGillivray, David, Michael B. Duignan, and Eduardo Mielke. "Mega Sport Events and Spatial Management: Zoning Space Across Rio's 2016 Olympic City." *Annals of Leisure Research* 23, no. 3 (2020): 280–303. https://doi.org/10.1080/11745398.2019.1607509

McGraw, Sarah, Christopher R. Deubert, Holly Fernandez Lynch, Alixandra Nozzolillo, and I. Glenn Cohen. "NFL or 'Not for Long?': Transitioning Out of the NFL." *Journal of Sport Behavior* 42, no. 4 (2019): 461–492. https://www.proquest.com/docview/2329189252?pq-origsite=gscholar&fromopenview=true&sourcetype=Scholarly%20Journals

Miller, Toby. *Greenwashing Sport.* Routledge, 2018.

Mitchell, Heather, and Mark Fergusson Stewart. "What Should You Pay to Host a Party? An Economic Analysis of Hosting Sports Mega-Events." *Applied Economics* 47, no. 15 (2015): 1550–1561. https://doi.org/10.1080/00036846.2014.1000522

Möhlenkamp, Stefan, Nils Lehmann, Frank Breuckmann, et al. "Running: The Risk of Coronary Events: Prevalence and Prognostic Relevance of Coronary Atherosclerosis in Marathon Runners." *European Heart Journal* 29, no. 15 (2008): 1903–1910. https://doi.org/10.1093/eurheartj/ehn163

Moore, Louis. *We Will Win the Day: The Civil Rights Movement, the Black Athlete, and the Quest for Equality.* University Press of Kentucky, 2021.

Morgan, William J. "Sports as the Moral Discourse of Nations." In *Values in Sport: Elitism, Nationalism, Gender Equality and the Scientific Manufacturing of Winners,* edited by Torbjorn Tännsjö and Claudio Tamburrini. Taylor & Francis, 2000.

Morris, Andrew D. "'The Communist Bandits Have Been Repudiated': Cold War–Era Sport in Taiwan." In *The Whole World Was Watching: Sport in the Cold War,* edited by Robert Edelman and Christopher Young. Stanford University Press, 2019.

Mousa, Salma. "Building Social Cohesion Between Christians and Muslims Through Soccer in Post-ISIS Iraq." *Science* 369, no. 6505 (2020): 866–870. https://doi.org/10.1126/science.abb3153

Müller, Martin. "After Sochi 2014: Costs and Impacts of Russia's Olympic Games." *Eurasian Geography and Economics* 55, no. 6 (2015): 628–655. https://doi.org/10.1080/15387216.2015.1040432

———. "How Mega-Events Capture Their Hosts: Event Seizure and the World Cup 2018 in Russia." *Urban Geography* 38, no. 8 (2017): 1113–1132. https://doi.org/10.1080/02723638.2015.1109951

———. "The Mega-Event Syndrome: Why So Much Goes Wrong in Mega-Event Planning and What to Do About It." *Journal of the American Planning Association* 81, no. 1 (2015): 6–17. https://doi.org/10.1080/01944363.2015.1038292

Müller, Martin, and Christopher Gaffney. "Comparing the Urban Impacts of the FIFA World Cup and Olympic Games from 2010 to 2016." *Journal of Sport and Social Issues* 42, no. 4 (2018): 247–269. https://doi.org/10.1177/0193723518771830

Mumford, Stephen. *A Philosopher Looks at Sports.* Cambridge University Press, 2021.

Mundim, Pedro Santos, and Gleice Meire Almeida da Silva. "The World Cup and Presidential Popularity in Brazil." *Brazilian Political Science Review* 13, no. 3 (2019): 1–32. https://doi.org/10.1590/1981-3821201900030001

Murray, Stuart, and Geoffrey A. Pigman. "Mapping the Relationship Between International Sport and Diplomacy." *Sport in Society* 17, no. 9 (2013): 1–21. https://doi.org/10.1080/17430437.2013.856616

Mwaanga, Oscar, and Kola Adeosun. "Reconceptualizing Sport for Development and Peace (SDP): An Ideological Critique of Nelson 'Madiba' Mandela's Engagement with Sport." *Sport in Society* 23, no. 5 (2020): 847–863. https://doi.org/10.1080/17430437.2019.1584184

Nagle, Kyle B., and M. Alison Brooks. "A Systematic Review of Bone Health in Cyclists." *Sports Health* 3, no. 3 (2011): 235–243. https://doi.org/10.1177/1941738111398857

Nicholson, Matthew, and Russell Hoye. "Sport and Social Capital: An Introduction." In *Sport and Social Capital,* edited by Matthew Nicholson and Russell Hoye. Routledge, 2008.

Nye, Joseph. *Soft Power: The Means to Success in World Politics*. PublicAffairs, 2004.

O'Reilly, Jean, and Susan K. Cahn. "Introduction." In *Women and Sports in the United States: A Documentary Reader*, edited by Jean O'Reilly and Susan K. Cahn. Northeastern University Press, 2007.

———. "Timeline: 125 Years of U.S. Women in Sports." In *Women and Sports in the United States: A Documentary Reader*, edited by Jean O'Reilly and Susan K. Cahn. Northeastern University Press, 2007.

Orttung, Robert W., and Sufian Zhemukhov. "The 2014 Sochi Olympic Mega-Project and Russia's Political Economy." *East European Politics* 30, no. 2 (2014): 175–191. https://doi.org/10.1080/21599165.2013.853662

Oshimi, Daichi, and Munehiko Harada. "The Effects of City Image, Event Fit, and Word-of-Mouth Intention Towards the Host City of an International Sporting Event." *International Journal of Sport Management, Recreation & Tourism* 24, no. 6 (2016): 76–96. https://doi.org/10.5199/ijsmart-1791-874X-24d

Oyer, Paul. *An Economist Goes to the Game: How to Throw Away $580 Million and Other Surprising Insights from the Economics of Sports*. Yale University Press, 2022.

Paolantonio, Sal. *How Football Explains America*. Triumph Books, 2015.

Papineau, David. "The Nature and Value of Sport." In *Games, Sports, and Play: Philosophical Essays*, edited by Thomas Hurka. Oxford University Press, 2019.

Park, Roberta J. "Sport, Gender, and Society in a Transatlantic Victorian Perspective." In *From "Fair Sex" to Feminism: Sport and the Socialization of Women in the Industrial and Post-Industrial Eras*, edited by J. A. Mangan and Roberta J. Park. Frank Class, 1987.

Parks, Jenifer. "Verbal Gymnastics: Sport, Bureaucracy, and the Soviet Union's Entrance into the Olympic Games." In *East Plays West: Sport and the Cold War*, edited by Stephen Wagg and David L. Andrews. Routledge, 2007.

Pauker, Ewa T. "Ganefo I: Sports and Politics in Djakarta." *Asian Survey* 5, no. 4 (1965): 171–185. https://doi.org/10.2307/2642364

Perales, José Raul. "Politics and Play: Sport, Social Movements, and Decolonization in Cuba and the British West Indies." In *Globalizations and Social Movements: Culture, Power, and the Transnational Public Sphere*, edited by John A. Guidry, Michael D. Kennedy, and Mayer N. Zald. University of Michigan Press, 2009.

Pfitzner, Rebecca, and Joerg Koenigstorfer. "Quality of Life of Residents Living in a City Hosting Mega-Sport Events: A Longitudinal Study." *BMC Public Health* 16, no. 1 (2016): 1–10. https://doi.org/10.1186/s12889-016-3777-3

Pinto, Gabriele. "Sports Nationalism and Xenophobia: When Cheering Turns into Violence." *Journal of Peace Research* 62, no. 3 (2025): 595–612. https://doi.org/10.1177/00223433241231177

Pollock III, Philip H. "Issues, Values, and Critical Moments: Did 'Magic' Johnson Transform Public Opinion on AIDS?" *American Journal of Political Science* 38, no. 2 (1994): 426–446. https://doi.org/10.2307/2111411

Pope John Paul II. "Homily Given at the Olympic Stadium in Rome." In *Blessed John Paul II Speaks to Athletes: Homilies, Messages and Speeches on Sport*, edited by Kevin Lixey, Norbert Müller, and Cornelius Schäfer. John Paul II Sports Foundation, 2000.

Potoski, Matthew, and Robert Urbatsch. "Entertainment and the Opportunity Cost of Civic Participation: Monday Night Football Game Quality Suppresses Turnout in US Elections." *Journal of Politics* 79, no. 2 (2017): 424–438. https://doi.org/10.1086/688174

Powers, Kathleen. *Nationalisms in International Politics*. Princeton University Press, 2022.

Preuss, Holger, and Christian Alfs. "Signaling Through the 2008 Beijing Olympics—Using Mega Sport Events to Change the Perception and Image of the Host." *European Sport Management Quarterly* 11, no. 1 (2011): 55–71. https://doi.org/10.1080/16184742.2010.537362

Prozumenshikov, Mikhail. "Action in the Era of Stagnation: Leonid Brezhnev and the Soviet Olympic Dream." In *The Whole World Was Watching: Sport in the Cold War*, edited by Robert Edelman and Christopher Young. Stanford University Press, 2019.

Pujadas, Xavier. "Sport Under Authoritarian Regimes in Times of Crisis." *Revista de Psicologia, Ciències de l'Educació i de l'Esport* 32, no. 2 (2014): 9–11.

Putnam, Robert D. *Bowling Alone: The Collapse and Revival of American Community*. Simon & Schuster, 2000.

Pyun, Hyunwoong. "Exploring Causal Relationship Between Major League Baseball Games and Crime: A Synthetic Control Analysis." *Empirical Economics* 57 (2019): 365–383. https://doi.org/10.1007/s00181-018-1440-9

Quigg, Zara, Karen Hughes, and Mark A. Bellis. "Effects of the 2010 World Cup Football Tournament on Emergency Department Assault Attendances in England." *European Journal of Public Health* 23, no. 3 (2013): 383–385. https://doi.org/10.1093/eurpub/cks098

Ralph, Michael. "'Crimes of History': Senegalese Soccer and the Forensics of Slavery." *Souls* 9, no. 3 (2007): 193–222. https://doi.org/10.1080/10999940701533340

Rees, Daniel I., and Kevin T. Schnepel. "College Football Games and Crime." *Journal of Sports Economics* 10, no. 1 (2009): 68–87. https://doi.org/10.1177/1527002508327389

Rider, Toby C. *Cold War Games: Propaganda, the Olympics, and U.S. Foreign Policy*. University of Illinois Press, 2016.

———. "In the 'Twilight Warzone': Overt and Covert Dimensions of the US Sports Offensive." In *The Whole World Was Watching: Sport in the Cold War*, edited by Robert Edelman and Christopher Young. Stanford University Press, 2019.

Ring, Jennifer. *A Game of Their Own: Voices of Contemporary Women in Baseball*. University of Nebraska Press, 2015.

———. *Stolen Bases: Why American Girls Don't Play Baseball*. University of Illinois Press, 2009.

Rosato, Sebastian. "The Flawed Logic of Democratic Peace Theory." *American Political Science Review* 97, no. 4 (2003): 585–602. https://doi.org/10.1017/S0003055403000893

Rosenzweig, Leah R., and Yang-Yang Zhou. "Team and Nation: Sports, Nationalism, and Attitudes Toward Refugees." *Comparative Political Studies* 54, no. 12 (2021): 2123–2154. https://doi.org/10.1177/0010414021997498

Ross, Michael L. "The Political Economy of the Resource Curse." *World Politics* 51, no. 2 (1999): 297–322. https://doi.org/10.1017/S0043887100008200

Ross, Stephen F., and Stefan Szymanski. *Fans of the World Unite. A Capitalist Manifesto for Sports Consumers*. Stanford University Press, 2008.

Rowley, Alison. "Sport in the Service of the State: Images of Physical Culture and Soviet Women, 1917–1941." *International Journal of the History of Sport* 23, no. 8 (2006): 1314–1340. https://doi.org/10.1080/09523360600922246

Ruck, Rob. "Deflected Confrontations: Cold War Baseball in the Caribbean." In *The Whole World Was Watching: Sport in the Cold War*, edited by Robert Edelman and Christopher Young. Stanford University Press, 2019.

Rugg, Caitlin, Adarsh Kadoor, Brian T. Feeley, and Nirav K. Pandya. "The Effects of Playing Multiple High School Sports on National Basketball Association Players' Propensity for Injury and Athletic Performance." *American Journal of Sports Medicine* 46, no. 2 (2018): 402–408. https://doi.org/10.1177/0363546517738736

Sagan, Carl. *Contact*. Orbit, 2020.

Sanderson, Jimmy, Evan Frederick, and Mike Stocz. "When Athlete Activism Clashes with Group Values: Social Identity Threat Management via Social Media." *Mass Communication and Society* 19, no. 3 (2016): 301–322. https://doi.org/10.1080/152054 36.2015.1128549

Sansone, David. *Greek Athletics and the Genesis of Sport*. University of California Press, 1988.

Scharpf, Adam, Christian Gläßel, and Pearce Edwards. "International Sports Events and Repression in Autocracies: Evidence from the 1978 FIFA World Cup." *American Political Science Review* 117, no. 3 (2023): 909–926. https://doi.org/10.1017/S0003055 422000958

Schlegel, Andrea, Rebecca Pfitzner, and Joerg Koenigstorfer. "The Impact of Atmosphere in the City on Subjective Well-Being of Rio de Janeiro Residents During (vs. Before) the 2014 FIFA World Cup." *Journal of Sport Management* 31, no. 6 (2017): 605–619. https://doi.org/10.1123/jsm.2017-0108

Schultz, Jaime. *Qualifying Times: Points of Change in U.S. Women's Sports*. University of Illinois Press, 2014.

———. *Women's Sports: What Everyone Needs to Know*. Oxford University Press, 2018.

Sekhon, Jasjeet S., and Rocío Titiunik. "On Interpreting the Regression Discontinuity Design as a Local Experiment." In *Regression Discontinuity Designs: Theory and Applications*, edited by Matias D. Cattaneo and Juan Carlos Escanciano. Emerald Publishing Limited, 2017.

Shaw, Duncan R. "The Political Instrumentalization of Professional Football in Francoist Spain 1939–1975." PhD thesis, University of London, 1988. https://qmro.qmul .ac.uk/xmlui/handle/123456789/1899

Sheldon, Kennon M., and Sonja Lyubomirsky. "Is It Possible to Become Happier? (And If So, How?)." *Social and Personality Psychology Compass* 1, no. 1 (2007): 129–145. https://doi.org/10.1111/j.1751-9004.2007.00002.x

Sherif, Muzafer, O. J. Harvey, B. Jack White, William R. Hood, and Carolyn W. Sherif. *Intergroup Conflict and Cooperation: The Robbers Cave Experiment.* Wesleyan University Press, 1988.

Shuman, Amanda. "Learning from the Soviet Big Brother: The Early Years of Sport in the People's Republic of China." In *The Whole World Was Watching: Sport in the Cold War*, edited by Robert Edelman and Christopher Young. Stanford University Press, 2019.

Singer, J. David, Stuart Bremer, and John Stuckey. "Capability Distribution, Uncertainty, and Major Power War, 1820–1965." In *Peace, War, and Numbers*, edited by Bruce Russett. Sage, 1972.

Sipes, Richard G. "War, Sports and Aggression: An Empirical Test of Two Rival Theories." *American Anthropologist* 75, no. 1 (1973): 64–86. https://doi.org/10.1525/aa.1973.75.1.02a00040

Sleifer, Jaap. *Planning Ahead and Falling Behind: The East German Economy in Comparison with West Germany 1936–2002.* Akademie Verlag, 2006.

Smith, Earl. *Race, Sport and the American Dream*, 3rd ed. Carolina Academic Press, 2014.

Smith, Lauren. "Stand Up, Show Respect: Athlete Activism, Nationalistic Attitudes, and Emotional Response." *International Journal of Communication* 13 (2019): 2376–2397. https://ijoc.org/index.php/ijoc/article/view/10027/2666

Steenveld, Lynette, and Larry Strelitz. "The 1995 Rugby World Cup and the Politics of Nation-Building in South Africa." *Media, Culture and Society* 20, no. 4 (1998): 609–629. https://doi.org/10.1177/016344398020004006

Storm, Rasmus K., and Tor Georg Jakobsen. "National Pride, Sporting Success and Event Hosting: An Analysis of Intangible Effects Related to Major Athletic Tournaments." *International Journal of Sport Policy and Politics* 12, no. 1 (2020): 163–178. https://doi.org/10.1080/19406940.2019.1646303

Storm, Rasmus K., Christian G. Nielsen, and Tor Georg Jakobsen. "The Impact of Formula One on Regional Economies in Europe." *Regional Studies* 54, no. 6 (2019): 827–837. https://doi.org/10.1080/00343404.2019.1648787

Sue-Chu, Malcolm. "Winter Sports Athletes: Long-Term Effects of Cold Air Exposure." *British Journal of Sports Medicine* 46, no. 6 (2012): 397–401. https://doi.org/10.1136/bjsports-2011-090822

Suggs, Welch. *A Place on the Team: The Triumph and Tragedy of Title IX.* Princeton University Press, 2005.

Suits, Bernard. *The Grasshopper: Games, Life and Utopia*, 3rd ed. Broadview Press, 2014.

Taylor, T. L. *Raising the Stakes: E-Sports and the Professionalization of Computer Gaming.* MIT Press, 2012.

Tenforde, Adam S., and Michael Fredericson. "Influence of Sports Participation on Bone Health in the Young Athlete: A Review of the Literature." *PM&R* 3, no. 9 (2011): 861–867. https://doi.org/10.1016/j.pmrj.2011.05.019

Tenforde, Adam S., Kristin Lynn Sainani, Lauren Carter Sayres, Charles Milgrom, and

Michael Fredericson. "Participation in Ball Sports May Represent a Prehabilitation Strategy to Prevent Future Stress Fractures and Promote Bone Health in Young Athletes." *PM&R* 7, no. 2 (2015): 222–225. https://doi.org/10.1016/j.pmrj.2014.09.017

Theberge, Nancy, and Susan Birrell. "Structural Constraints Facing Women in Sports." In *Women and Sports in the United States: A Documentary Reader*, edited by Jean O'Reilly and Susan K. Cahn. Northeastern University Press, 2007.

Thistlethwaite, Donald L., and Donald T. Campbell. "Regression-Discontinuity Analysis: An Alternative to the Ex Post Facto Experiment." *Journal of Educational Psychology* 51, no. 6 (1960): 309–317. https://psycnet.apa.org/doi/10.1037/h0044319

Timm, Annette F. "'The Most Beautiful Face of Socialism': Katarina Witt and the Sexual Politics of the Cold War." In *The Whole World Was Watching: Sport in the Cold War*, edited by Robert Edelman and Christopher Young. Stanford University Press, 2019.

Tomlinson, Alan, and Christopher Young. "Culture, Politics, and Spectacle in the Global Sports Event—An Introduction." In *National Identity and Global Sports Events: Culture, Politics, and Spectacle in the Olympics and Football World Cup*, edited by Alan Tomlinson and Christopher Young. State University of New York Press, 2006.

Tomporowski, Phillip D., and Caterina Pesce. "Exercise, Sports, and Performance Arts Benefit Cognition via a Common Process." *Psychological Bulletin* 145, no. 9 (2019): 929–951. https://psycnet.apa.org/doi/10.1037/bul0000200

Torres, Cesar R. "Morally Incompatible? An Analysis of the Relationship Between Competitive Sport and International Relations at the Olympic Games." *SAIS Review of International Affairs* 31, no. 1 (2011): 3–16. https://doi.org/10.1353/sais.2011.0016

Trendl, Anna, Neil Stewart, and Timothy L. Mullett. "The Role of Alcohol in the Link Between National Football (Soccer) Tournaments and Domestic Abuse—Evidence from England." *Social Science & Medicine* 268 (2021): 113457. https://doi.org/10.1016/j.socscimed.2020.113457

Tuchman, Gaye. "The Symbolic Annihilation of Women by Mass Media." In *Hearth and Home: Images of Women in the Mass Media*, edited by Gaye Tuchman, Arlene Kaplan Daniels, and James Walker Benét. Oxford University Press, 1978.

Tunis, John R. "The Dictators Discover Sport." *Foreign Affairs* 14, no. 4 (1936): 606–617. https://www.foreignaffairs.com/articles/russian-federation/1936-07-01/dictators-discover-sport

Vamplew, Wray. *Games People Played: A Global History of Sport*. Reaktion Books, 2021.

Van der Meij, Leander, et al. "Testosterone and Cortisol Release Among Spanish Soccer Fans Watching the 2010 World Cup Final." *PLoS ONE* 7, no. 4 (2012): e34814. https://doi.org/10.1371/journal.pone.0034814

Vincent, John, Edward Kian, Paul Pedersen, Aaron Kuntz, and John Hill. "England Expects: English Newspapers' Narratives About the English Soccer Team in the 2006 World Cup." *International Review for the Sociology of Sport* 45, no. 2 (2010): 199–223. https://doi.org/10.1177/1012690209360084

Vlachopoulos, Dimitris, et al. "Effect of a Program of Short Bouts of Exercise on Bone Health in Adolescents Involved in Different Sports: The PRO-BONE Study Proto-

col." *BMC Public Health* 15, no. 1 (2015): 1–10. https://doi.org/10.1186/s12889-015-1633
-5

Wagg, Stephen, and David L. Andrews. "Introduction: War Minus the Shooting." In *East Plays West: Sport and the Cold War*, edited by Stephen Wagg and David L. Andrews. Routledge, 2007.

Ware, Susan. *Game, Set, Match: Billie Jean King and the Revolution in Women's Sports.* University of North Carolina Press, 2011.

Wenn, Stephen R., and Robert K. Barney. *The Gold in the Rings: The People and Events That Transformed the Olympic Games.* University of Illinois Press, 2020.

Widener, Daniel. "Race and Sport." In *The Oxford Handbook of Sports History*, edited by Robert Edelman and Wayne Wilson. Oxford University Press, 2017.

Wiggins, David K., and Patrick B. Miller. *The Unlevel Playing Field: A Documentary History of the African American Experience in Sport.* University of Illinois Press, 2003.

Will, George F. "A Train Wreck Called Title IX." In *Women and Sports in the United States: A Documentary Reader*, edited by Jean O'Reilly and Susan K. Cahn. Northeastern University Press, 2002.

Xu, Xin. "Modernizing China in the Olympic Spotlight: China's National Identity and the 2008 Beijing Olympiad." *Sociological Review* 54 (S2) (2006): 90–107. https://doi.org/10.1111/j.1467-954X.2006.00655.x

Yu, Haiqing. "Game On: The Rise of the Esports Middle Kingdom." *Media Industries Journal* 5, no. 1 (2018): 88–105. https://doi.org/10.3998/mij.15031809.0005.106

Zang, David. "An Interview with Calvin Hill." In *The Unlevel Playing Field: A Documentary History of the African American Experience in Sport*, edited by David K. Wiggins and Patrick B. Miller. University of Illinois Press, 2003.

Zerhouni, Oulmann, Laurent Bègue, and Kerry S. O'Brien. "How Alcohol Advertising and Sponsorship Works: Effects Through Indirect Measures." *Drug and Alcohol Review* 38, no. 4 (2019): 391–398. https://doi.org/10.1111/dar.12929

Zhang, Hao, Siyuan Liu, Dazhong Yuan, and Chunyan Miao. "Ping Pong: An Exergame for Cognitive Inhibition Training." *International Journal of Human–Computer Interaction* 37, no. 12 (2021): 1104–15. https://doi.org/10.1080/10447318.2020.1870826

Zimbalist, Andrew. *Circus Maximus: The Economic Gamble Behind Hosting the Olympics and World Cup.* Brookings Institution Press, 2020.

———. "The Economic Legacy of Rio 2016." In *Rio 2016: Olympic Myths, Hard Realities*, edited by Andrew Zimbalist. Brookings Institution Press, 2017.

Zirin, Dave. *Bad Sports: How Owners Are Ruining the Games We Love.* New Press, 2012.

———. *Brazil's Dance with the Devil: The World Cup, The Olympics, and the Struggle for Democracy*, updated Olympics ed. Haymarket Books, 2016.

———. *Game Over: How Politics Has Turned the Sports World Upside Down.* New Press, 2013.

———. *Jim Brown. Last Man Standing.* Blue Rider Press, 2018.

———. *The Kaepernick Effect: Taking a Knee, Changing the World.* New Press, 2021.

———. *What's My Name, Fool? Sports and Resistance in the United States.* Haymarket Books, 2005.

INDEX

Note: Page numbers in italic type indicate figures or tables.

The authorized representative in the EU for product safety and compliance is:
Mare Nostrum Group
B.V Doelen 72
4831 GR Breda
The Netherlands

www.ingramcontent.com/pod-product-compliance
Lightning Source LLC
Chambersburg PA
CBHW030817270326
41928CB00007B/775